Accounting and Society

The Chapman & Hall series in Accounting and Finance

Consulting editors
John Perrin, Emeritus Professor of the University of Warwick and Price Waterhouse Fellow in Public Sector Accounting at the University Exeter; Richard M.S. Wilson, Professor of Management and Accounting at the University of Keele; and L.C.L. Skerratt, Professor of Financial Accounting at the University of Manchester.

'The *Dutch Students' Manual* to accompany the third edition of *Management and Cost Accounting* by Colin Drury, is not published by Chapman & Hall, but is available from Interfaas, Onderzoek en Advies, Postbus 76618, 1070HE, Amsterdam. Tel. (020) 6 76 27 06.

ACCOUNTING AND SOCIETY

R.W. Perks

Sainsbury Professor of Business Studies
Birkbeck College
University of London
UK

CHAPMAN & HALL
University and Professional Division
London · Glasgow · New York · Tokyo · Melbourne · Madras

Published by Chapman & Hall, 2-6 Boundary Row, London SE1 8HN

Chapman & Hall, 2-6 Boundary Row, London SE1 8HN, UK

Blackie Academic & Professional, Wester Cleddens Road, Bishopbriggs, Glasgow G64 2NZ, UK

Chapman & Hall GmbH, Pappelallee 3, 69469 Weinheim, Germany

Chapman & Hall USA., One Penn Plaza, 41st Floor, New York, NY10119, USA

Chapman & Hall Japan, ITP - Japan, Kyowa Building, 3F, 2-2-1 Hirakawacho, Chiyoda-ku, Tokyo 102, Japan

Chapman & Hall Australia, Thomas Nelson Australia, 102 Dodds Street, South Melbourne, Victoria 3205, Australia

Chapman & Hall India, R. Seshadri, 32 Second Main Road, CIT East, Madras 600 035, India

First edition 1993
Reprinted 1994

© 1993 R.W. Perks

Typeset in 10/12 pt Times by EXPO Holdings, Malaysia
Printed in Great Britain by Page Bros (Norwich) Ltd, Norwich

ISBN 0 412 47330 5

A Catalogue record for this book is available from the British Library

Library of Congress Cataloging-in-Publication Data available

∞ Printed on acid-free paper, manufactured in accordance with ANSI/NISO Z39.48-1992 and ANSI/NISO Z39.48-1984 (Permanence of Paper)

Dedicated to Kevin,
Michael and Julia
because I love them

Contents

Introduction

This book is intended to provide a highly readable, interesting and controversial overview of the role of accounting in society. In the last few years there has been a substantial increase in literature that is critical of accounting, but much of it is inaccessible and difficult to read, and such work is often written from rigid, narrow theoretical perspectives. This text is intended to provide a more balanced introduction to many challenging ideas and to a wealth of critical literature.

It is a book about ideas, intended to stimulate thought, discussion and controversy. Students used to conventional financial accounting calculations, and the idea of single, correct solutions to problems, will be disturbed by their absence. Unlike most accountancy books it includes no calculations and almost no figures. Readers who are unfamiliar with accounting will probably discover that there is a lot more (or perhaps a lot less!) to the subject than they had previously thought, and that it can actually be interesting. Readers who think that they are familiar with conventional accountancy may find their eyes opened to very different ways of seeing their subject.

The book should be of interest to those who want some understanding of the role of accounting, and to think about what accounting is all about, rather than for those who are intending to become professional accountants. It might even put them off their chosen career path! Its approach is academic, theoretical and journalistic; it is not a training manual. It will find a place on the third year of many business, social science and accounting degree courses where the intention is to encourage thought, discussion, argument and further reading.

It is a book to read, savour and think about. Each chapter raises interesting and controversial ideas and provides a wealth of challenging, exciting essay and discussion topics.

Readers may take different views as to what they mean by 'accounting', and the book does not attempt to deal with all of the roles of accountancy. It concentrates on financial reporting and accountability rather than on management accounting and control. Similarly readers may take different views of what they mean by 'society', but the book does not view society as a whole, echoing Mrs Thatcher's view that there is no such thing as society. Instead, society is seen as a collection of different and overlapping groups and individuals, each with its own interests. There are rarely solutions to problems that are 'best' for society. More usually one set of arrangements benefits some groups in society more than it benefits others; or it benefits one group at the expense of others.

The book begins by questioning the role of professionals in society. But what do we mean by a 'profession'? The first chapter outlines some of the characteristics of various professionals and how these apply to accountancy. To some extent these characteristics operate for the benefit of society; but readers are also encouraged to consider the possibility that professions might be a 'conspiracy against the laity' (George Bernard Shaw).

Perhaps professionals – and other powerful groups – should be made more accountable to society. But what do we mean by 'accountability'? The accountancy profession has for years earned its bread and butter from its involvement in the idea that the directors of companies are accountable to their shareholders. The second chapter examines what we mean by accountability and some of the limitations of the approach that accountants usually take. It also explores some wider interpretations of the idea of accountability.

Accountants often see accountability as involving little more than providing an 'account', a report expressed mainly in financial terms. But who determines what is in that account and what is going to be the official picture of an organization? In an era of 'creative accounting' there is a need for independent verification of the directors' version of events. But do auditors satisfactorily fulfil this role? Chapter 3 provides a critical assessment of the conventional audit function; it recognizes that there are major differences between what society expects from auditors, and what they actually do, particularly because of their lack of independence. Major changes are required if auditors are to deliver anything like what society might reasonably expect from them. Interesting comparisons are made between conventional private sector auditing and approaches to auditing in the public sector.

The conventional 'account' that accountants provide, intended mainly for investors and creditors, is inadequate in many respects. Many other groups in society want information about the performance of companies and other organizations, and they are not just interested in profits and financial position. Chapter 4 explores the possibilities of corporate reports being extended to cover a wide range of issues (such as the environment, safety and employment) that would be of interest to many different groups in society.

It sometimes seems that almost the only thing that matters in accounting is profitability. Profit is seen as encompassing all aspects of performance. Chapter 5 takes us beyond profit and explores other approaches to performance measurement. It discusses value for money auditing and the development of performance indicators relating to economy, efficiency and effectiveness.

Conventional accountants may feel safer with the reliability of profit as a measure of performance. But how reliable is profit measurement? The accountancy profession has a long history of trying to establish 'rules', or accounting standards, to determine how profit should be measured and how financial position and performance should be reported. Chapter 6 reviews outlines these attempts, and some of the recurring failures to deal with particular problems. There is still no agreed, workable definition of basic concepts like 'profit', 'asset', 'liability', 'income' or 'expenditure'. From time to time the accountancy profession has produced apparently acceptable definitions and rules, and an accounting standard is established. But it is not long before someone dreams up some new scheme to bypass the standard and the profession has to start tackling the problem all over again, researching, reporting, exposing, discussing, then specifying – only to have to start revising all over again when some new loophole has become evident leading to public controversies and scandals.

Why do all the problems of creative accounting arise? In part it is because the accountancy profession cannot effectively enforce its standards. But the standards themselves are often inconsistent and debatable. Why is this? If financial accounting is based on fundamental principles, all society needs is some detailed rules to apply those principles to particular situations. But – alas – there are no fundamental accounting principles! Chapter 7 examines the search for a conceptual framework that could provide a basis for financial accounting, and questions whether accounting can ever be based on meaningful principles.

In the absence of principles, perhaps financial reports can never be more than whatever it is that the most powerful parties involved want them to be. But who are the most powerful parties? Companies Acts clearly exert a powerful influence over the form and content of annual reports, and there is usually comparable legislation for other types of organization. But directors and chief executives can also have a powerful influence on the form, content and presentation of annual reports. Their power is to some extent limited by legislation and other official requirements – and by their accountants and auditors. But how powerful are auditors and the accountancy profession and what do we mean by power?

Chapter 8 explores various approaches to the concept of power. Are accountants as powerful as they appear to be? Are they powerful in unseen ways? In examining the role of accounting in society, the interplay of power relationships is a recurring theme: the power of professionals; attempts to use accountability mechanisms to control the power of those who might abuse it; the power of official reports and the struggle to control their form and content.

Accounting plays a role in almost all organizations in society, but its growth, assumptions and traditions have developed primarily from the private sector, and from its role in the accountability relationship between directors and shareholders. The baggage that accountants bring from these private sector traditions is often inappropriate, and against the interests of many in society. Conventional private sector accountancy emphasizes profitability and accountability through the provision of a financial account. Auditors are there to enhance the credibility of these accounts. These conventional approaches are increasingly colonizing public sector and not-for-profit organizations where, from a societal viewpoint, other accountability mechanisms would be more appropriate.

There are serious weaknesses in accountancy even in its most traditional roles. Although the accountancy profession began with work in bankruptcies it soon moved into financial accounting and auditing as its main areas of work. The original accounting and auditing requirements were intended to make the directors of companies more accountable to their shareholders and to improve the ways in which companies were run. But 'corporate governance' still leaves much to be desired, and even the recent proposals of the Cadbury Report do little to alter the balance of power and wealth in society. The book's concluding section discusses ways in which accounting might contribute to this.

1 Professions, society and accountancy

INTRODUCTION

This chapter is concerned with the role of professions in society and it considers the characteristics of professions particularly in relation to the accountancy profession. It defines the word 'profession' and examines the various characteristics that are attributed to professions. There is widespread agreement about some of these characteristics, but others are debatable. The various characteristics may be seen as defining a profession to assist in determining whether or not a particular occupational group has a legitimate claim to such status; or they may be seen as stages in development towards professionalism. Some may be seen as operating for the benefit of society while others operate in the interests of the professionals themselves. And some may be seen mainly as enhancing the power of the professionals. Different interpretations of the role of professions in society are then discussed. The historical development of professional accountancy bodies in the UK is then outlined and related to the development of professions in society generally. The chapter concludes by questioning the implication that society will continue to become increasingly professionalized.

WHAT IS A PROFESSION?

Accountancy is usually regarded as being a 'profession' although there is no agreement on exactly what it means to be a 'profession' or to have 'professional status'. A profession may be defined as a vocation in which a professed knowledge of some department of learning is used in its application to the affairs of others or in the practice of an art founded upon it. Traditionally the term is particularly applied to the three 'learned' professions, Divinity, Law and Medicine, and also to the military profession.

It is necessary to distinguish between a 'professional' (in the sense that a person can be a professional footballer or singer) and a 'profession' in the sense of a grouping of persons following a similar occupation. In the above definition the reference to 'the affairs of others' implies the existence of clients, and those who work in a profession tend to see themselves as meeting the needs of their individual (and corporate) clients. Abbott (1988) uses a loose definition of professions: they are 'exclusive occupational groups applying somewhat abstract knowledge to particular cases'.

The word is generally used to imply some favourable status and many different occupations aspire to professional status. Few would doubt that doctors are truly 'professionals', and other occupations, such as lawyers or architects, have similar high status. Accountants may worry whether they have comparable status as professionals and it is worth questioning the nature of their knowledge, the identity and interests of their clients, and whether accountancy is a 'vocation'. But in the hierarchy of professions accountants have less to worry about than teachers or nurses (who generally earn salaries rather than fees from clients) or others who aspire to professional status (e.g. funeral directors).

CHARACTERISTICS OF PROFESSIONS

This section outlines a number of characteristics which may be seen as being applicable to professions. Different writers take different views on the importance, if any, to be attached to particular characteristics. There is widespread agreement about the importance of the first few items listed (skill based on theoretical knowledge, professional association, institutionalized training, testing of competence, licensing, work autonomy, code of ethics, self-regulation), but some of the other characteristics listed are more controversial.

It is usually claimed that accountancy is a profession, and some indication is given in this section of the extent to which each characteristic applies to accountancy. These characteristics are interesting and important in relation to a number of other questions, including the following.

1. How does accountancy 'score' on this list: how strong is its claim to be a profession?
2. Do they indicate a number of 'stages' through which an occupational group must pass on the way to becoming a profession?
3. To whose advantage does each of these characteristics operate?
4. Do these characteristics make professionals more powerful in society?

1. Scoring

It may be tempting to use this list to 'score' the extent to which accountancy, or any other occupation, complies with this list, and then to assess whether or not these occupations may properly be called professions. One problem with this approach is that there is no definitive set of characteristics that determines whether or not nursing, architecture or school teaching, for example, are 'professions'. Different studies of different professions or occupations adopt different criteria, sometimes apparently intended to include or exclude particular occupations. Law and Medicine are always seen as being 'true' professions, with Dentistry, Civil Engineering, Architecture and then Accountancy not far behind. There is less agreement on military occupations (what do 'professional' soldiers have in common with members of the legal or accountancy profession?), civil servants, the clergy and a range of other occupational groups. Some writers even refer to the 'semi-professions', such as teachers, nurses and social workers (Etzioni, 1969), and have clear-cut views of which occupations merit the title profession and which do not. Goode (1969) considered that many occupations that aspired to professional status (such as school teaching, nursing, librarianship, pharmacy, stockbroking, advertising and business management) would never reach the levels of knowledge and dedication to service that society considered necessary for a profession. He stated that a number of occupations had become professions in the last generation (such as dentistry, certified public accountancy, clinical psychology, and engineering) but that most such occupations would 'continue to be seen as qualitatively different from the four great person professions: law, medicine, the ministry, and university teaching'.[1] A further set of semi-professions would achieve professionalism over the following generations: social work, marital counselling and perhaps vetinary medicine and city planning. And he stated that some occupations would not become professional: osteopathy, nursing, chiropractic, pharmacy, school-teaching and librarianship. Such judgements depend, of course, on which particular characteristics one chooses to emphasize in deciding what is meant by a 'profession'. Goode considered that the two main qualities are (1) a basic body of abstract knowledge, and (2) the ideal of service. But other writers emphasize different characteristics.

---

[1] Goode was, of course, a university teacher!

2. Stages

Another approach to the study of professions is to see them as developing through a series of stages to maturity. Buckley and Buckley (1974) show Accounting as the most recent of the 'established' professions. The main milestones in becoming established are identified as being when:

1. it became a full-time occupation;
2. the first training school was established;
3. the first university school was established;
4. the first local professional association was established;
5. the first national association was established;
6. the codes of professional ethics were introduced;
7. state licensing laws were established

Their 'ranking' of the 'established' professions on this basis in the USA shows Medicine first, followed by Law, Dentistry, Civil Engineering, Architecture, then Accounting. They then refer to other occupations in process of becoming professions, some of which are only marginal. The oldest established of these are Pharmacy and School-teaching, closely followed by Vetinary Medicine, Nursing, Librarianship, Optometry and Social Work, all of which could claim to be professions under most of the headings identified by 1900. They refer to City Management, City Planning and Hospital Administration as being 'new' professions, and Advertising and Funeral Direction as being 'doubtful' professions.

Buckley and Buckley's work is derived from Wilensky (1964) who also referred to a number of other stages including the redefinition of the core task so as to give the 'dirty work' over to subordinates; conflict between old-timers and the new men who seek to upgrade the job; competition between the new occupation and neighbouring ones; and political agitation in order to gain legal protection.

Just as some professions rise in status and power through various stages, so others may decline. Zola *et al.* (1977) see the influence of **religion** being overtaken by **law** in about the eighteenth century and law being overtaken by **medicine** in the twentieth century. This is characterized by the red cloaks of bishops giving way to the black cloaks of lawyers and then to white cloaks of doctors. The relative status of different professions is subject to constant change and it is worth considering whether accountancy has peaked or whether it might yet overtake medicine as financial considerations and 'economy, efficiency and effectiveness' become increasingly emphasized in health care.

3. Who benefits?

To whose advantage do these characteristics operate? To what extent do they benefit the individual professionals and their status and income? To what extent do they benefit other groups in society?

Writers such as Buckley and Buckley appear to assume that it is a 'good thing' for accountancy, and presumably other occupations, to achieve professional status. They portray the profession as dealing with complex problems requiring a wide range of disciplines and specialists, but

> These diverse backgrounds are welded together by learning the common body of knowledge in accounting by qualifying for membership in terms of academic standards and by demonstrating proficiency through professional examination ... It is, however, the set of unique problems and **adherence to a common service ideal** [emphasis added] which bind the diverse members of the profession (Buckley and Buckley, 1974, p. 16).

It is a common theme in the literature on professions that writers on particular occupational groups appear to be defenders of those groups, selecting particular attributes to demonstrate that their chosen calling can rightly claim the high status of being a profession, and that it performs valuable services for society. But not everyone takes the same view of the role of professions in society. It is presumably to the advantage of accountants to achieve professional status, but whether or not it is an advantage to others in society is more debatable.

4. Power

To what extent do these characteristics increase the power of professionals in society at the expense of others? A common theme in the literature on professions is the idea that society is becoming increasingly professionalized, that professions are becoming increasingly powerful in society and may even be a threat to democracy. Illich *et al.* (1977, pp. 21–2) sees professions as self-accrediting élites and 'democratic power is subverted by an unquestioned assumption of an all embracing professionalism'. According to McKnight (Illich *et al.*, 1977) professionals see deficiencies as being the **client's** (rather than society's) and solutions are seen in the **tools** that professionals have to offer for individual clients; in this way professions are sidestepping economic and social problems that require political solutions.

In examining the various characteristics that are attributed to professions we can ask which characteristics seem to make those professions powerful. For example, it might be postulated that the greater the apparent knowledge of a particular profession and the greater its exclusivity, the greater its power in society is likely to be. With each of these characteristics, do they seem more likely to protect society from charlatans and incompetents? Or are they more likely to enhance the power of professionals to protect themselves from interference from society and to impose their own views and interests?

The list of characteristics that follows is extensive, but does not claim to include every characteristic that has ever been attributed to professions. And the various characteristics are not mutually exclusive. The existence of a professional body, for example, tends to be associated with formal examinations, codes of ethics and the licensing of practitioners, but all of these features do not necessarily apply in every professional body.

1. Skill based on theoretical knowledge   Professionals are assumed to have extensive theoretical knowledge (whether of medicine, law, the Bible or engineering) and to possess skills based on that knowledge that they are able to apply in practice. Those with theoretical knowledge, but who are unable to apply it in practice, or those who have extensive practical skills that are not based upon their own theoretical knowledge, would not generally be regarded as professionals. Accountants are assumed to have skills and knowledge in a wide range of financial and business matters. Although there is obvious expertize (e.g. in tax computations) the nature of accounting knowledge may be questioned (Hines, 1989) especially as major international accountancy firms now take on assignments in a wide range of consultancy from counting votes to designing golf courses. She argues that

> one of the main obstacles against which accountants have continually had to struggle in their professionalisation quest has been the threat of an apparent absence of a formal body of accounting knowledge, and that creating the perception of possessing such knowledge has been an important part of creating and reproducing their social identity as a profession.

Her argument continues that in the eighteenth century accountants relied on various disparate skills (such as diligence and honesty, penmanship, accuracy and orderliness, arithmetic, and recording skills) rather than a formal body of knowledge; and that even by the early twentieth century it was difficult to identify exactly who was an accountant because of the varied nature of their work and their emphasis on personality characteristics. Many writers on the professions (e.g. Goldstein, 1984, p. 125) argue that 'professionalism is dependent on the intellectual core'. Hines (1989, p. 79) takes a contrary view and sees professionalization in accountancy as a 'social process by which members aspiring to professionalization laid claim to general qualities such as common sense, diligence, respectability, honesty, independence, ... penmanship, arithmetic and calculation' rather than a formal body of knowledge. The search for such a body of knowledge came later as a defence of their status and privileges.

2. Professional association   Professions usually have professional bodies organized by their members. These professional associations are intended to enhance the status of members and have carefully controlled entrance requirements. They try to ensure that only members of that body can have the exclusive, truly professional label. In accountancy there has been a plethora of organizations for 'professional' accountants, and anyone can call themselves an 'accountant'. Much of the history of professional accountancy bodies may be interpreted as attempts to establish an exclusive body for 'reputable' (e.g. 'chartered') accountants (Willmott, 1986).

3. Extensive period of education   The most prestigious professions usually require at least three years at university and it sometimes seems that the longer the period of university education the more prestigious the profession. Medics would no doubt argue that there is so much to learn about medicine that even a three-year degree course is not enough. The accountancy profession has gradually become almost the exclusive preserve of graduates, although they do not need to be accountancy graduates! The route is still open for 'non-relevant' graduates, who tend to be the majority in England and Wales.

4. Testing of competence   Before being admitted to membership of a professional body there is usually a requirement to pass prescribed examinations that are based mainly on theoretical knowledge. Some 'lesser' professional bodies (and almost all in their early years) have admitted members without passing examinations. Such bodies then have difficulty in attaining respectability until their membership is seen to be overwhelmingly on the basis of 'proper' qualifications. Examinations are usually set by the professional bodies with some exemptions available to those who have passed appropriate degree courses. The extent of such exemptions varies, but British accountancy bodies appear to be more reluctant to allow such exemptions than their opposite numbers in, for example, the medical profession, or accountancy bodies in many other countries.

5. Institutionalized training   In addition to examinations there is usually a requirement for a long period of institutionalized training where aspiring professionals acquire specified practical experience in some sort of trainee role before being recognized as a full member of a professional body. This may be justified on the grounds of the need to acquire extended experience before being able to operate as an unsupervised professional. It may also be seen as a way in which established professionals exploit their juniors to carry out much of their day-to-day work; or it may be seen as a way in which aspiring professionals are socialized into accepting the norms and attitudes of their superiors before being accepted as one of them.

6. Licensed practitioners   Professions seek to establish some sort of register or membership so that only those individuals so licensed are recognized. The three main chartered accountancy bodies (ICAS, ICAEW and ICAI) maintain a monopoly for their members on the use of the word 'chartered accountant' and have resisted attempts by the Chartered Institute of Management Accountants to use the designation 'chartered management accountant'. The final part of this chapter provides a brief introduction to the history of the professional accountancy bodies in the UK.

7. Work autonomy   Professionals tend to retain control over their own work, even when they are employed outside the profession. Organizations may be seen as power hierarchies where those in higher ranks control and co-ordinate the activities of those in lower ranks. But Professionals in an organization are assumed to have individual expertise and creativity which

> can only to a very limited degree be ordered and coordinated by the superior in rank ... the ultimate justification of a professional act is that it is, to the best of the professional's knowledge, the right act. He might consult his colleagues before he acts but the decision is his. If he errs, he still will be defended by his peers. The ultimate justification of an administrative act, however, is that it is in line with the organization's rules and regulations, and that it has been approved – directly or by implication – by a superior rank (Etzioni, 1964).

Lawyers, accountants and other professionals who join large (e.g. commercial or public sector) organizations outside public practice tend to be more powerful, in the sense of having more control over their work and greater ability to make independent decisions, than those who are seen primarily as dependent for their position on a managerial hierarchy and who are there to carry out tasks set and controlled by that hierarchy.

8. Code of professional conduct or ethics   Professional bodies usually have codes of conduct or ethics for their members and disciplinary procedures for those who infringe the rules. One sometimes hears of members of the various professional bodies being 'struck off' for various infringements. Sometimes professional bodies are criticized for being slow or reluctant to 'discipline' members and it is suggested that professionals should be subject to more public scrutiny. But it can be claimed that a high level of expertise is required to assess whether or not a professional has acted against the requirements of the appropriate code of professional conduct. Only another heart surgeon can judge whether or not heart surgery has been carried out competently; the fact that the patient died is irrelevant! Similarly, only fellow accountants can judge whether or not accounting standards have been complied with. Such claims for judgement by fellow professionals and protection from public scrutiny can, of course, be carried too far.

9. Self-regulation   Professional bodies tend to insist that they should be self-regulating and independent from government. A good example of this is the setting of accounting standards where the main professional accountancy bodies have combined to retain control.

10. Public service and altruism   Most of us would accept that good health and justice are in the public interest and those who are religious would defend 'professionals' in the church on similar grounds. This does not mean that doctors or other professionals are purely altruistic and not interested in earning their fees. It means that the earning of fees for services rendered can be defended because those services are seen to be in the public interest.

The accountancy profession may not at first sight appear to be particularly altruistic, but it can still be defended as being in the public interest. Professional accountancy may be seen as protecting shareholders and creditors, preventing and detecting fraud, making individuals and organizations 'accountable', providing information that influences share prices and so, in turn, the allocation of resources in the economy, and providing information to make organizations more 'efficient'. The extent to which these are achieved in practice is debatable, but professionals are likely to see their position as being strengthened if they can be presented as being in the public interest (although the interest of the 'client' who pays the fee also has to be considered!).

11. Exclusion, monopoly and legal recognition Professions tend to exclude those who have not met their requirements and joined the appropriate professional body. The accountancy profession still struggles to retain such exclusivity. Their monopoly is threatened as long as any individual can describe her/himself as an accountant and prepare accounts and tax returns and give financial advice. Chartered accountants' monopoly on the right to conduct company audits is not quite complete: members of the Chartered Association of Certified Accountants can also be recognized as auditors; individuals can be authorized by the Secretary of State for Trade and Industry, for example if they have appropriate overseas qualifications; and the Association of Authorised Public Accountants has about 1000 members who are individually authorized statutory auditors.

Although professional bodies insist on their independence from government they welcome official recognition of their monopoly. Doctors have been particularly successful in this respect. Recently solicitors have lost their monopoly on conveyancing, but the position of accountants has, if anything, been strengthened. The virtual monopoly on auditing remains and there is now a requirement that investment advisers and insolvency practitioners are officially registered. In some countries there is official recognition of taxation practitioners.

12. Control of remuneration and advertising Where levels of remuneration are determined by government (e.g. medicine, teaching, dentistry) professional bodies are active, like trade unions, in negotiating remuneration packages for their members. In other professions (e.g. architecture, surveyors, solicitors) professional bodies have set standard scale fees, but government advocacy of competition means that these are no longer generally followed. Restrictions on advertising were presumably based on the idea that all members of a professional body were properly qualified and individuals should not put themselves forward as being 'better'. A sound reputation and increasingly profitable business may be the reward for years of not ruffling the comfortable feathers of senior members of the profession. But recent emphasis on competition has swept away many such restrictive practices and professional services are more likely to be advertised and seen in the market place.

13. High status and rewards   The most successful professions achieve high status and rewards for their members. Some of the factors included in this list contribute to such success.

14. Individual clients   Many professions have individual fee-paying clients. In accountancy 'the profession' is usually taken to refer to accountants in professional practice who have individual and corporate clients, rather than accountants who are simply employees of organizations (such as industrial companies or public sector bodies) that are not primarily concerned with offering professional accountancy services. Lawyers, architects and surveyors are often in professional practice in this way and many doctors still have private practices with private patients. Whether a doctor is less 'professional' if s/he works full-time for the National Health Service is debatable. Similarly, it could be argued that a management accountant who works full-time for ICI is no more 'professional' than any other ICI employee. It might be claimed that school teaching is not a profession where the teachers are simply employees with no individual clients. University teachers may be seen as being professionals to the extent that they have individual 'clients' when they undertake private research, writing and consultancy; to the extent that they merely carry out functions allocated to them by university management they are in the same boat as other employees. Some universities are now trying to impose regimes where 'permission' is required for any outside work, and increasing teaching and administrative burdens, together with requirements to 'perform' in research in accordance with criteria set by others, may be seen as deprofessionalizing (and destroying?) academic life. Insofar as academic staff have 'clients' they are seen as clients (or customers) of the institution rather than as clients of individual academic staff.

Although many professionals have individual clients, it should not necessarily be assumed that professionals are simply trying to serve the best interests of their clients. Professionals tend to encourage client dependence upon them. One writer, Illich (Illich *et al.*, 1977), concentrates on the idea of 'disabling professions', arguing that professionals tell you what you need and claim the power to prescribe. 'In any area where a human need can be imagined these new professions, dominant, authoritative, monopolistic, legalized – and, at the same time, debilitating and effectively disabling the individual – have become exclusive experts of the public good.' To McKnight (Illich *et al.*, 1977) the main disabling influences of professionals are their prerogative to define both the problem and the solution on behalf of the client. Both the problems and the solutions become technical matters with which the professional can deal, and are expressed in technical language that is incomprehensible to ordinary citizens. The result is that the client can neither understand the problem that the professional has attributed to her/him, nor the solution. As a result only the professional can determine whether or not the solution has been successful.

15. Middle-class occupations Traditionally many professions have been seen as 'respectable' occupations for middle and upper classes. Long ago the younger sons of landed families would enter the Church or the army as the main acceptable occupations. In Britain 'trade' or industry was somehow unacceptable to upper-class families but other professions emerged, particularly in the nineteenth century, as respectable outlets. Although the professions have increasingly been opened up to working-class people, they still tend to be dominated by the middle classes. Insofar as upper-class people occupy more powerful positions in society than working-class people, professionalism can support this class position, just as class position can support professionalism.

16. Male-dominated The highest status professions tend to have been male-dominated. The proportion of women in school-teaching has increased as its status has declined, and women are being admitted to the priesthood now that its status has declined relative to other professions. Nursing is female-dominated and is subordinate to the medical profession. Etzioni (1969) argues that

> tensions that may seem a result of the clash between professional and organizational principles actually may be the result of the composition of the labour force ... It is difficult to believe that many of the arrangements we found in the relations between doctors and nurses, social workers and their supervisors, teachers and principals, would work out if, let us say, 90 per cent of the nurses and of the supervised social workers were male, especially lower middle class, as are so many of the females employed in these positions.

Class and gender[2] dominance and professionalism may be seen as reinforcing each other. Although the proportion of women in the accountancy profession is increasing they still represent a very small minority of those in powerful positions in the profession. If there are to be more women in powerful positions in the accountancy profession, more general questions about the position of women in society must be addressed. It could happen that, as women become more powerful within the profession, so the profession will become less powerful in society.

17. Offer reassurance It sometimes appears that, in view of the authority that they possess, professionals are able to offer reassurance to clients that although there appear to be problems, everything is 'normal' or being dealt with properly.

---

[2] Similar arguments apply to race: women, ethnic groups and working-class people are no less disadvantaged in most professions than they are in society generally.

Such reassurance may be offered rather than solutions to particular problems. Sick people often visit doctors to find that they are suffering from something called 'there is a lot of it about' and to be reassured that they will probably be better in a few days. Treatments such as recommending no food for 24 hours to cure diarrhoea, or keeping warm, resting and drinking plenty of fluids to deal with a cold, are much more reassuring from a doctor with a black bag and a stethoscope than from a book of old wives' tales.

18. Ritual   Many professional practices include an element of ritual. The Church, and legal procedures in Court, are the most obviously ritualistic, but there is also an element of ritual in medical examinations. At first sight accountancy may not appear to be particularly ritualistic, but many conventional accounting procedures are well-established and are seen to be appropriate regardless of the particular circumstances. Budgetary control systems and cash-flow forecasts are rituals that add credibility to management forecasts, and the credibility of accounting calculations is enhanced if they are produced by a computer that is seen as being capable of magical rituals. The audit process may be seen as a ritual that serves 'to create a reality in which financial statements are perceived to be credible', and 'to mask conflict in order to maintain social order and to legitimize the profession's actions' (Mills and Bettner, 1992).

19. Legitimacy   Professionals have clear legal authority over some activities (e.g. certifying the insane, or auditing company accounts) but are seen as adding legitimacy to a wide range of related activities. Doctors are seen as legitimate advisers on any health matters; accountants on any financial matters; and lawyers on any legal matters. As most issues in society have potential health, financial and legal implications, these professionals are well placed to sell their services. And as there are often no clear-cut 'right' answers to problems in society (e.g. whether to close a production facility or to legalize cannabis) it is a bold decision-maker who chooses to implement a particular decision without its being 'legitimated' and supported by professionals who are seen to be relevant and appropriate.

20. Inaccessible body of knowledge   In some professions the body of knowledge is relatively inaccessible to the uninitiated. Medicine and Law are typically not school subjects and have separate faculties and even separate libraries at universities. School subjects **contribute** to the understanding of the various bodies of knowledge required for particular professions, but it is unusual for schools to teach particular occupational requirements, although word processing and accountancy are more commonly taught than plumbing or architecture. For many years the Church was seen as a high-status profession, particularly when priests were a fairly exclusive group who could read and apparently understand the Bible; once schooling became compulsory and most people could read the Bible for themselves, the exclusivity of the knowledge of the priesthood declined, as did their status and power. To some extent it seems that professions with the highest status have the least accessible body of knowledge. To what extent the various professionals have deliberately sought to make their knowledge inaccessible is debatable, but it would be difficult to argue that schools simply offer what people need or demand: we are all more likely to have to deal with medical problems than speak French, or with legal problems than with calculating the surface area of a sphere; yet mathematics and French are principal school subjects, and law and medicine are scarcely taught at all.

21. Indeterminacy of knowledge   Jamous and Peloille (1970) argue that professional knowledge includes (a) technical elements that can be mastered and communicated in the form of rules, and (b) indeterminate elements that escape rules and are attributed to the 'virtualities' of the producers. This indeterminacy allows secrecy and means that control over these professional skills remains in the hands of practitioners, and they can choose the apprentices to whom they wish to pass on those skills. Non-professionals can acquire the technical skills, but only the invited and initiated will be seen as possessing the indeterminate skills (e.g. professional judgement and experience). Low-level technical skills can be hived off to 'sub-professionals' (e.g. nurses or accounting technicians) and this can further raise the status of the 'real' professional.

It might be argued that the greater the indeterminacy, the greater the prestige of the profession. But professionals who lack effective technical skills are in danger of being seen on a par with priests or witch doctors. 'Indeterminacy' can be interpreted as meaning that the professional has no effective answer to particular problems or that the answers are effective only if the client is prepared to believe in them. On the other hand, if professionals possess technical skills alone, anyone can learn them and so undermine the market for professional services. Armstrong (1985) argues that engineers attempted to install themselves at the top of the managerial apex by using 'scientific management'; 'but these techniques proved too lucid and could too easily be detached from the ambitions of engineers'; this proved to be to the advantage of accountants who took over such techniques as costing, which began as a technical skill but has become more mystical and indeterminate as different approaches develop and it is seen that there are no 'right' answers.

22. Mobility   The skill, knowledge and authority of professionals belongs to the professionals as individuals and not to the organizations for which they work. They are therefore relatively mobile in employment opportunities as they can move to other employers and take their talents with them. Standardization of professional training and procedures enhances this mobility.

A number of different authors have identified the various 'traits' that they consider characterize professions. Millerson (1964) lists 14 such traits that have been included by 21 different authors. The traits that were most frequently identified were as follows:

Organized	13 authors
Professional code of conduct	13 authors
Skill based on theoretical knowledge	12 authors
Required training and education	9 authors
Competence tested	8 authors
Altruistic service	8 authors
Applied to affairs of others	5 authors

Traits that were mentioned by only two authors each were: indispensable public service; licensed community sanction; definite professional client relationship; fiduciary client relationship; best impartial service given; loyalty to colleagues; predetermined basis of remuneration (e.g. fee). Other attributes that were mentioned only occasionally include: members prepared to contribute to professional development; independence; non-manual; profits not dependent on capital; and recognized status.

Many of these attributes may be seen as demonstrating the benefits that professionals bring to society. But some characteristics of professions may be interpreted, or applied in practice, in ways that suggest that they benefit the professionals themselves more than they benefit others in society.

ROLE OF PROFESSIONS IN SOCIETY

The idea that various characteristics of professions have developed in response to the needs of society, and for the benefit of society is consistent with a 'functionalist' interpretation of the role of professions. Willmott (1986) identifies two other interpretations. The three interpretations are (1) a functionalist interpretation, (2) an interactionist approach and (3) a more critical approach.

1. Functionalist interpretation   A traditional functionalist interpretation of professionalism would explain the characteristics of professions as being necessary for society to obtain the benefits of the services of professionals. Professional activity is seen as being in the interests of society (which needs health, justice, education, truth and fairness, and perhaps even divinity). But society also needs to be protected from exploitation by unqualified charlatans and quacks who do not have the expertise that they claim. Professional bodies therefore undertake responsibility for testing and registering members and disciplining members who are guilty of malpractice. The professional body is thus seen as protecting the public both from the unqualified and from exploitation by its own members.

2. Interactionist interpretation The interactionist approach studies 'professions as interest groups that strive to convince others of the legitimacy of their claim to professional recognition' (Willmott, 1986, p. 557). Professional work is seen 'as a process of constructing and maintaining an occupational role which enables them to "get by" and "make out"'. The professional body helps to secure a respectable and valued social identity; relevant symbols and beliefs are constructed and projected; and interactionists see professional bodies as including competing interest groups. But 'they omit consideration of the **structural conditions** of relative success or failure'. The role of professions in society cannot be understood except in relation to a particular view of how society is structured and operates.

3. Critical approach Here professionalism 'is understood as a strategy for controlling an occupation, involving solidarity and closure which regulates the supply of professional workers to the market and also provides a basis for the domination of institutions, organizations and other occupations associated with it'. Control of entry is achieved through training and qualifications. Professionals are seen as being powerful because they are involved with and supported by more powerful groups in society, whether the state or powerful corporations. The market for professional services is not seen as one where skills are bought and sold because skills are not seen as individual possessions but as being produced by social power, including the power of the state to grant or deny monopolies. In this Marxist interpretation professions are seen as promoting monopolies and scarcities in the labour market; and the role of professional bodies is seen in terms of the social division of labour and the structure of the labour market rather than in terms of the traits of professionalism.

There is, of course, some truth in each of these interpretations. Professions would not survive and prosper unless they were seen as providing something valuable to society. But they do, of course, look after their own interests. Professional accountants are likely to be as interested as pop singers, golfers or plumbers in participating in various activities designed to add to their market value. And the power of accountants and other professional groups is likely to be greater if they can carve out a monopolistic niche for themselves, particularly if it is in alliance with more powerful groups in society.

DEVELOPMENT OF UK PROFESSIONAL ACCOUNTANCY BODIES

In attempting to understand the role of accounting in society and to provide some insight into likely future developments, some knowledge of the existing professional bodies is useful. It is particularly relevant to notice how many different professional accountancy bodies have come into being and how some have been more successful in enhancing their status than others, partly through selective mergers and partly through restrictions on the use of the term 'chartered accountant'.

In 1993 there were six major professional accountancy bodies in the British Isles, namely

The Institute of Chartered Accountants of Scotland (ICAS)
The Institute of Chartered Accountants in England and Wales (ICAEW)
The Institute of Chartered Accountants in Ireland (ICAI)
The Chartered Association of Certified Accountants (ACCA)
The Chartered Institute of Public Finance and Accountancy (CIPFA)
The Chartered Institute of Management Accountants (CIMA).

Table 1.1 shows the membership of each body in 1992–93, the date when each body began and the date when the existing body was established.

Table 1.1 The six major British professional accountancy bodies

Body	*Membership 1992–3*	*Date of origin*	*Date established*
ICAS	13 300	1854	1951
ICAEW	102 000	1870	1880
ICAI	8 000	1888	1888
ACCA	39 750	1891	1939
CIPFA	11 200	1885	1885
CIMA	33 700	1919	1919

Institute of Chartered Accountants of Scotland originated with the Edinburgh Society of Accountants (1854), the Glasgow Institute of Accountants and Actuaries (1854) and the Aberdeen Society of Accountants (1867), each of which was granted a royal charter almost from the beginning. The three bodies merged in 1951.

The Institute of Chartered Accountants in England and Wales was established by royal charter in 1880. It was formed from the five bodies that existed in England at the time: the Incorporated Society of Liverpool Accountants (January 1870); the Institute of Accountants in London[3](November 1870); the Manchester Institute of Accountants (February 1871); the Society of Accountants in England

---

[3] 'in London' was dropped in 1872.

(1872); and the Sheffield Institute of Accountants (1877). The ICAEW merged with the Society of Incorporated Accountants[4] (1885) in 1957.

The Institute of Chartered Accountants in Ireland was established in 1888, before the island was partitioned, and continues to operate both north and south of the border.

The Chartered Institute of Public Finance and Accountancy (previously known as the Institute of Municipal Treasurers and Accountants) was established in 1885.

The Chartered Association of Certified Accountants was established as the Association of Certified and Corporate Accountants in 1938. It was formed by the amalgamation of two bodies:

1. The Corporation of Accountants (Glasgow, 1891);
2. The London Association of Accountants (1904).

A third body joined in 1941:

3. The Institute of Certified Public Accountants which originated in 1903 and had amalgamated in 1932 with the Central Association of Accountants (originated in 1905).

The Chartered Institute of Management Accountants was founded in 1919 as the Institute of Cost and Works Accountants.

A number of themes emerge from the study of the development of professional accountancy bodies in the UK. There is a recurring move towards monopoly. This can be seen in a number of the amalgamations that took place. The original London Institute of Accountants rapidly dropped the 'London' label to attract other members, but the Society of Accountants in England attracted more members and the Institute rapidly arranged an amalgamation which, at the time, included all the accountancy bodies in England. There were also (unsuccessful) attempts at establishing a national register of accountants. The ICAEW, ICAS and ICAI were successful in establishing a monopoly of the label 'chartered accountant' and as each operated in a different part of the United Kingdom there was little real competition between them. These 'superior' bodies were rather dismissive of the claims to respectability of the various lesser bodies.

When any new professional body is established it usually sets up a system of qualifying examinations, but the founders obtained their membership before the examinations existed. There is usually some doubt about the value of 'qualifications' in a newly established body if many of its members have passed no examinations, especially if there is a comparable body which has for a long period

---

[4] The 'Society of Incorporated Accountants and Auditors' dropped the 'and Auditors' in 1954.

required examinations to be passed as a condition of membership. In spite of such initial reservations about new bodies, further mergers were eventually proposed. Both the Incorporated Accountants and the ACCA represented major competitors in the main work of chartered accountants. The former merged with the ICAEW in 1957, but a merger with the latter fell through in 1970 because members of the ICAEW voted against giving equal status to a body that they saw as having lower status. Members of both CIMA and CIPFA could call themselves 'accountants' and were members of a chartered professional body of accountants, but they could not call themselves 'chartered accountants'; they were not able to undertake audits of companies; and they did not tend to set themselves up in practice offering professional accountancy services in competition with 'chartered accountants'. They were therefore essentially complementary rather than competing accountancy bodies.

In England the first accountancy bodies to be established came together in 1870 to form the ICAEW. Most of the next wave of accountancy bodies, founded between 1885 and 1919, achieved comparable status with ICAS and ICAEW by 1970 in the Consultative Committee of Accountancy Bodies. CIPFA, ICAI, ACCA and CIMA became members of the CCAB; the Incorporated Accountants had joined ICAEW; and four bodies had joined together in the ACCA. The next wave of accountancy bodies has so far been less successful. The Society of Company and Commercial Accountants (7200 members) dates from 1923 and the Association of International Accountants (2000 members) from 1928; the Association of Cost and Executive Accountants (3500 members) began in 1942 as the Institute of Industrial and Commercial Accountants.

The Institute of Financial Accountants (8000 members), which began in 1916 as the Institute of Bookkeepers, may be seen as the first 'technician' or lower-level accountancy body. Just as doctors are supported by nurses, and solicitors by legal executives, so accountants are supported by bookkeepers and others. Developing such second-tier bodies may be seen as a natural stage in the development of a profession. For many years trainees or apprentices did much of the low-level work in return for modest salaries. In 1980 the five CCABs based in Britain set up the Association of Accounting Technicians to provide a junior level of qualification. This may be seen as an attempt to attract aspiring accountants who have not succeeded in attaining the envied 'chartered' status, and to retain them within the monopolistic CCAB framework. In this way the competitive pressures from the various 'lesser' accountancy bodies is reduced. The Accounting Technicians route can lead to full CCAB qualification, and so the door, in theory, remains open to all. But it is a long and difficult road to achieve the status of 'chartered accountant'; the Association of Accounting Technicians effectively enhances the status of 'chartered accountant', and provides a home for those who might otherwise join professional bodies that could undermine the status of the CCABs.

Other professional accountancy bodies exist which may be seen as competing with the CCABs in various specialist areas. The Institute of Taxation was established in 1930 and is often seen as a more advanced, specialist qualification for those who have already achieved CCAB membership. The Institute of Internal Auditors was established in Britain in 1948 as part of an international (American-based) body that is achieving increasing recognition. The Association of Corporate Treasurers was established in 1979 and also represents significant competition for the established professional accountancy bodies.

A recurring theme of the study of professional bodies is their constant struggle to maintain the status and exclusivity of their members. Doctors have tended to absorb such occupations as psychiatry and counselling and to fight off others such as chiropractic, homeopathy and faith healing. The accountancy profession came into being partly because lawyers failed to maintain their monopoly of bankruptcy work, and accountants and lawyers still compete with each other in areas such as taxation. Accountants have to a large extent absorbed computing expertise, but the battle continues.

As new occupational groupings emerge, established professionals may attempt to discredit them or to compete with them directly by offering the same professional service. Some professional bodies in accountancy are providing very different services from the established bodies of chartered accountants (CIPFA, CIMA); others are offering much the same (ACCA). In both cases there is a continuing interest in merger: the established bodies wish to protect the name 'chartered accountant' or even 'accountant'; the other bodies wish to acquire that status.

In 1970 the ICAEW proposed a merger of the three 'chartered' bodies (Scotland, England and Wales, Ireland) and the 'certified' (or 'the Association'), CIPFA and the ICMA. After this proposal had been accepted by five of the bodies and rejected by the membership of the ICAEW, prospects of merger faded. Since the major merger proposal in 1970 various other mergers have been proposed (including ACCA and CIMA; ICAEW and ICAS; and ICAEW and CIPFA), but each of these has fallen through. ICAS and ICAEW are now more directly in competition with each other and there is no real difference between the work formed by their respective members. The legal and medical professions have been relatively successful in maintaining professional unity while accepting many, very different specialisms. In the accountancy profession there has been some unity of action through the Consultative Committee of Accountancy Bodies and in the promulgation of accounting standards. But there are still separate professional bodies, some with different specialisms and some with little difference other than their geography and history.

THE DEVELOPMENT OF PROFESSIONAL FIRMS

Many lawyers, accountants, architects, surveyors and others work in professional practices of varying sizes. There are still many sole practitioners and some partnerships have only a handful of partners and a dozen or so employees. But the accountancy profession, unlike any other, is increasingly dominated by a small number of international professional practices with annual revenues measured in billions of pounds and offices throughout the world. Through a series of dramatic mergers the accountancy profession is now dominated by the 'big six' professional firms that operate world-wide. In the UK alone each has annual revenues measured in hundreds of millions of pounds and is larger than most of their clients. The largest professional firms are powerful because of the resources that they command and the status and credibility that they bring to their work. If one of these major firms is the auditor of a company's accounts or lends its name to their profits projections, cash-flow forecasts, tax returns or fund-raising activities, then that company benefits from the prestige and status of the international accounting firm. The power of accountancy in society is enhanced by its ability to mobilize high-calibre professional resources on a scale that would impress most companies and even governments.

THE DECLINE OF PROFESSIONALISM?

If professionalism is seen in terms of altruism and public service or in terms of individual professionals providing a service to individual, fee-paying clients, the professionalism of accountants seems to be declining. The larger firms of accountants are mopping up an increasing share of the work that is available and they are increasingly seen as 'big business', mainly interested in generating revenues and profits.

Much of the literature on professions traces the steady rise of different professional groups and the increasing numbers of groups that lay claim to professionalism. Acquiring professional status is sometimes seen to be the result of passing through a series of stages as if, in due course, almost every occupational group will become 'professionals'. But if every occupation was seen to be a 'profession', then the label 'profession' could come to mean no more than 'occupation'. There will always be some occupations that require more knowledge and expertise than others, and that have more status, power, prestige and privilege than others.

While some professions increase in status, others decline. Accountancy seems to have been rising while school-teaching and the Church have declined. Which professions have the highest status at any particular time will vary, but it should not be assumed that professions as we know them will always exist. If they are seen to be a threat to democracy, politicians may seek to limit their influence. If professionals employed within organizations are seen to be too independent, then managerialists may seek to curtail them. There is evidence of creeping managerialism reducing the authority of ministers, university teachers, and doctors in the Church, universities and the National Health Service. And monopolies of expertise can easily be eroded or ended. Who relies on a priest for advice if they have read the Bible themselves and found it wanting? Who would rely on a doddery GP if a computer-based expert system can produce a more reliable diagnosis? For how long would we continue to pay expensive lawyers' fees if it were revealed that their learning was more apparent than real and that they could not provide clear-cut answers to our legal problems? And who will use accountants if a simple computer system will produce more reliable tax computations or other accounting information? If education continues to become less 'academic' and more relevant to the 'real world', more and more potential clients will realize the limitations of the professionals. But if accountancy continues to be badly taught and little understood, the role of the accountancy profession will be somewhat protected!

FURTHER READING

Berlant, J. L. (1975) *Profession and Monopoly: A Study of Medicine in the US and GB*, Berkeley, University of California Press.
Brown, R. (ed.) (1905) *A History of Accounting and Accountants*, Edinburgh, Jack.
Dingwall, R. and Lewis, P. (eds) (1983) *The Sociology of the Professions*, London, Macmillan.
Elliott, P. (1972) *The Sociology of the Professions*, London, Macmillan.
Larson, M. S. (1977) *The Rise of Professionalism: A Sociological Analysis*, Berkeley, University of California Press.
Millerson, G. (1964) *The Qualifying Associations: A Study in Professionalization*, Routledge & Kegan Paul, New York.

ESSAY AND DISCUSSION TOPICS

1. Which professions have the highest status? Draw up a list of professions and rank them in order of status. Why do some professions have higher status than others?
2. Why does a claim to be a 'professional musician' sound more credible than a claim to be a 'professional plumber'?
3. Which profession(s) are the most powerful in society, and why? Are some professions becoming more powerful while others are becoming less powerful?
4. Why do some writers regard university teaching as being a profession, but not school-teaching?
5. When a large firm of chartered accountants is recruiting graduates, what are they looking for? Personality characteristics or a formal body of knowledge?
6. Will the status and power of the accountancy profession decline as the subject becomes increasingly available in schools and as part of business and management studies courses?

7. Would you like to see the power and status of the accountancy profession reduced? Why (or why not)?
8. What factors (if any) are likely to lead to a reduction in the power and status of the accountancy profession?

REFERENCES

Abbott, A. (1988) *The System of Professions: An Essay on the Division of Expert Labour*, University of Chicago Press, p. 8.

Armstrong, P. (1985) Changing management control strategies: the role of competition between accountancy and other organizational professions, *Accounting, Organizations and Society*, **10**(2), 132.

Buckley J. W. and Buckley, M. H. (1974) *The Accounting Profession*, Melville, Los Angeles.

Etzioni, A. (1964) *Modern Organizations*, Prentice Hall, p. 76.

Etzioni, A. (ed.) (1969) *The Semi-Professions and Their Organization: Teachers, Nurses, Social Workers*, Free Press, New York.

Goldstein, I. (1984) Foucault among the sociologists: the 'disciplines' and the history of the professions, *History and Theory*, 170–92.

Goode, W. J. (1969) The theoretical limits of professionalization, in Etzioni (1969), op. cit.

Hines, R. D. (1989) Financial accounting knowledge, conceptual framework projects and the social construction of the accounting profession, *Accounting, Auditing and Accountability Journal*, **2**(2), 72–92.

Illich, I. (with Zola, I. K., McKnight, J., Caplan, J. and Shaiken, H.) (1977) *Disabling Professions*, Marion Boyars Publishers, New York and London.

Jamous, H. and Peloille, B. (1970) Changes in the French university-hospital system, in *Professions and Professionalization* (ed. J. A. Jackson), Cambridge University Press, p. 113.

Millerson, G. (1964) *The Qualifying Associations: A Study in Professionalization*, Routledge & Kegan Paul, New York.

Mills, S. K. and Bettner, M. S. (1992) Ritual and conflict in the audit profession, *Critical Perspectives on Accounting*, **3**(2), 185–200.

Wilensky, H. L. (1964) The professionalisation of everyone?, *American Journal of Sociology*, **70**, Sept., 142–6.

Willmott, H. (1986) Organising the profession: a theoretical and historical examination of the development of the major accountancy bodies in the UK, *Accounting, Organizations and Society*, **11**(6), 555–80.

Zola, I. K. (1977), Healthism and disabling medicalization, in Illich *et al.* (1977), op. cit.

2 Accountability

INTRODUCTION AND DEFINITION

This chapter begins with a definition of accountability. It then outlines the relatively straightforward version of accountability upon which accountancy is based. Some of the limitations of this approach are then explored. Other views of accountability are discussed, including the view taken by the corporate report; approaches to accountability in the public sector; and managerial accountability. The final part of the chapter explores changing concepts of accountability.

Accountability sounds like a good thing – something that we can all be in favour of. There is likely to be widespread agreement that companies, directors, universities, bureaucrats, local authorities or central government should be made more accountable. But what do we mean by 'accountability'?

For simplicity the concept of accountability will be introduced as if there are only two parties involved: directors may be accountable to shareholders, politicians to the electorate, secretaries to managers, or children to parents. In practice, individuals and organizations may be accountable to a number of different parties. Accountability means the obligation to give an account. The extent to which the form and content of that account is defined will vary from one relationship to another. To clarify what is meant by accountability in a particular situation we should ask (1) **who** is accountable (2) **to whom**, (3) **how** (by what means) and (4) **for what**? Those who argue for greater accountability may be arguing for any one or more of these: (1) more people or organizations in society should be made accountable; (2) they should be made accountable to a wider group, or to 'society' generally; (3) accountability should be more effective and enforceable; or (4) the organizations concerned should be made accountable for a wider range of activities.

The two parties involved in a particular accountability relationship will be referred to in this chapter as the **Principal** (the accountee, e.g. shareholders) to whom the account is due; and the **Agent** (the accountor, e.g. directors) from whom the account is due. In practice there may be several different parties involved. In the 1970s and 1980s it became fashionable to describe this accountability relationship in terms of 'agency theory'. A company's shareholders are seen as being the Principal, and the company directors are their 'Agents'. The Principals pass control of their resources to the Agents on the basis of a contractual relationship that requires information to be provided; this is governed by legislation. But the relationship implies much more: shareholders expect not only that good care will be taken of their money, but also that the company will be profitable and perhaps 'efficient' and 'effective'.

Whether or not we are in favour of increased accountability is likely to depend on whether we see ourselves as being the Principal or the Agent in a particular relationship. We are likely to favour increased accountability if we think of ourselves as representing society; that we are the Principals; and that powerful individuals (whether politicians, directors, trade union bosses or university vice chancellors) should be more accountable to us. But if we see ourselves as being the Agent (accountable to our boss, parents, electorate or the public) we are less likely to favour any effective system of accountability that restricts our freedom of action. If we think of particularly powerful groups or individuals in society as being (if only potentially) our, or society's, Agents, there may be widespread agreement that such Agents should be made more accountable to society. In this scenario accountability implies that society places restrictions upon the powerful by requiring that they give an account of their actions. We are likely to favour others being made more accountable to us, or to society; we are less likely to favour restrictions being put upon ourselves to make us more accountable to others. We are concerned that 'they' might do things that are against our interest, and that if they are made more accountable to us then their ability to act against our interests is restricted. We are less likely to want ourselves to be made more accountable to 'them'. However, some people may not want power and responsibility; they may be happy to give an account of their activities to someone who takes responsibility for them.

Those who are in positions of power are likely to be less keen to be made accountable and are likely to struggle to retain their freedom of action. Where others attempt to impose accountability systems upon them, they are likely, if they wish to remain powerful, to subvert, bypass and control any accountability systems that are imposed upon them.

An examination of how systems of accountability operate is therefore likely to include an examination of a struggle for power. It is worth asking who is calling for greater accountability and for what reasons. Those who call for increased accountability often see themselves as being the Principal and are likely to be advocating a shift in power to themselves from those who they think should be their Agents.

Most definitions of accountability emphasize **information**. Jackson (1982), for example, defines accountability as 'explaining or justifying what has been done, what is currently being done and what is planned ... [and] ... involves therefore, the giving of information'. Gray *et al.* (1987, p. 2) define accountability as 'the onus, requirement or responsibility to provide an account (by no means necessarily a **financial** account) or reckoning of the actions for which one is held responsible'.

Accountability that ends with the provision of information or an account, is, however, incomplete and likely to be ineffective. What happens if the Principal is dissatisfied with the Agent's account? In addition to information, accountability requires that Principals have effective **sanctions** that can be used when Agents are not meeting the Principal's requirements.

In dealing with **public accountability** *The Corporate Report* (ASSC 1976) stated that

> public accountability does not imply more than the responsibility to provide general purpose information. Whether or not subsequent questioning of action results will depend on the circumstances ...

Stewart (1984), however, recognized that public accountability required both (1) the provision of information and (2) evaluation of the action to be taken as a consequence, in other words 'holding to account', which may involve approval or blame (with consequent reward or penalty), dismissal, renewal of confidence or perhaps no action.

THE ACCOUNTANTS' TRADITIONAL MODEL

The accounting model of accountability is based on the idea that, in companies, the owners (or shareholders) are separate from the managers or directors and that there is a need for directors to be **accountable** to shareholders. The model originates in respect of companies, and company terminology is used in this section of the book. But the same model is often assumed to be applicable in a variety of different organizations: trade union officials are assumed to be accountable to their members, and local authorities to the local community (whether to voters or to local tax-payers). One of the defences of the ill-fated community charge (or 'poll tax') was that it would make local authorities more accountable. It was argued that local authorities should be accountable to those who paid local taxes, and as everyone had a vote and made use of local services everyone (however poor) should pay towards local authority expenses. As a result, voters (= local tax payers) could make the local authorities more accountable for how their money was spent. But the 'accountability' argument came from central government and may be seen as attempting to make local authorities more accountable to central government; this would have the effect of transferring some power to central government from local authorities.

There may be calls for greater 'public' accountability, but with some organizations it is less clear to whom accountability is due. Universities and churches may be accountable to their students, congregations and local communities; but accountability may also be due to a Higher Authority.

ORIGINS OF THE ACCOUNTANTS' MODEL

Accountability came to be important with the development of companies in the nineteenth century, such as those established to build railways, which required substantial capital. As large numbers of shareholders hand over control of their funds to directors whom they do not even know, there is a need for some mechanisms to monitor the directors' stewardship of those funds. Many early companies had unlimited liability[1] which meant that, if the companies found themselves in financial difficulties, their creditors could call upon the shareholders to put in more money. Investors could therefore find themselves losing not only their original investment but a great deal more. In such circumstances it was important that investors could trust the competence of the directors that they elected to manage their companies; individuals would not want to risk incurring unlimited losses in an organization where there were few safeguards. There is also the possibility that directors would prove to be fraudulent or more interested in their own remuneration, comforts, security and reputation than in satisfying the objectives of shareholders. Shareholders needed to make directors more 'accountable' to them.

When companies with limited liability could easily be established, following the 1855 Joint Stock Companies Act, there was an increased need to protect creditors. Shareholders were to some extent protected by the fact that they could lose

---

[1] Prior to 1844 companies could be established only by royal charter, or a special Act of Parliament, and there were no general requirements for accounting. The Joint Stock Companies Act of 1844 enabled companies with unlimited liability to be established by registration and included basic accounting requirements.

no more than the price of the shares in which they invested. If the company became insolvent, no call could be made on shareholders for more funds than they had originally committed and it was the creditors who would suffer. In this situation there is a case for accountability to creditors as well as to shareholders. The origins of the accountant's role in accountability can be seen in terms of providing information and reassurance to shareholders and to creditors.

The origins of the conventional accountants' model of accountability may be interpreted as if the shareholders (and perhaps the creditors) set up accountability mechanisms to serve their interests. An alternative view is that the accountability mechanisms are operated by the directors in their own interests: to be able to attract funds from shareholders and provide them with reassurances about their investment; to satisfy creditors of their company's financial reliability; and to legitimate their own actions.

The main elements of accountability were established by the various Companies Acts, beginning with the Joint Stock Companies Act, 1844, which introduced general incorporation by registration and also established the three elements of accountability that are central to modern accountancy.

ELEMENTS OF ACCOUNTABILITY

The main elements of accountability established by company law are (1) the production, (2) the audit and (3) the publication of accounting information and (4) the possibility of sanctions against directors.

1. The production of accounting information

The earliest companies acts required that adequate accounting records should be kept and that a balance sheet should be produced showing a true statement of capital stock and credits, property belonging to the company, debts due by the company and a distinct view of the profit or loss made during the preceding period. Subsequent legislation has steadily and substantially increased the amount of information that companies are required to produce. This has, to some extent, been supplemented by the various recommendations and standards produced by the professional accountancy bodies.

2. The audit of accounting information

The earliest companies acts required that balance sheets should be audited, although it was not specified who could be an auditor or that they should have any particular qualifications. More recent companies acts have established qualifications for auditors and controls on their activities, and made provisions to demonstrate their independence from directors. The role of the auditor is considered more fully in Chapter 3.

3. The publication of accounting information

The earliest legislation required that the balance sheet should be presented at annual general meetings, sent to every shareholder and filed with the Registrar of Joint Stock Companies. Company annual reports are 'published' in the sense that they are made public by being accessible at Companies House on payment of a nominal fee. With improvements in communications and the establishment of commercial organizations that will do 'searches', company accounts have steadily become more accessible.

The general trend of companies legislation since the 1844 Act has been to provide for additional information to be published and to strengthen the audit requirements. But there have been exceptions. In the late nineteenth century political attitudes favoured *laissez-faire* and it was increasingly left for companies themselves, their directors and shareholders, to determine the accounting and auditing requirements that they would adopt. The twentieth century has seen a steady series of Acts strengthening accounting and auditing requirements. The 1929 Act introduced the requirement to publish profit and loss accounts. The 1948 Act introduced substantial changes with new requirements for additional disclosure, the production of consolidated accounts and the need for auditors to be qualified. The 1967 Act required turnover to be disclosed for the first time and additional information had to be disclosed in the Directors report, including political and charitable contributions, and market values of investments. The 1980 Act laid down detailed requirements for determining the amount of profits that is available for distribution as dividends. The 1982 Act implemented the EC's Fourth Directive; it required standard formats for accounts for the first time, specified fundamental accounting principles and valuation rules and extended disclosure requirements. The 1985 Act was a major consolidating piece of legislation. The 1989 Companies Act implemented the Seventh and Eight Directives of the EC which deal with group accounts and the qualifications of auditors.

Although the Thatcher government (1979–90) espoused free market economics rather than state regulation, the trend to extend Companies Act requirements continued, to some extent influenced by the European Community. The only slackening was with regard to abbreviated accounts. The 1985 Act allowed small and medium-sized companies to file only abbreviated financial statements with the Registrar of Companies (although full accounts still have to be provided for shareholders). Small companies need not deliver a profit and loss account or a directors' report and may omit all information relating to directors' remuneration. Medium-sized companies can submit an abbreviated profit and loss account. The 1989 Act introduced a provision that allows listed companies to issue summary financial statements to shareholders, although they still have the right to receive full sets of accounts. Summary financial statements are much fuller than the abbreviated accounts that small companies can file with the registrar. Making use of this provision is likely to lead to substantial savings for companies, such as those privatized by the government, with very large numbers of shareholders.

At the time of writing there are continuing pressures for strengthening accounting, disclosure and audit requirements, particularly for listed companies. There are also pressures to exempt small companies from the substantial accounting requirements that are really designed for large companies and perhaps even to remove the audit requirement for small companies.

4. Sanctions

Some accountants may consider that the production of information that is audited and published (i.e. the rendering of an account) fulfils the requirements of accountability. But what happens if the account demonstrates that the directors' stewardship of the company has been a disaster? If the shareholders have no sanction against the directors, then they are unable to hold the directors to account in any meaningful way and it would be misleading to pretend that directors are accountable to shareholders.

If shareholders are dissatisfied with the directors' account, there are a number of sanctions that they can apply:

1. they can sell their shares;
2. they can express their dissatisfaction at the company's annual general meeting and seek to influence future actions by the directors and employees of the company; or
3. they can not re-elect the directors of the company.

5. Other elements

Some writers argue that the notion of accountability includes other elements in addition to those set out above. Sherer and Kent (1983), for example, following Tocher (1970), argue that there are three main elements to accountability: the organization; a statement about objectives; and information and the monitoring mechanism. This approach may be attractive to accountants as it can give the accountability role to the accountancy profession. Once they know what the organization is supposed to be doing, they can report on the success or otherwise in achieving that. The Principals and Agents may be effectively excluded from the process. The approach in this book is that accountability should involve the Principal having some power over the Agent; it is not sufficient for a third party to be able to give an account in accordance with their understanding of what is required and their understanding of what the Principal's objectives are, or should be. The Agent is not accountable unless the Principal can influence the account that is provided, as well as having some sanction if s/he considers the account to be unsatisfactory.

LIMITATIONS OF THE ACCOUNTANTS' MODEL

The accountants' model of accountability can be effective only if the four elements on which it is based operate adequately. In practice accountability is often less effective than might be expected. The **information** produced may be inadequate or misleading; the **auditing** may be subject to severe limitations; the information may be **published** in such a way that it is inaccessible to those to whom the company is supposed to be accountable; and there may be no effective **sanctions** against Agents (directors), even when the information produced shows that they are not doing what the Principal(s) want. The potential weaknesses of each of the four elements will now be considered in turn.

1. The information

When politicians seek re-election they produce election manifestos and election addresses that include whatever information they wish, selected and presented however they wish. Even if their record is generally very poor, it is always possible to select some statistics, comparisons, or periods where their performance looks good. The chairman's statement and some other parts of a company's annual report and accounts often look like an election address (as in a sense they are), with statistics selected to give a good impression of management. If Agents (whether politicians or directors) are free to select and present information in their own way, the 'account' is unlikely to be satisfactory from the Principal's point of view. Accountability is weakened to the extent that Agents control the content of the account. Effective accountability depends on the information being reliable and appropriate for controlling Agents. One of the main functions of the accounting profession, the Companies Acts and of the profession's accounting standards is to try to ensure that the information that has to be disclosed is established by law and by the accountancy profession and that directors cannot easily avoid disclosing uncomfortable facts. The accountancy profession's role in setting accounting standards is examined in Chapter 6.

There are, of course, weaknesses in the prescription of the information that has to be disclosed. It is often argued by particular groups in society that additional information ought to be disclosed to enable corporate activities to be assessed from the point of view of society, not just of investors. Each successive Companies Act, and most new accounting standards, require additional information to be disclosed. Within the accountancy profession there are recurring pressures for more or better information to be disclosed to meet a particular need or to deal with a particular problem. Each new accounting standard, and the discussion documents and exposure drafts that precede them, attempts clearer specifications of the information that should be disclosed.

There is, however, still considerable scope for 'creative accounting', and published accounts can be manipulated to present an unrealistically favourable view of a company's position and performance. Questionable aspects of the company's finances are often tucked away in obscure notes to the accounts, while the more favourable aspects of performance are portrayed in glowing terms, and illustrated with pictures, graphs and diagrams, often selected with the help of public relations experts. Extensive information is available, but it is often not as true and fair as shareholders would like, and needs to be interpreted with care.

2. The audit

Audited information is probably 'better' than unaudited information. If information is to be the basis on which directors are made accountable, that information must be credible (and perhaps even true!). If no one checked up on the directors' version of events they could more easily mislead investors into thinking that they were doing a good job on behalf of the shareholders and they could hide the extent to which they line their own pockets at the shareholders' expense.

The limitations of conventional audits, and the 'expectations gap' between what the public seem to expect of auditors and what auditors think that their role should be, are discussed in Chapter 3. In terms of the effectiveness of accountability it is particularly worth mentioning the following two points.

1. The question of auditor independence. If auditors are concerned about earning additional fees by providing non-audit services to the company, their independence may be compromised. Auditors who insist on exposing to shareholders any possible wrong-doing by directors, such as taking undisclosed perks, are less well placed to earn additional fees than those who see it as being their main function to please the directors.
2. Pressure on fee income. In an increasingly competitive climate there is a tendency for auditors to be forced to 'bid' to retain clients and to tender very low figures. In this situation it may be that the quality of the audit suffers.

Directors can reduce the power and independence of the auditors by keeping audit fees as low as possible and keeping them sweet with the prospect of remunerative additional work in tax, consultancy and so on.

It seems that in most cases auditors play a valuable role in inhibiting the worst excesses of creative accounting. But there are serious questions about auditor independence. It sometimes seems as if directors have colonized or taken control of the accountability mechanisms that are supposed to control them. If the directors exert too powerful an influence over accounting and auditing, then these functions can serve to legitimate and defend the directors and, in effect, make them less accountable to shareholders or to anyone else.

3. Publication

If Agents are to be accountable to Principals there must be appropriate and credible information that is **available** to the Agents. As company annual reports are published in the sense that they are sent to shareholders, and publicly available at Companies House, they are sufficiently available to shareholders. But companies are also in a sense accountable to creditors and perhaps to other groups in society, and it could be argued that it is an inconvenience to have to go to Companies House to see their annual reports. In the case of smaller companies they might have to rely on abbreviated accounts that contain less information than is available to shareholders. Recent changes have therefore reduced the effectiveness of publication of accountability information, particularly for non-shareholders.

The effectiveness of annual reports as accountability mechanisms is also limited by the fact that they are not usually available until some months after the year end and the information that they contain is necessarily dated.

Company annual reports and accounts may be inaccessible in that the terminology and assumptions upon which they are based are difficult and obscure for all but the expert reader. In some cases it seems that parts of annual accounts, particularly obscure footnotes, are deliberately written in such a way as to conceal information. Accounting expertise to some extent protects directors and others from being made accountable – except to those with equivalent expertise. Attempts by Principals to obtain a satisfactory account may be frustrated if the Agent can hide behind jargon, expertise and special knowledge. In director–shareholder relationships it is frequently the case that directors' power is enhanced by their access to information and expertise that it is more difficult for their Principals to obtain. Information can enhance directors' power; and directors' power enhances their ability to obtain superior information.

Accountability depends on appropriate information being made available, but a published annual report of the sort with which accountants are familiar is not the only way of achieving this. More general rights of access to information are discussed on p. 42.

4. Sanctions

If shareholders of a listed company do not like what they read in their company's annual report and accounts they can simply sell their shares; or they can express their dissatisfaction and seek to influence directors' future behaviour; or they can oppose the re-election of directors. In practice each of these has particular difficulties.

In an unlisted company there may be no ready market for the shares and it may be very difficult to sell them. In a listed company it is easy to sell the shares, but as soon as there is bad news in the wind, share prices tend to fall. By the time the individual shareholder receives and studies a company's annual report and accounts, and concludes that s/he wants to sell them, the stock market will already be reflecting the new interpretations of the company's prospects and the share price will already have reacted. The new share price may be so low that the shareholder has already lost out and may prefer not to sell.

Selling shares can be an effective sanction against directors who perform badly. If enough people sell and the share price falls substantially, the company may become the target for a takeover bid. If the bidder is not satisfied with the directors' performance, the directors may soon find themselves without the remuneration and perks that they previously enjoyed. Selling shares, and a low share price, may indicate a lack of confidence in directors and lead to difficulties in the company obtaining capital, and perhaps even in surviving.

But selling shares is only an indirect influence on directors. It is more like withdrawing from a situation because you are unable to make your Agents effectively accountable. Longstreth (1990) notes that 'shareholders of public corporations are becoming less and less able to hold management to account', and that it is becoming easier just to 'exit' partly because of the 'multiplicity of interests within the "ownership" group [that] create diffusion and increased potential for conflicts, [and so] shareholders are becoming less and less interested in holding management to account'.

It is difficult to have a direct influence on directors' behaviour, particularly for small shareholders (Cruickshank, 1991). It is possible to speak and vote at annual general meetings, but the directors usually have sufficient proxy votes in their pockets to prevent anything that happens at the meeting from affecting the out-come. It is also difficult to have a direct influence on the composition of the board of directors, for similar reasons; contested elections are extremely rare and a board of directors tends to be a self-perpetuating group. The board is likely to be concerned to keep a small number of major shareholders happy, particularly institutional shareholders. Where there are individuals who own significant numbers of shares, for example where family companies are involved, they are likely to be represented on the board.

Major institutional shareholders can influence company policy, and the com-position of the board. The relationship between directors and such investors is sometimes criticized for being too cosy. The favoured few investors may be invited to special lunches and briefings, and there is the danger that they could use any information gained to their advantage in dealing in the company's shares. Such 'insider dealing' is illegal, but is hard to detect. Powerful institutional investors may be interested in developing a close relationship with particular companies in order to make the directors more accountable; they could also be interested in gaining whatever advantages there may be for themselves in such relationships. Jensen (1989) argues that the high costs of being an active investor have left institutions almost completely uninvolved in the major decisions and long-term strategies of the companies their clients own. There may be exceptions to this but, in general, provided directors can avoid the threat of a hostile take-over bid, they remain secure in their positions.

The conventional accounting model of accountability tends to assume that directors and shareholders are on different sides; that directors might use their shareholders' money to line their own pockets instead of acting in the best interests of the shareholders. The established accountability mechanisms restrict most such excesses. But there are sometimes criticisms that directors' remuneration is excessive; that they have extravagant lifestyles at the company's expense; that they use company resources to further their own ambitions instead of maximizing the wealth of their shareholders; that when the company is doing well they reward themselves through generous 'incentive' payments, and share option schemes that are intended to enable them to buy shares in the company at favourable prices; that when the company does badly their remuneration tends not to be reduced accordingly; that even when they are no longer competent their fellow directors reward them with massive golden handshakes; and that they sometimes use 'creative accounting' techniques to give an unduly favourable impression of the company's performance. All of this, however, does not necessarily work to the shareholders' disadvantage. Provided the company can maintain a reasonable growth record in dividends, the appearance of increasing profits and confidence in the share price, then any 'excesses' by the directors may not matter to the shareholders. In order to keep share prices high, shareholders may be happy to collude in the myth that the directors are doing a splendid job. If a chairman or director's performance turns out to be a disaster, share prices may be adversely affected if this is admitted; it may be better to give him or her a generous golden handshake as a reward for good service.

Directors are generally also shareholders in the company that they run, and may have options to buy shares. They are likely to be at least as interested as other shareholders in maintaining and increasing share prices, by whatever means are likely to be successful. It is therefore unrealistic to assume that directors and shareholders necessarily have different interests, and accountability mechanisms should be designed with this in mind. It may even be that shareholders have an interest in colluding with ineffective accountability mechanisms. Those who claim to represent a society may call for full disclosure of 'the facts' when a company gets into financial difficulties, or has used creative accounting to exaggerate its profits, or is attempting to buy another company on the cheap, using their own company's overvalued shares as paper currency. But directors and shareholders may both be interested in keeping these matters quiet. They are also likely to be in favour of impressive looking Companies Act disclosure requirements and published accounts verified by auditors if these serve to legitimate the version of events that they wish to present.

In a small, family-run company there may be real dangers that the few directors who manage the company could use the company's limited resources for their own benefit at the expense of other shareholders. The difference between directors' remuneration of £30 000 per annum and £60 000 per annum may be the difference between profit and loss, dividends and no dividends. In a major listed company, however, the difference between £30 000 remuneration and £300 000 remuneration may have no effect on shareholders' wealth. The amounts of directors' remuneration are unlikely to reduce the amount of dividends paid, or the share price. It may even be that stock-market investors have more confidence in companies that are run by prestigious directors who are able to command such high salaries.

The accountability mechanisms that emerged in the nineteenth century no longer seem appropriate for major companies where share price appears to be more important to shareholders than the fear that directors will enrich themselves at the company's expense. Although the traditional model of accountability has succeeded in removing the worst excesses, in many ways companies and their directors have become too powerful in society and there are no effective accountability mechanisms to control their excesses. Rubner (1965) was concerned about 'our modern managerial autocrats who are driven by vanity, paternalism or intoxication for power to oppress and deceive their shareholders'. His thesis was that directors should not have the freedom to retain profits for their own purposes; all profits should be paid out to the shareholders, and it was for the shareholders, not the directors, to decide whether such profits should be reinvested in the company. More recently Sibley (1990) referred to ethical investors who may wish to avoid companies that are run by a single powerful individual who 'could be accused of megalomania, of rampant greed, of inordinate arrogance ... [or] ... of running a public company as a personal fief'. After the death of Robert Maxwell there was some evidence that shareholders were avoiding investing in such companies, and their share prices suffered accordingly. It seems that share price can be a more effective restriction on the activities of directors than the accountants' traditional accountability mechanisms.

There have been some attempts by groups of shareholder activists to influence company policy and to elect directors other than those (re)nominated by existing directors. But such attempts are exceptional and rarely successful. An attempt by an activist group of members of the Abbey National Building Society ('Abbey Members Against Flotation' or AMAF) to oppose their directors' proposal to convert the society to a company and a bank failed, as did their attempt to secure the election of their nominees to the board. AMAF argued (Perks, 1991) that their failure was due to the power that the directors had to present their own case, and to obstruct AMAF's attempts to present a different view to members, rather than to the case itself. The directors were able to use the Society's funds to contact all members of the Society, to employ public relations consultants, to produce expensive literature and to pay for advertising; their case was also legitimated by lawyers and accountants, although their case was seriously flawed and was subsequently severely criticized by the Building Societies Commission. The legal and accounting mechanisms that AMAF thought were there to protect members from directors were used by directors to their own advantage. AMAF's request for a Special General Meeting of members was refused by the directors on a legal technicality; and AMAF had insufficient resources to challenge this, or to circulate members. The directors refused to give AMAF's address to members who requested it. Although the directors were required to distribute statements by AMAF candidates seeking election to the board to all members of the society, they arranged dates of meetings and distributions so that most members would have voted on the proposed conversion before they received AMAF statements. The directors were able to use their position to ensure that most members received only the official point of view, powerfully presented. Although there are differences between company law and building society law, the case does illustrate how difficult it is for shareholders to challenge the position and view of the board.

In a democratic society it is assumed that those in a position of power are accountable to society. As major international corporations become more powerful, sometimes more powerful than national governments, we need to consider the accountability of those who control such organizations. The question of accountability to society is considered in Chapter 4. But there appear to be serious weaknesses in the accountability of companies and directors even to their own shareholders.

OTHER VIEWS OF ACCOUNTABILITY

The term 'accountability' is used in a wide range of different contexts other than the traditional accounting model, which is concerned with directors' stewardship of shareholders' resources, as outlined above. Accountants are involved in many of these other systems of accountability.

THE CORPORATE REPORT

The Corporate Report adopted a very wide view of accountability. The authors' proposals applied not only to companies but to every significant economic entity. All such entities were seen as having an implicit responsibility to report publicly, whether or not this was required by law or regulation. They saw responsibility for **public accountability** as being in addition to legal obligations, and argued that it 'arises from the custodial role played in the community by economic entities'. They worked on the assumption that an all-purpose report should seek to satisfy, as far as possible, the information needs of a wide variety of different 'users' of such reports.

The various user groups identified by *The Corporate Report* were so extensive as to include just about everyone. The **equity investor group** included existing and potential shareholders. The **loan creditor group** included existing and potential holders of loan stock. The **employee group** included existing, potential and past employees. In addition there was an **analyst adviser group** that included financial analysts, economists, statisticians, researchers, trade unions, stockbrokers, and credit rating agencies. The **business contact group** included customers, trade creditors and suppliers, competitors, business rivals and those interested in mergers and takeovers. **The government** included the tax authorities and departments of central and local government. And, in case there was anyone left who had not been included (at least once!) in the above groups, there was **the public**, including taxpayers, ratepayers, consumers and other community and special interest groups such as political parties, consumer and environmental protection societies and regional pressure groups. All of these were seen as having a reasonable right to information, and corporate reports were expected to deal with their information needs.

After identifying the users *The Corporate Report* went on to identify their information needs. As the users seemed to be just about everyone, so their information needs seemed to be just about everything. In particular *The Corporate Report* recommended that six additional statements should be published as follows:

1. a statement of value added;
2. an employment report;
3. a statement of money exchanges with the government;
4. a statement of transactions in foreign currency;
5. a statement of future prospects; and
6. a statement of corporate objectives.

The extent to which these have been implemented in practice varies. The first two may be seen as aspects of corporate social reporting and have at times been the fashion of the day; their rise and fall is discussed in Chapter 4. The second two have made little progress, but information appropriate for the final two has at times been included in company annual reports. *The Corporate Report* made a valuable contribution to the debate on widening the involvement of accountants in the accountability of many different organizations in society to many different interest groups in society. It relied exclusively on the publication of general purpose annual reports that were expected to meet the many different needs of various user groups identified. The ideas of corporate social reporting that are implicit in *The Corporate Report* are examined in Chapter 4.

ACCOUNTABILITY IN THE PUBLIC SECTOR

The term **public accountability** may be applied to any entity where it is assumed that there is a responsibility to the public. This is most clearly established, and most wide-ranging, in public sector organizations. Accountability may be at a relatively low level. Fiscal accountability, for example, is concerned with whether the funds were spent as stated and on the project for which they were intended. Or it may be at a higher level: for achieving objectives and ultimately to the electorate for the policies pursued. Stewart (1984) presents this as a 'ladder of accountability' with each step dealing with different bases of accountability, as follows:

1. accountability for probity is concerned with avoiding malfeasance;
2. accountability for legality is concerned with ensuring that the powers given by the law are not exceeded;
3. process accountability is concerned with efficiency and ensuring that resources are not wasted; and with avoiding maladministration, particularly that leading to injustice;
4. performance accountability is concerned with whether performance meets required standards;
5. programme accountability is concerned with the effectiveness of programmes in achieving the objectives set for them;
6. policy accountability is concerned with the setting of policy for which accountability is to the electorate.

This form of presentation has the advantage of distinguishing between the lower rungs of the ladder and the higher rungs. Accountability on the lower rungs is more likely to be achieved through accounting mechanisms and standards; the higher rungs are more dependent on personal judgement. In the public sector there is increasing emphasis on the higher rungs, and concern with economy, efficiency and effectiveness and performance measurement are dealt with more fully in Chapter 5. In the private sector accountants are more concerned with the lower rungs of the ladder and it is often assumed that market forces protect the public and avoid the need for the sorts of accountability shown on the higher rungs of the ladder.

MANAGERIAL ACCOUNTABILITY

Managerial accountability is concerned with the relationship of subordinates to their 'superiors' in hierarchical organizations. Employees are seen as being accountable to their bosses for performing particular tasks. Management accounting systems, such as budgetary control, are often involved in monitoring their performance. The organization is expected to operate on the basis of a coherent plan; any deviations from that plan are monitored; and responsibility or blame can be attributed to the individual responsible for budget concerned. Accounting systems can reinforce this simplistic view of management, and senior managers are likely to favour a system that attributes blame to more junior colleagues when things go wrong.

In the accountability relationship between directors (the Agents) and shareholders (the Principals), the agents are in a powerful position to influence the flow of information to the Principal. In managerial situations the superiors (Principals) are usually more powerful than their subordinates (Agents). The provision of accounting information therefore serves to enhance the power of the Principals over their Agents (the bosses over their subordinates). In providing information to shareholders the position is more likely to be the other way around: the Agents have more power over the information supplied and the accountability process can enhance the power position of the directors (Agents) over the shareholders (Principals). In both situations the processes of accountants and accountability tend to support the power position of directors and senior management.

In a hierarchical situation subordinates may attempt to reduce the extent to which they are controlled by the accountability systems that are imposed by their superiors. Managerial accountability can be undermined if subordinates are able to influence the information that is supplied. In some situations it may be possible for divisional managers, for example, especially if situated a long way from the managers to whom they report, to have a major influence on the accounting reports that they produce. They may hope that they will have earned promotion to another position before their apparently successful record is questioned. In a managerial hierarchy there may be a continuing struggle between superiors and subordinates to gain control over the mechanisms of accountability.

THE DEVELOPING CONCEPT OF ACCOUNTABILITY

There have been important changes in the ideas associated with accountability. In the 1970s, for example, there were pressures to widen accountability: more and more organizations were expected to be accountable to an increasingly wide range of different interest groups, and even to society as a whole. In the 1980s there were also calls for increased accountability, and the term public account-ability was much in evidence. Central government saw itself as representing the public interest, and organizations such as universities, local authorities and poly-technics were expected to be more publicly accountable for the resources that they used. But the emphasis was on the provision of information to central government rather than to a wider public.

Those who call for increased accountability usually see themselves as being the Principals, and they expect that those who they consider should be their agents should be made more accountable to them. A call for increased account-ability is a call by Principals for more power over Agents. The 1970s version of accountability was a call for all those with an interest in organizations, whether as employees, consumers, local residents or investors, to have more control over those organizations. The 1980s version of accountability was a call for central government to have more power over the various organizations that receive public funds.

The implication of this argument is that accountability is a subjugating force; that it tends to reduce the freedom of those who can be controlled by Principals. Employees may be increasingly restricted and frustrated by managerial controls that are intended to make them more accountable to their superiors. Attempts to impose increased accountability on employees may result in taking responsibility away from them and lead them to be more interested in complying with the requirements that the bureaucratic controls impose than with taking responsibility for their actions.

Some writers (Roberts, 1991; Roberts and Scapens, 1985; Arrington, 1990) take the view that the process of being held to account determines, reflects, reifies, strengthens and solidifies power relationships between Principals and Agents, and this may be seen as an odious activity – exploitative and suppressive. But this does not have to be the case. Roberts (1991) would prefer to 'recover accountability from the apparently mesmeric grip of Accounting' and to see less hierarchical forms of organizational accountability that give more recognition to interdependencies within organizations. Authors such as Gray (1991) see accountability as 'an emancipatory concept helping to expose, enhance and develop social relationships through a re-examination and expansion of established rights to information'. They recognize the difficulty in determining some empirical base for such rights, as opposed simply to asserting what one's own faith demands as rights. Extending rights of access to information may prove to be liberating and emancipating. But traditional models of accountability, largely determined and operated by accountants and based on the publication of annual reports, are not well suited to this objective.

An increase in accountability is likely to lead to a shift in power from Agents to Principals. Whether and where increases in accountability are desirable depends on the view taken about the power positions of different groups in society. Central government and directors of companies are both in powerful positions over others, if only because of the substantial resources that they can command. If they are seen as being too powerful there will be calls for them to be made more accountable, whether to Parliament, the public, shareholders, or whatever interest group is represented by those calling for increased accountability. An area of future concern may be the extent to which directors should be made accountable to governments. It may even be that some companies will sometimes expect some governments to be more accountable to them!

Employees who see accountability mechanisms taking power and responsibility away from them are likely to want to be less accountable, or to turn managerial hierarchies on their head. Perhaps 'superiors' in an organization should be made accountable to their 'subordinates' to help the latter achieve their objectives. Employees may seek to improve their position through trade unions, but those who fear trade unions becoming too powerful are likely to want to make them more accountable; whether to their members, the public or the government hardly matters: if they are more accountable they are less powerful.

Accountants tend to assume that accountability is concerned with the provision of information by accountants in a fairly standard format. The involvement of accountants inevitably results in such information reflecting the assumptions and position of accountants: conventional accounting formats predominate, and the information can be biased by those who have power over the accountants. If accountability is to be an emancipatory concept that helps to liberate those in society who are less powerful, it is important that information is made available in accordance with their needs, without being biased by intermediaries. But as the various different individuals who may wish to be Principals are likely to want different information, it is not possible to produce a single account that satisfies all needs. It may therefore be more appropriate if Principals had open access to information so that they can obtain whatever information they wish.

The idea of freedom of access to information for individuals is a more emancipatory concept than accountability mechanisms that are ordained by accountants. But many would argue that it is impractical, and that is why accountants and auditors have taken on the roles that they do. In the United States, however, the principles of freedom of information regarding government activity are seen as an important democratic right. In the UK local residents have extensive rights of access to financial information in local authorities. And the Data Protection Act allows people the right of access to information about themselves that is kept on computer records by any organization. In practice there do not appear to be problems with too many people trying to obtain too much information. Few people in practice take up their rights. The argument that allowing freedom of access to information would be too costly or impractical is, to some extent, an excuse put forward by those who do not want to see their freedom of action circumscribed by others having the right to know what they are doing.

Most people are not well placed to determine and understand the information that they want, but, when issues of public concern arise, politicians and investigative journalists tend to unearth and make use of whatever information is available. The conventional accounting model tends to assume that information is provided to users who then make decisions on the basis of that information. One of the problems with this is that by the time a user has received the information it is often too late to do anything with it. A more effective restriction on the activities of powerful individuals is the knowledge that some of the things that they do can eventually become public. Anti-social activities are more likely if they can be kept secret. The fear of disclosure can be a powerful deterrent.

SUMMARY AND CONCLUSIONS

Power and accountability are intertwined. Attempts to impose accountability are attempts to restrict power. But the way in which accountancy operates tends to mirror and enhance existing power relationships. The extent to which accountants' approaches to accountability can **change** power relationships is limited. There are important differences between the ways in which accountability operates in (1) director–shareholder relationships in companies; (2) managerial relationships; and (3) the public sector.

1. In director–shareholder relationships the accountability mechanisms are largely controlled by the directors, and do little to restrict the powers of directors. The directors are well placed to embroider the account of their activities that they give to shareholders; they use auditors to add credibility to their account; and they are usually (re-)elected unopposed. Directors use the argument that they are accountable only to their shareholders to avoid other restrictions and to frustrate attempts to impose wider accountability responsibilities upon them.

2. In managerial relationships accounting information is often central to the accountability relationships. The 'subordinate' is accountable, in a hierarchical relationship, to the 'superior'. The superior usually controls the form of the account, and the subordinate's power is effectively restricted.

3. In the public sector the various organizations are accountable to the public. But the public is too large and diffuse to have an effective say on how accountability should operate. The most powerful party, central government, acting in the name of the public, calls for increased accountability (from local authorities, hospitals, universities and so on) to central government.

If we think of Agents as being accountable to Principals, there are three possibilities: (1) the Principals control the process; (2) the Agents control the process; and (3) it is unclear who controls the process and there is a struggle between Principals and Agents. In any of these situations either party may call for increased accountability to strengthen its position, but it is likely to be most obvious in the third situation. The conventional accounting model derives mainly from the accountability of the directors of companies to their shareholders. Major companies and their directors have become increasingly powerful in society, and corporate governance, accountability and the actual and potential role of auditors in this are becoming major issues for society. These are addressed in the following chapters.

Accountability, seen as a process that involves a relationship between Principals and Agents, may be dominated by (1) Principals, or (2) Agents, or it may be (3) a continuing power struggle between the different parties. Another possibility is (4) that it may be dominated by an independent third party. Auditors may be expected to fulfil this role. The way in which they do so and differences between the public sector and the private sector are examined in the following chapter. Broader aspects of accountability in relation to employees, the environment and so on are dealt with in Chapter 4.

Accountancy and accountability can be compared with the strings that are used to control a marionette puppet. Companies and major organizations are assumed to be the puppets that need to be controlled. Shareholders and society are assumed to be pulling the strings – and ensuring that their puppets do as they wish. Academics and the accountancy profession are busy studying and redesigning the strings. But some are beginning to notice that the puppets are gaining control of the strings. The mechanisms of accountability, which are assumed to control Agents, are being colonized by the Agents. Agents can use accountability as a mask which legitimates and hides their activities and protects them from external control.

FURTHER READING

Accounting Standards Steering Committee (ASSC) (1975) *The Corporate Report*.

Gray, R., Owen, D. and Maunders, K. (1987) *Corporate Social Reporting, Accounting and Accountability*, Prentice Hall.

Sherer, M. and Kent, D. (1983) *Auditing and Accountability*, Pitman, London.

Journals

Financial Accountability and Management, Basil Blackwell; mainly public sector and charities.

Accounting, Auditing and Accountability Journal, MCB University Press; more general.

ESSAY AND DISCUSSION TOPICS

1. In the conventional accounting model who is the Principal and who is the Agent? Why is the Agent accountable to the Principal?
2. If you were the major shareholder in a company (but too busy as a student to take part in running it), in what ways would you want the management of the company to be accountable to you?
3. How would you know if the management of a major listed company were useless? What sanctions can be operated against them?
4. In what ways do accountants and auditors make accountability more effective than it might be without them? In what ways do they make it less effective?
5. To whom are the following accountable?

    (a) a university professor;
    (b) a bishop;
    (c) the finance director of a listed company;
    (d) a police officer.

    What form of account might be appropriate to discharge that accountability?
6. How does accountability in the public sector differ from accountability in the private sector?

7. Assess the contribution of *The Corporate Report* to the concept of accountability.

REFERENCES

Accounting Standards Steering Committee (ASSC), (1975) *The Corporate Report.*

Arrington, E. (1990) Intellectual tyranny and the public interest: the quest for the grail and the quality of life, *Advances in Public Interest Accounting*, 1–16.

Cruickshank, J. (1991) The small shareholder and the big company, *Management Accounting*, Jan., 20–1.

Gray, R. (1991) Accounting and environmentalism: an exploration of the challenge of gently accounting for accountability, transparency and sustainability. University of Dundee Discussion Paper, July.

Jackson, P. M. (1982) *The Political Economy of Bureaucracy*, Philip Allan.

Jensen M. C. (1989) *Harvard Business Review*, Sep./Oct.

Longstreth, B. (1990) Takeovers, corporate governance and stock ownership: some disquieting trends, *Journal of Portfolio Management*, **16**(3), 54–9.

Perks, R. W. (1991) The fight to stay mutual: Abbey Members Against Flotation versus Abbey National Building Society, *Annals of Public and Co-operative Economics*, **62**(3), 393–429.

Roberts, J. (1991) The possibilities of accountability, *Accounting, Organizations and Society*, **16**(4), 355–70.

Roberts, J. and Scapens, R. (1985) Accounting systems, and systems of accountability, *Accounting, Organizations and Society,* 443–56.

Rubner, A. (1965) *The Ensnared Shareholder: Directors and the Modern Corporation*, Macmillan, London.

Sherer, M. and Kent, D. (1983) *Auditing and Accountability*, Pitman, London.

Sibley, A. (1990) The City's conscience, *The Accountant's Magazine*, Jan.

Stewart, J. D. (1984) The role of information in public accountability, in *Issues in Public Sector Accounting* (eds A. Hopwood and C. Tomkins), Philip Allen, Oxford.

Tocher, K. (1970) Control, *Operational Research Quarterly*, June, 159–80.

3 The role of auditing in society

ORIGINS AND DEFINITION OF AUDITING

The terms 'accountancy profession' and 'auditing profession' are sometimes used almost interchangeably and auditing has provided the bread and butter of the accountancy profession for the best part of a century. But this was not always the case. Most of the major international accountancy firms can trace their origins back to the 1840s in London and the first professional accountancy bodies began in 1854 (Scotland) and 1870 (England). But most of their early work was in insolvencies and accountancy rather than in auditing. The pre-eminence of auditing within the accountancy profession was not established until towards the end of the nineteenth century.

> *The Accountant* began to appear in 1874, and ... in its first half-a-dozen years the reader must look closely to find material in its pages which is not to do with insolvencies. (Kitchen, 1982)

In the 1860s professional auditors were the exception; accountants were generally seen as being associated with, and dependent upon insolvency work (Cooper 1921).

Kitchen states that the first book on auditing came out in 1881 and that probably the first fully reported lecture on auditing was in 1882. By the time Brown's *History of Accounting* appeared in 1905 the author was able to state that most accountants would regard their auditing department as the most regular and, on the whole, the most remunerative portion of their practice. He added that this was certainly not the case twenty or thirty years earlier (Brown, 1905).

The origins of auditing are, however, much older than the accountancy profession, and can be traced at least as far back as biblical times. For as long as accounting records have been kept and the stewardship of resources was entrusted by their owner to another, it seems likely that there was some sort of checking of the records kept by the steward. Mills (1990) states that

> historians have long held that the audit has been a valued activity throughout recorded history and that 'every society which has developed systematic record keeping has also produced some kind of account verification'. (Chatfield, 1977)

The word derives from the Latin *auditus*, meaning hearing, and early audits, for example in medieval England, were based on an annual hearing of the accounts.

The modern form of statutory audit began with the 1844 Companies Act which required the annual appointment of auditors by shareholders. Very often the shareholders simply appointed one of their own number, probably not an accountant, and these 'auditors' had the right to inspect the companies' books, and to receive assistance from the companies' employees in conducting the audit. Subsequent legislation extended the remit and provisions to protect the independence of the auditor, and professionally qualified accountants steadily took over the auditing function. It was the 1948 Companies Act that first established professional accountancy qualifications as a requirement to become a company auditor.

An audit is based on an official examination of accounts with verification by reference to witnesses and vouchers. The accountancy profession has tended to dominate the meaning of the word 'audit' and there is a danger that those who study the subject may simply accept that auditing is, and should be, as it is laid down by the accountancy profession. But meanings of words change over time, and various different groups in society advocate different kinds of audit at different times. To some extent the profession responds to such changing shifts and may become involved in social audits, energy audits, environmental audits, perhaps audits of citizen's charters and whatever else may be the concerns of the day. But we should not assume that the only approach to auditing is that carried out by professional accountancy firms in relation to company accounts.

Within the subject areas of accountancy the term 'audit' is most commonly used in connection with the verification of published financial statements as an element of the process of accountability. Chapter 2 introduced the idea of accountability in terms of Principals (to whom accountability is due) and Agents. It was concerned that Agents might dominate the accountability process and so limit its effectiveness. One way to avoid the process being dominated by either Principals or Agents is to place it largely in the hands of a third party, such as the auditors. This chapter is concerned with the involvement of accountants as auditors in the process of accountability.

Accountants are also very much involved in the areas of **internal audit, management audit, social audit** and **value for money audit**.

Internal auditing is conventionally seen as an element of the internal control system set up by the management of an organization to review accounting, financial and other operations. External auditors take account of the work done by internal auditors, and a company's management may hope that, if an internal audit department does a good job, then the external auditors' fees may be reduced accordingly. But internal auditing is also an emerging profession in its own right. It is seen as

> an independent appraisal function established within an organization to examine and evaluate its activities as a service to the organization. The objective of internal auditing is to assist members of the organization in the effective discharge of their responsibilities. To this end, internal auditing furnishes them with analyses, appraisals, recommendations, counsel and information concerning the activities reviewed. (IIA, 1981)

Management audit takes a wider view than internal audit. It is intended to be an independent review of the performance of management with a view to making recommendations for improvements in policies and procedures. A management audit is likely to have more credibility if it is undertaken by external auditors or consultants than if it is undertaken internally by a group who will be assumed by many to have their own axes to grind.

The idea of **social audit** is concerned with appraising and reporting on the social impacts of an organization, and particularly with verifying such reports. It is discussed in Chapter 4. **Value for money audit**, which is concerned with monitoring an organization's economy, efficiency and effectiveness, is examined in Chapter 5.

THE OBJECTIVES OF AUDITING

Auditors are not noted for being of a philosophical disposition and are more inclined to get on with the job of auditing, and vaguely assume that it must fulfil a valuable purpose rather than question what the objectives of an audit might be. But auditing texts often include some discussion of the objectives of audit, although it is hard to see how an audit, or auditing, can have objectives. The

auditor may have objectives (such as earning a living); governments may have objectives in establishing legislation requiring audits (such as preventing financial scandals); **professional bodie**s may have objectives in establishing guidelines and standards for the conduct of audits (such as enhancing the reputation of auditors); **company directors** may have objectives in dealing with auditors (such as persuading auditors to support the directors' point of view). But auditing itself can hardly have an objective. The distinction is important because if we are to understand how auditing operates in society we must understand that what actually happens is the result of interplay between different groups in society who may have different objectives.

The formal role of the auditor in society is determined mainly by company law. The duty of auditors, as laid down by the Companies Act 1985 (Section 237) is 'to carry out such investigations as will enable them to form an opinion as to ... whether proper accounting records have been kept, [and] whether the ... balance sheet and profit and loss account are in agreement with the accounting records and returns'.

If the auditors are of the opinion that proper accounting records have not been kept, or that the balance sheet and profit and loss account are not in agreement with those records, or if they fail to obtain all the information and explanations which, to the best of their knowledge and belief, are necessary for the purposes of their audit, they should state the fact(s) in their report.

The Companies Act gives substantial powers to auditors in the carrying out of their duties. They have the right of access at all times to the company's books, accounts and vouchers, and are entitled to require from the company's officers such information and explanations as they think necessary for the performance of their duties.

Auditors are required to make an annual report to members of the company stating whether the financial statements have been properly prepared in accordance with the Companies Act (1985), and

> whether in their opinion a true and fair view is given –
> (i)   in the balance sheet, of the state of the company's affairs at the end of the financial year [and]
> (ii) in the profit and loss account ... of the company's profit or loss for the financial year (Section 236)

There is also specific legislation about the appointment of auditors and their removal; there are provisions to safeguard their independence; and there are provisions allowing auditors to present their case to shareholders where auditors leave office following disagreements with directors. The legal position regarding some matters likely to be of concern to society is less clear; some of these are examined in the following sections.

If the auditing function is to be justified in society it must serve some purpose(s) other than meeting Companies Act requirements: governments must have good reasons for passing Companies Acts with provisions for auditing. The conventional explanation in auditing texts, and in the profession's literature, is that the main function of auditing is to add credibility to financial statements. But accounts cannot portray a single, undeniable version of the truth; they can only reflect a particular view of financial performance and position. There are advantages in having a single version of a company's accounts produced, provided it has credibility. If there were a number of different versions in circulation, the information would be less useful. Which should investors and creditors believe? Adding credibility to financial statements can be seen as being a valuable part of the operation of a private enterprise system in which investments are made in shares on the basis of credible information that is made publicly available.

FRAUD AND ERROR

Society may expect auditors to help to detect and prevent fraud and accounting errors, but the auditor's role in relation to this is not clear-cut and has changed over time. If there is fraud and error of such magnitude as to mean that the financial statements do not show 'a true and fair view', it is clear that the auditor must disclose this. But what constitutes 'a true and fair view' is less clear; this is discussed below. It may be unrealistic to expect the auditor to discover every little error, fraud and petty theft, and it is difficult to establish a point at which such matters are so large that only an incompetent auditor would fail to notice them. If it is the directors or senior management of the company who are guilty of fraud or of misrepresenting the company's financial position and performance, then the auditor's position is particularly difficult.

The first Companies Act (1844) required the audit report to state whether or not the company's balance sheet gave a 'full and fair' view – a phrase which was generally taken to mean that the company's solvency was properly portrayed from the point of view of the company's creditors (Lee, 1972). But an 1859 judgment stated that it was part of the auditor's duties to discover fraudulent misrepresentations and this 'was the start of fraud and error detection as the major company audit objective for the next eighty years of so' (Lee, 1972). There was increasing recognition that auditors could not be expected to discover **all** fraud, and in the famous *Kingston Cotton Mill Co.* [1896] case the judge remarked that the auditor's role was more akin to that of a watch-dog than that of a bloodhound. But the discovery of fraud was still a primary objective of the audit.

In the period between the two world wars there was increasing recognition of the importance of providing information to investors and by 1948 it was recognized that the auditors' main role was in relation to the credibility of financial statements rather than in the detection of fraud.

If, however, auditors do discover fraud by employees they have a responsibility, in accordance with the accounting profession's Auditing Practices Committee guidelines, to report such fraud to management. A qualified audit report would be required by law if proper accounting records had not been maintained, or if the auditor had not been able to obtain all necessary information and explanations (or if the fraud was such that the financial statements did not portray a true and fair view). Otherwise there is generally no requirement for auditors to report fraud outside the company. No responsibility to society is assumed. In some circumstance auditors may wish to disclose wrongdoing if only for fear of legal action by aggrieved parties who felt that they had been misled by the auditor's report. But as the auditor also owes a duty of confidentiality to the company, s/he can be in a difficult position in disclosing wrongdoing. The professional bodies have attempted to seek legal clarification, and to issue guidance to their members, but the position regarding disclosure of wrongdoing by directors is still not clear-cut. It is clear, however, that auditors do not at present have a legal duty to society to discover and report on fraud.

New legislation in 1986 and 1987 in relation to the financial sector gave auditors the right to report their suspicion in relation to possible fraud by senior management to appropriate public regulatory bodies. But there is not yet an equivalent provision for the generality of companies. However, the Cadbury Committee has recommended that the Government should consider introducing legislation allowing auditors to report reasonable suspicion of fraud to government authorities without breaching client confidentiality rules (Cadbury, 1992).

A TRUE AND FAIR VIEW

Earlier Companies Acts have required a full and fair view (1844), or a 'true and correct view' (1929). But since 1948 the phrase 'a true and fair view' has been crucial. There is no suggestion that financial statements should show **the** true and fair view; the Companies Act in a sense recognizes that there is likely to be more than one view that is 'true and fair'. And the accounts presented are the directors', not the auditors'. The auditors have expressed only the 'opinion' that the accounts give a true and fair view. But is this an opinion?

In the following exchange the auditor does not appear to be expressing an opinion:

> Auditor: What is your opinion about the capitalization of interest?
> Director: In my opinion, the capitalization of interest is wrong.
> Auditor: In my professional opinion, that is an opinion.

In relation to company accounts the auditor's opinion, expressed as follows, appears similar:

> Auditor: What is your view of the year's profit?
> Director: My view is that the profit for the year was £1.5 million.

Auditor: In my professional opinion, that is a view.

The auditor appears to be stating nothing more than that the director has expressed a view; we do not know whether or not the auditor agrees with that view. Of course the auditor does not say merely that the financial statements are a view, s/he also states that they are a true and fair view. But what does 'true and fair' mean?

Chambers (1965) criticized the fact that professional recommendations permitted many different principles to be used in producing accounts. Dealing with stocks alone he stated

> Given three bases, four cost methods, three methods of finding cost (i.e. of treating overheads) and three methods of choosing the final figure, there are $3 \times 4 \times 3 \times 3 = 108$ explicitly permitted methods.

He went on to summarize different permitted methods of dealing with fixed assets and depreciation, and the treatment of investments and concluded that, even if only stocks, three classes of fixed assets and three classes of investments are considered,

> The number of possible methods, or sets of rules , for obtaining the aggregate amount of the assets of the company is $108 \times 24 \times 48 = 124\ 416$. And this is only a conservative estimate, which, by considering alternatives implicit in some of the rules such as those for deprecation, could be increased at least ten-fold.

> A million sets of mutually exclusive rules, each giving a true and fair view of a company's state of affairs and its profits!

But Chambers was considering only the 'rules'. Even when the rules are agreed there are likely to be problems with estimates. It might be agreed, for example, that a provision for bad debts should be created based on previous experience of bad debts. But different interpretations of past experience could produce very different estimates of future bad debts and so, in turn, a wide variety of profit and asset figures.

If we accept that there may be a million different true and fair views, then the auditor's report states no more than that the view presented is only one of a million possible versions. And that version is selected mainly by the directors – it is **their** opinion. What is the auditor's opinion? The auditor seems to be saying no more than 'in our opinion these accounts are an opinion'. This seems not to be an opinion at all.

If the above conversation continued as follows, the auditor would be expressing an opinion:

Director: What is your view of the year's profit?
Auditor: In my view the profit for the year was £1.1 million.

This might be better expressed as

> Auditor: In my view, the profit figure that most closely follows the requirements of the Companies Act, and the requirements of accounting standards, is £1.1 million

In this situation, auditors, using their professional judgement and experience, would actually be expressing an opinion. Although it might seem eminently reasonable to suggest that an opinion ought really to be an opinion, this is unlikely to be acceptable because

1. it would highlight the fact that there is no single correct profit figure; that profit is a matter of opinion; and
2. it would sometimes lead to conflicts between auditors and directors.

In common with many professionals, an auditor's opinion can command a high fee. But, unusually among professionals, the main part of the auditor's opinion is not an opinion at all! It merely states that the accounts are an opinion. This may seem to be rather an extreme view. If the phrase 'a true and fair view' means anything, then the auditor is expressing the opinion that the financial statements represent such a view.

The auditor also has to state whether the annual accounts have been properly prepared in accordance with the Companies Act, and this may be the most valuable part of the audit report. But the Act, and most discussion of the audit 'opinion', particularly emphasizes the 'true and fair view' aspect. Williams (1985) quotes various legal authorities that indicate that the phrase has no clear meaning.

> It seems that, despite the test of truth and fairness, or truth and correctness, having been imposed on British companies for over half a century ... no lawyer can tell you what it means beyond the statement that its meaning is a question of law. But it is a law that only one person has ever been prosecuted for breaking, and one that courts do not enforce through civil actions.

He concludes by asking if we do not know what it means and do not seem to need to know what it really means, is the test itself of any value? Apart from auditors, who benefits from the existing system? And for whose protection does it exist? Such awkward questions challenge the very nature of auditing, and Williams's contribution was excluded from the second edition of Sherer and Turley's book!

Within accountancy and auditing circles it is usually assumed that the term 'true and fair' has some meaning and may even be seen as being of great importance. But it does not seem to mean very much in legal circles. If we accept that a number of different views are possible, and that accounts may be used by a number of different people for a number of different purposes, then we can say that one view is more 'true and fair' than another only if we know for what purpose the accounts are to be used. Accountants tend to see their statements as having many different users but in terms of legal liability the purposes for which accounts are produced and audited are very restricted. The following section examines to whom the auditor has a legal liability.

RESPONSIBLE TO WHOM?

Conventional accounting texts are littered with references to the 'users' of accounts. Even the narrowest interpretation accepts that shareholders and creditors are legitimate users of published accounts in making decisions whether to invest in a company, or to lend to it or to allow credit as a supplier. Some writers provide a much fuller list of 'users' of accounts, including employees, customers, competitors and so on, as shown on pp. 36–37. Few, if any, are likely to suggest that **existing** shareholders are the only legitimate users. How can we argue that financial statements are of use in making investment decisions if only existing shareholders have access to them? How can potential creditors assess whether or not a company is creditworthy if they do not have access to financial information about the company? The fact that company accounts are made accessible to the public at Companies House suggests that the law assumes a range of users beyond existing shareholders (who can receive a personal copy of the financial statements).

If we assume that the auditing function has some value, it seems reasonable to assume that the various users would place some reliance on the fact that financial statements are supported by an audit report. It might also seem reasonable to assume that auditors have a legal duty to carry out their audits with reasonable skill and care. It might therefore be expected that any investor or creditor, and perhaps others, who suffer loss as a result of placing reliance on an audit report could expect damages from the auditors if s/he could show that the audit was not carried out with reasonable skill and care. Auditors could be liable for substantial damages in such circumstances and this has often been the case in the USA. Liability insurance premiums became unduly burdensome and in conducting audits there was increasing emphasis in documentation of the work that had been done. This involved producing files that could be used in defence of the auditors' work in case of subsequent legal action.

The matter became of increased concern in the UK following the *Hedley Byrne* v. *Heller* (1963–64) case where the House of Lords decided that a duty of care was owed to a party which has suffered economic loss as a consequence of reliance upon a negligently made statement. Subsequent cases confirmed the interpretation that auditors had a wider liability for negligence than had previously been assumed, subject to conditions such as that the person bringing the action is in a sufficient relationship of proximity, and that the possibility of loss as a result of carelessness might reasonably be foreseen. The auditor was not being made responsible to society as a whole, but might be held responsible for losses suffered by those in society who used and placed reliance upon the audit of published financial statements. But the *Caparo Industries v. Dickman* (1990) case appears to have changed all this.

In 1984 Caparo took over a company called Fidelity. Fidelity's profit for the year just ended was shown as £1.3 million, and the audit report was unqualified. Caparo's investment in Fidelity did not turn out well and Caparo issued a writ against Caparo's auditors alleging that they had suffered loss as a result of negligence in performing the audit. They argued that the auditors had failed to detect various irregularities such as the overvaluation of stock, and that Fidelity had made a loss of £400 000 in the previous year, not a profit of £1.3 million. The case went all the way to the House of Lords and the Law Lords ruled, in effect, that auditors had no duty to investors. The Law Lords were against a general duty of care in respect of anyone who placed reliance on a statement that might have been given for a different purpose, and stated that each case needs to be examined to see if a duty of care exists. They therefore examined the purpose for which an audit report is produced, basing their arguments on the Companies Act (1985, Part VII). Lord Jauncey stated that there is nothing in the Companies Act

> which suggests that the accounts are prepared and sent to members for any purpose other than to enable them to exercise class rights in general meeting. I therefore conclude that the purpose of annual accounts, so far as members are concerned, is to enable them to question the past management of the company, to exercise their voting rights, if so advised, and to influence future policy and management. Advice to individual shareholders in relation to present or future investment in the company is no part of the statutory duty of the preparation and distribution of the accounts.

This view of the purpose of annual accounts is extremely narrow and effectively excludes the possibility of any investors taking action against auditors for negligence in the performance of their duties. Auditors appear to be responsible in law only to shareholders **as a whole**, rather than to any individual shareholders, and only to enable them to exercise their rights in general meeting. It seems that auditors are protected from a very wide range of actions against them and that they have no legal responsibilities to the main users of accounts. Auditors may be responsible to individual investors for specific advice and information given but, in respect of the general purpose audit report, they are responsible only to the company (shareholders) as a whole.

We cannot reasonably expect auditors to be liable for all losses incurred by all those who place reliance on audited published financial statements, especially if those individuals are far removed from the company, and their decisions and actions are hard to predict. It does seem, however, that the law is excessively protective of auditors and that, in the public interest, it ought to be possible to take action against them if they have been negligent in the performance of their duties. It is unlikely that shareholders as a whole would take legal action against their auditors and if individual shareholders are unable to do so it begins to look as if auditors are responsible to no one but themselves. The Caparo judgment seriously weakens the position and credibility of the audit function in society.

INDEPENDENCE

It is important that the auditor, whose job it is to check and verify accounts and other statements that are produced by someone else, is seen to be **independent** from that person. According to Flint (1988) 'It is primarily on the basis of its independence that the audit derives its authority and its acceptance.'

It is often asserted, particularly by auditors, that independence is a state of mind (Flint, 1988, p. 59; Moizer, 1985, p. 34; Lee, 1982, p. 89), implying that the personal qualities of the auditor are important in determining their independence. But few would claim that personal qualities alone can provide sufficient reassurance that auditors are free from influence by powerful interest groups. Flint accepts the need for supervision of auditor behaviour and the administration of sanctions and suggests that 'this may be imposed by a self-regulatory system as in the United Kingdom, or by a state agency'. Many auditors seem to believe that they are a self-regulating profession, free from interference by the state. A more realistic interpretation is that the state has recognized the need for statutory provisions to guarantee some measure of independence for auditors. From time to time various problems and scandals have indicated that these measures are inadequate; the profession may then respond by establishing procedures to enhance the auditor's real or apparent independence, or the state may intervene by extending statutory provisions. The fear of state interference is often sufficient to encourage the profession to take some sort of action.

The Companies Acts make provisions that are intended to ensure that auditors are to some extent independent from directors. The auditor cannot be an officer or servant of the company, or an employee or partner of an officer or servant of the company. It is normally the shareholders, rather than the directors, who appoint the auditors and determine their remuneration. And there are restrictions on getting rid of auditors. The directors cannot sack them; removal from office requires a resolution at a company general meeting, and the auditors have the right to attend and be heard at general meetings. The directors may propose the appointment of a new auditor when the existing auditor's (one-year) term of office expires, but this requires special notice of a resolution at a general meeting of the company, and the auditors have the right to have their point of view circulated to shareholders.

Even if the auditor resigns voluntarily, s/he must **either** state that there are no circumstances connected with the resignation that ought to be brought to the attention of the shareholders or creditors of the company, **or** make a statement of such circumstances.

In spite of these provisions to strengthen the position of the auditor *vis á vis* the directors, the directors' position is still very powerful. It is the directors rather than the shareholders who appoint a company's first auditors before a general meeting has taken place and it is the directors who appoint the auditor when a casual vacancy arises. In practice shareholders are unlikely to overturn the directors' appointment or to defeat a resolution proposed by the directors. The Companies Act specifies that auditors' remuneration is 'fixed by the company in general meeting, or in such manner as the company in general may determine'. Again it is likely to be the directors who determine the outcome.

It would be unusual for directors openly to attempt to replace auditors because of a difference of opinion or because auditors were attempting to disclose matters that the directors wanted to keep quiet. Any such differences are usually dealt with in private. Auditors do not want to get a reputation of being 'difficult' with directors; other companies might be reluctant to employ auditors with such a reputation. And directors do not want to be 'exposed' as engaging in dubious accounting practices or in being reluctant to follow auditors' recommendations. Auditors may threaten to expose any dubious matters and this can be a powerful weapon. But it can be countered by the directors' threat to put the audit out to tender with the risk that either the existing auditor would be replaced or could continue in office only if fees were substantially reduced. It may be that in some situations agreement is quietly reached that innocuous disclosures are made that can be deemed to comply with the standards that auditors are supposed to uphold; and the cosy relationship between auditors and directors continues, with an acceptable increase in fees proposed for the following year.

Criticisms of auditor independence

The auditors' apparent lack of independence has often been criticized. Schandl (1978) recalls his own days as a practising auditor. 'I remember very well the instructions received from the managing partners while I was in public practice: "You can do anything with our clients, but don't lose them." Where was our independence?' More recently the Chairman of the British Accounting Standards Board, David Tweedie, said that he was 'very concerned about who appoints the auditor and whether the client can threaten to put the audit out to tender whenever a problem with the accounts arises' (Biennial Conference of CIMA September 1991).

There seems to be a growing practice of opinion shopping. When a company does not like the recommendations of a particular firm of auditors they 'shop around': they ask the opinions of different firms of auditors until they find one that they like.

Excessive dependence on a few large clients is also seen as a threat to auditor independence, as is the cosy relationship that sometimes develops between the clients and the auditor when there has been no change in the auditor for a number of years. It is sometimes suggested that recent mergers among the major international accountancy firms increases auditor independence because the fees of audit clients now represent a smaller proportion of the fee income of the enlarged accountancy firms. But even the largest accountancy firms are likely to wish to maintain good relationships with client companies.

The case against statutory provisions

It can be argued that there is no need for institutional mechanisms to safeguard auditors' independence. This argument rests on the assumption that both share-holders and auditors have an economic interest in maintaining independence and so would be inclined to do so even if there were no statutory provisions. It does not rest on the idea that auditors should be some sort of saints who always act in the public interest rather than simply trying to maximize their fee income!

At first sight this might seem unlikely. It seems more likely that auditors have an economic interest in going along with what the directors want, not rocking the boat, not challenging questionable interpretations, not exposing dubious prac-tices, and quietly picking up their fees. Auditors with a reputation for being 'diffi-cult' with directors would gradually be replaced by those who are more compliant.

But a good, independent audit has an economic value to shareholders which ought to be reflected in share prices. Although auditing may not always be as effective as some might wish, it can produce positive benefits: errors are sometimes found and corrected; auditors' recommendations can lead to improvements in systems and internal controls; the fear of errors and dubious practices being discovered must cause some people to avoid improper behaviour; and discussions between directors and auditors sometimes lead to companies adopting accounting policies and practices that are more consistent with generally accepted accounting principles than would otherwise be the case. All of this should improve the usefulness of published accounts to investors and creditors, and if an audit succeeds in removing any doubts about the soundness and performance of the company, this would lead to higher share prices than would otherwise be the case. From the point of view of investors the value of an independent audit report is that it reduces the degree of risk attached to an investment. In theory, the value of the audit service, and of an independent audit report, must be greater than its cost, otherwise shareholders would not want to pay for it.

Auditors have an economic interest in trying to ensure that the financial state-ments that they have audited are not misleading because (a) there is a possibility of litigation; and (b) the amount of fees that they can earn is related to the value of their reputation. There is evidence that some audit firms have better reputa-tions than others (Moizer, 1989). In a way the fee for auditing may be seen as being based on renting out that reputation. Auditors therefore have an economic interest in high reputations so that they can command high fees. If their reputations can be enhanced, so can the fees that they are able to command. If their reputation is tarnished, then, in theory, their fee levels are likely to suffer.

The assumption that shareholders have an economic interest in an independent audit is difficult to demonstrate as they have no choice in the matter. Auditing, as practised by professional accountants, is compulsory. Presumably the legal requirements were introduced because, without them, not enough shareholders were choosing to have effective audits. Shareholders are also forced to choose as auditors a firm of accountants that is in business to sell a range of different services and this is a threat to their independence. If shareholders could choose between being audited by completely independent auditors or by one of the existing accountancy firms, we might get some indication of the extent of their interest in independence.

If we assume that auditing firms are motivated primarily by economic self-interest, then they need to maintain their reputation for independence. But they are also interested in maximizing fee income, a matter which is largely in the hands of the senior management and directors of companies. They are therefore likely to favour measures which increase the **appearance** of independence and which enhance their reputations. They are less likely to favour measures that jeopardize their good relationships with directors or which restrict their freedom to increase their fee income, whether by being 'helpful' with audits or by providing other services. They are therefore likely to favour provisions to demonstrate independence that are established by the professional accountancy bodies.

The need to maintain the appearance of independence is recognized within the professional accountancy bodies and they issue extensive ethical guidance to their members. To avoid becoming too dependent on one client, auditors should endeavour to ensure that the recurring fees paid by one client do not exceed 15 per cent of their fee income. The staff of a firm of auditors should not hold beneficial shareholdings in a company which the firm audits or in a company on which they report. Where the Articles of Association of a company prescribe that the company's auditors must also be shareholders, they should hold no more than the minimum number of shares required. Auditors should not make or guarantee loans to clients. Auditors should not accept goods or services from clients on terms more favourable than is available to the client's employees. Where auditors earn commission as a result of advice given to clients, the facts should be disclosed to clients. Conflicts of interest, for example where there are clients competing with each other, should be avoided. It is accepted that auditors can do non-audit work for audit clients but there are provisions to avoid some of the worst threats to independence.

The profession's guidance does not change the basic position that compromises the auditor's independence: that auditors need the support of directors and senior management if they are to retain their audit work, increase their audit fee income and have opportunities to earn fees for non-audit work in such areas as taxation, accountancy, systems and consultancy.

Many of the arguments against statutory safeguards for auditor independence are ideological. Some market economists see market solutions to most problems and oppose state involvement. There is the danger that introducing public sector mechanisms can result in costly bureaucracies which can become more interested in perpetuating their own existence, expansion and career prospects than in protecting the public interest. Those who see existing arrangements for protecting auditor independence as being less than satisfactory may argue for more effective ethical guidance and enforcement mechanisms from the professional accountancy bodies; or they may argue for new legislation and increased state involvement.

Strengthening auditor independence

One way of strengthening auditor independence would be to continue to revise and strengthen the profession's guidelines and perhaps to give legal backing to them. But more substantial suggestions for change have been made, such as the following.

1. The audit fee should be established by national scales or by an independent body so that auditors are not compromised in their dealings with management by having to negotiate their fees. Such an arrangement would also remove the possibility of directors getting rid of uncooperative auditors by putting audit work out to tender.
2. Auditors should not be allowed to undertake non-audit work for audit clients. Companies are now required to disclose any fees paid to their auditors for services other than audit.[1] This disclosure suggests that in some cases auditors' independence appears to be compromised by substantial non-audit earnings; and it might discourage audit firms from taking on excessive amounts of such work.

   In 1992 some disclosures on non-audit earnings were made for the first time. Lea and Bagnall showed that a number of companies paid twice as much to their auditors for non-audit work as they did for auditing. These companies included Anglian Water, BAA, Guinness and Sainsbury.

   > PW received the biggest fee for non-audit work from their client drinks giant Guinness. The massive £4.75m fee for tax and consultancy work far outstripped the audit fee of £2.34m. In the previous year, the company paid non-audit fees of £2.04m in top of audit fees of £1.8m. This may go some way to debunk the profession's assertions that firms do not rely on the auditors to bring in the more valuable consultancy work.(Lea and Bagnall, 1992)

[1]Statutory Instrument, Companies Act 1989 (Disclosure of Remuneration for Non-Audit Work) Regulations 1991. Small companies are exempt from this.

The requirement to disclose does not change the basic position that auditors are usually interested in earning some additional fees and their independence may be compromised in this situation.

3. Separate audit committees (comprising largely or entirely non-executive directors) should be established to deal with the appointment and remuneration of auditors. This could be seen as enhancing the auditor's position by removing senior management from decisions in relation to auditors' employment. The extent of an audit committee's independence from the rest of the board is, however, questionable.

4. Rotation of auditors: there should be a requirement that a company changes its auditors every, say, three to five years. This would have the advantage of preventing the relationship between directors and auditors becoming too cosy. It would also strengthen the position of auditors *vis á vis* directors if it were clear that they would lose the audit in any case at a predetermined time. Such a proposal would further strengthen the position of the auditor if it were virtually impossible for the company to get rid of the auditors before the end of the period.

    The possibility of requiring a rotation of auditors was considered by the Cadbury Committee (1992), but rejected. They did, however, recommend a gesture in that direction: they urged the accountancy profession to draw up guidelines to guarantee a periodic change of partners involved in the preparation of any particular company's audit over a period of years. This proposal may have some cosmetic appeal but would do nothing to enhance the independence of the auditing firm from the client company.

5. A State Auditing Board. One way of enhancing the independence of auditor would be for the state to take over the auditing function. The implication of this is that auditing should be clearly seen to function in the **public** interest, rather than the present unclear situation.

The creation of a State Auditing Board was proposed by Lyall and Perks (1976). It was intended primarily to develop, promulgate and enforce accounting standards and to license and employ state licensed auditors. They argued that if accounting standards were to be in the public interest they should not be set by professional accountancy bodies who had a vested interest in maintaining the existing position of auditors. The ASC was not in a position to develop or enforce clear-cut accounting standards if the directors of powerful companies did not want to follow them. A State Auditing Board would establish the independence both of auditors and of standard setters from companies and their directors.

The idea was taken up in Parliament by Ivor Clemitson, MP who sought to introduce an Audit Reform Bill on 22 March 1977

> to establish a public audit board for the purpose of providing an independent auditing service to companies, financed by a levy on such companies.

In support he quoted from *The Times* in September 1976 saying that this was

a time of growing public disquiet about the role and responsibilities of auditors.

He referred to particular problem companies of the day including SUITS and Lonrho. He argued that

the fact that auditors are appointed by companies and not to them militates against the independence of auditors that is at the heart of the function of auditing. (Hansard, 1977)

The Bill was drafted by Ivor Clemitson jointly with David Lyall and Bob Perks of Strathclyde University. It was intended to strengthen the independence of auditors and would have established a public auditing board which would include representatives from the professional accountancy bodies, the TUC and the CBI. The Board would have three functions:

1. to provide an auditing service to companies using the Board's own employees who would be professionally qualified auditors;
2. to devise accounting standards, in consultation with the professional accountancy bodies, with a view to giving such standards more weight and more teeth; and
3. to give advice on accounting and auditing practices.

The board would have the right to audit any company.
It was opposed by John Wakenham who argued that

the independence and objectivity of auditors has been called into question in no more than a handful of cases in the last 10 years

and that

No nation in the EEC has found it necessary to establish a public audit board.

The Bill was defeated by 194 votes to 159 votes, but was supported by a number of Cabinet ministers and by John Smith who was subsequently to become leader of the Labour party.

It seems unlikely that any EEC country would adopt exactly the form of public audit board suggested in Clemitson's Audit Reform Bill, but other EEC countries were concerned that auditing should be a separate activity from the other types of work that accountancy firms undertake. Turley and Sherer (1991) state that

Direct state control of auditing could take a number of forms, for example passing legislation to specify how an audit should be conducted and restricting the type of non-audit work which can be performed by the auditor; or even making auditors employees of the state, as in France where the *commissaires aux comptes* are responsible to the Ministry of Justice.

The idea that the independence of auditors has never seriously been called into question is disingenuous, but popular with accountants. Russell (1991) states that

> DTI investigations have never seriously questioned the independence of auditors, although inspectors have been critical of auditors who failed to stand up to company chairmen with strong personalities.

This seems to suggest that auditors can be independent when companies have weak chairmen, but that it is difficult to stand up to strong ones!

More recent criticisms of auditor independence and EC concerns about their position suggest that Wakenham's arguments against the Audit Reform Bill were not altogether 'true and fair'. But they were credible and effective!

The EC is still concerned about inadequate auditor independence in the UK but so far the British accountancy profession has succeeded in fighting off serious threats to its present arrangements. Auditor independence may eventually be enhanced by legislation, perhaps as a result of EC influence. In the mean time the professional bodies will, no doubt, continue to issue guidelines and codes of practice designed to maintain the appearance of independence. Even the Cadbury Committee was concerned that the relationship between company directors and the senior partners in their audit firms might appear too close.

But market forces are likely to prove more powerful than either legislation or professional guidelines. If we believe in market forces, and if there really is a demand in society for organizations (and their directors) to be subject to audit by people who are genuinely independent of the directors, we should expect some-one to emerge to meet this demand. There is a need for a 'Campaign for Independent Auditors' to mobilize support for such a proposition. Such a campaign could aim to establish a Society of Independent Auditors; membership would be confined to qualified auditors who undertook only auditing work; who were not available for other related work in taxation, consultancy and so on; and who agreed to work for fees established by the Society in a predetermined way that could not be influenced by the company being audited. It may be that investors and other stakeholders in many companies and other organizations, particularly where there are suspicions that directors may be abusing their position, would argue for the appointment of such genuinely independent auditors. Directors who still chose to have 'their' companies audited by auditors who were not so clearly independent might be forced to defend their position: how can they justify being audited by firms of accountants who could be influenced by the directors' offers of additional fee income when there is a genuinely independent alternative?

THE EXPECTATIONS GAP

The 'expectations gap' has been of concern to the accountancy profession since the 1970s. The phrase originated in the United States but there are similar concerns on this side of the Atlantic. Crudely, one might say that society expects a great deal from auditors, but in practice auditors fall far short of what is expected of them. This oversimplification has some truth in it and to some extent it is inevitable. This chapter has already examined areas where society might be disappointed by current auditing arrangements: their limited responsibility for detecting and reporting fraud; the lack of meaning of the phrase 'a true and fair view'; the limited nature of auditors' legal responsibilities; and doubts about auditors' independence. Legislative changes and reforms could reduce the expectations gap to some extent, but it could not be completely eliminated.

Society consists of many different individuals and groups, each with different interests and expectations; it is to be expected that there are differences between (a) what auditors do and (b) what some individuals and groups expect of them.

Criticisms that auditors have failed to come up to expectations often arise in connection with highly publicized frauds or company failures. It is perhaps inevitable that, from time to time, a company will publish an apparently sound set of financial statements, supported by an unqualified audit report, and then, within a few months, get into financial difficulties and collapse. It is also inevitable that, from time to time, senior management will be guilty of major fraud or of misleading the auditors, and that the auditors will fail to detect or report these matters.

When a company's financial statements are given an unqualified audit report, this is frequently seen as being a clean bill of health for the company or as indicating that all is well. But what expectations are reasonable when there is an unqualified audit report?

Most accountants would probably agree that an unqualified audit report indicates what the Companies Acts require: that proper accounting records have been kept; that the financial statements are in agreement with those records; that the auditors have received all information and explanations that they considered necessary; that the financial statements have been properly prepared in accordance with the Companies Acts; and perhaps that they represent 'a true and fair view' (whatever that means!).

But accountants would generally not agree with what they regard as unrealistic and inappropriate expectations, such as those listed below. In examining this list of possible expectations it is worth considering whether, from the point of view of others in society, such expectations are realistic, desirable and attainable.

1. The financial statements are prepared by the auditors, and the auditors agree with and are responsible for what they contain

In large companies the financial statements are prepared by the company's own accounting staff. It is only in small companies, where few if any accounting staff are employed, that the financial statements are prepared by the auditors. In both large and small companies, these statements are the responsibility of the directors, not of the auditors. The auditors have been remarkably successful in avoiding responsibility for the statements to which they put their name.

2. The financial statements are correct and accurate; that another auditor would produce the same financial statements from the same basic information

The financial statements show a particular view from a range of possible views, valuations, estimates and assumptions that are acceptable as being in accordance with normal accounting practice. It is unlikely that two different accountants would produce the same financial statements from the same basic information, except perhaps in highly simplified situations.

3. The financial statements show what the company is worth; that assets have been properly valued

A balance sheet is not intended to show what the business is worth as a whole, or even what individual assets are worth. Some assets are specifically valued at a particular date (e.g. property, investments). Other assets are shown on various different bases, such as at cost, at cost less various provisions (e.g. for depreciation, or for bad debts), at face value (e.g. some investments), at the lower of cost and net realizable value (e.g. stocks) or as a result of various arcane accounting manipulations (e.g. goodwill). The business as a whole, or its separate assets, may well be worth much more, or much less, than the amounts shown on the balance sheet. It is almost certainly impossible for a balance sheet to show the 'true' value of a business (except perhaps at a single moment when a valuation is agreed at the time when a business is sold).

4. The auditors have checked and ascertained that no significant fraud or irregularities have taken place

Auditors are not primarily concerned with seeking out fraud. A reasonably competent audit is likely to uncover major frauds or irregularities, but most frauds, particularly relatively small ones, will probably not be detected by the auditor. Even where frauds are found, any report by the auditors is likely to be to the management, and the company's accounts will still have a clean audit report.

5. The business is a going concern and is not likely to collapse or fail in the foreseeable future

Financial accounts are prepared on the assumption that the company is a going concern, unless it is stated otherwise. But any statement that the going concern assumption is not applicable is likely to become a self-fulfilling prophecy and result in the company collapsing! Auditors are therefore caught in a difficult position. If a company receives a clean audit report, and subsequently collapses, the auditors will be criticized for failing to highlight the weaknesses. But if the auditors did highlight the weaknesses, creditors might all press for immediate payment and so bring about the company's collapse. Many companies survive temporary financial difficulties if they can retain the confidence of their creditors, and a clean audit report is an important ingredient of this.

So what should the auditor do if there are financial difficulties and there is a possibility of the company collapsing? The problem is the over-simplistic assumption that either a company is sound financially or it is about to collapse. In practice many companies lie between these extremes.

The Cadbury Committee has recommended that directors should state that the business is a going concern, with supporting assumptions or qualifications as necessary and that the auditors should report on this statement. The committee also recommended that the accountancy profession should develop guidance for such statements. It considered the possibility of legislation to make this effective, but concluded that this should be decided in the light of experience.

6. The management of the company are reputable, competent, efficient and effective

It is not at present part of the auditor's responsibility to examine and report on the competence of management. Auditors may suspect or know that some chairmen and chief executives are too powerful, dubious, or even outright crooks, but that does not prevent a clean audit report being given. Many in society may condemn the activities of some company directors, but a change in the law would be required to expand auditors' responsibilities to include checking on the reputability and competence of management. In the present situation, where company management can exert very powerful influences over auditors, it is unlikely that auditors would feel able to make any significant criticisms of management, and a management audit is likely to be of little value unless conducted by a genuinely independent outside body.

7. The audit report draws attention to any doubts about the company's finances

Audit reports normally use brief, standard wording, and do not usually draw attention to any unusual or questionable aspects of the company's annual report and accounts. Where there are difficulties any reference in the audit report is likely to be brief, and difficult for the uninitiated to interpret.

What can be done?

What can be done about the expectations gap? The accountancy profession's response is that the public should be educated so that they can understand what the auditor really does. In some respects public expectations are unreasonable and unattainable; the auditor cannot, for example, predict all company collapses. But in other respects more might be expected of auditors than they currently deliver, and changes to deal with some of society's expectations of auditors could be incorporated into future legislation. It has to be recognized, however, that the accountancy profession manages to be quite effective in warding off such public interference in their affairs. Sikka *et al.* (1992) argue 'that the expectations gap cannot be eliminated in a society which is marked by competing worldviews, contradictory institutional structures and an unequal distribution of power, wealth and influence'. Although the accountancy profession's view of the meaning and expectations of auditing sometimes seem to dominate, there are prospects for reform as argued by, for example, Mitchell *et al.* (1991), Humphrey *et al.* (1992) and Cadbury (1992).

Humphrey *et al.* (1992) offer three positive suggestions to reduce the expectations gap:

1. clarifying that the auditor has a duty to detect fraud;
2. auditors' responsibility should be extended by statute so that it clearly includes responsibility to shareholders, creditors and **potential** shareholders;
3. setting up an independent Office for Auditing to enhance auditor independence by acting as a buffer between the auditor and the management of the client company, freeing the auditor of worries about fee income, and the possibility of losing the audit.

As long as auditors are concerned about fee income, and the possibility of losing the audit, and as long as these matters are largely in the hands of company management, there is no possibility that auditors can be independent from management. But Humphrey *et al.* shy away from dealing with this problem. They say that 'consideration should be given' to setting up an Office for Auditing, but it is not at all clear how it would operate, what its powers would be, or how it would be independent (from the profession and/or from company managements). This proposal echoes the 1976 proposed State Auditing Board, but it seems unlikely to be effectively implemented. Who could do it? Such an office could only be effective in safeguarding independence if it were free from influence by the profession; if it had the responsibility to decide who should audit particular companies and what their fees should be; and if audit firms were forbidden from undertaking non-audit work for audit clients.

THE ROLE OF THE AUDITOR IN THE PUBLIC SECTOR

The bodies responsible for public sector auditing are (1) **the National Audit Office** and (2) **the Audit Commission.**

1. *The National Audit Office (NAO)* is responsible for the auditing of central government. It was established in 1984, taking over responsibilities from the old Exchequer and Audit Department. It is controlled directly by Parliament rather than by the Treasury; the independence of its head, the Comptroller and Auditor General, is protected by the fact that he is appointed by the Crown and can be removed only by an address presented to the Queen by both Houses of Parliament. The NAO reports directly to the House of Commons, and its published reports are widely reported in the press and form the basis of much of the work of Parliament's Public Accounts Committee.

2. *The Audit Commission* was established by the Local Government Finance Act, 1982, and is responsible for appointing the external auditors of local authorities. The auditor may be one of the Commission's own staff or an outside firm of accountants. Before 1982 local authorities themselves were responsible for appointing their external auditors and most local authority auditing was undertaken by the district audit service. Since the 1972 Local Government Act local authorities were able to choose whether to use the district audit service or other approved auditors. The district audit service had its origins in the Poor Law Amendment Act of 1844 which established a central body, the Poor Law Commissioners, to regulate the administration of the Poor Law, including the keeping and auditing of accounts. The Commissioners could make local guardians appoint and pay auditors. The duties of these district auditors were extended by subsequent legislation to include the accounts of local highway, education and health bodies. The district audit service was, in effect, taken over by the Audit Commission (the Audit Commission for Local Authority Accounts in England and Wales) under the 1982 Act, and its remit has been extended to include the National Health Service.

There are therefore three distinct strands in the development of auditing in the UK: private sector auditing, mainly of companies, undertaken by firms of professional accountants (Chartered or Certified); central government auditing originating with the Exchequer and Audit Department, now the National Audit Office; and local government auditing, originating with the district audit service, now under the Audit Commission. Auditing in the public sector appears to have been well established before the professional accountancy bodies came into being and long before auditing became the bread and butter of the accountancy profession. Public sector auditing was therefore, for many years, largely insulated or protected from the influences of private sector auditing. In some ways this continued to be the case until the 1960s or 1970s. Since then we have seen increasing emphasis on professional accountancy qualifications in the public sector; increased involvement by CIPFA (the public sector accounting body) with the rest of the accountancy profession, including merger talks and joint action on accounting and auditing standards; and increased use of professional accountancy firms by local authorities and the National Health Service in external auditing (subject to appropriate supervision and review), and by central government (though mainly in consultancy rather than auditing).

Important differences between public sector and private sector auditing are as follows:

1. In the public sector it is part of the auditor's job to check that public funds are spent only on the specific purposes for which they were authorized. In local authorities this tradition began with the first district auditors, appointed under the Poor Law Amendment Act (1844); they were expected to disallow any payments made by local guardians which did not conform with the Poor Law Commissioners' regulations. Any person making such an unauthorized payment could be surcharged or required to pay back the amount involved. This tradition of ensuring that public funds are spent only on the specific purposes for which they were authorized, and surcharging those who fail in this duty, lives on as an important ingredient of public sector auditing. Auditors no longer have the right to impose surcharges themselves but if an item appears to be contrary to the law they may apply to the court for a declaration accordingly and the court may require an amount to be repaid and, if appropriate, disqualify a councillor from holding office.

    In the private sector there is no real equivalent. It is possible that a company may engage in activities that are *ultra vires*, but companies usually give themselves wide enough powers to make this unlikely, and it is not part of the auditor's job to check for such activity. Directors have very wide discretion on how they manage and spend the company's resources. Auditors are often concerned to check on the company's internal controls, including the authorization of expenditure, and they need to check that particular expenditures (on directors' remuneration, for example) are properly disclosed. But they have no interest in finding unauthorized expenditure so that they can report the matter to the courts, or surcharge directors, or to attempt to disqualify them from office.

2. Most of those who audit the public sector are employees of the public sector; the interests of public sector employees are likely to be different from those in the private sector. It would be too crude to suggest that public sector employees are concerned mainly with the public interest, whereas private sector employees are interested mainly with increasing fees, profits and their own remuneration. Public sector employees are also concerned about their own remuneration! Private sector auditors are also concerned about their own reputations; the market value of their services is influenced by perceptions about the quality of their work. But there are serious questions about auditor independence in the private sector, about the priority given to not losing clients and about the extent to which auditors may wish to keep problems quiet rather than risk rocking the boat. In the private sector the directors or senior management of the company that is being audited are often seen as being the client, and the auditor is usually keen to keep the client happy.

In the public sector the senior management of the organization being audited is not usually seen as being the client and there is less emphasis on keeping them happy. The managers of the organization are unlikely to be involved in appointing the auditor, or in offering additional fee-paying work, and they are not in a position to determine the fees. In local authority audits the fees are set by the Audit Commission; in central government audits the costs are borne by National Audit Office and fees are not normally charged. In public sector audits it is less likely that the auditor's position will be compromised by the need to tout for business. And public sector auditors are more likely to have a positive incentive to embarrass the management of the organization that they are auditing by disclosing questionable practices. National Audit Office reports often receive national publicity and form the basis of careful questioning in Parliament's Public Accounts Committee. Members of Parliament are often very keen to see wrongdoing uncovered and National Audit Office staff are often keen to be more like bloodhounds than watchdogs in searching for information that will enhance their reputation and the attention that their reports receive.

3. Public sector auditors are to some extent involved in monitoring the quality of the management of the organizations that they audit. They have a specific responsibility for value for money auditing: for seeing that mechanisms are in place to check that economy, efficiency and effectiveness are achieved. Effectiveness deals with checking that the organization's objectives are achieved. Value for money auditing is discussed in Chapter 5. In the private sector it is not part of the auditor's job to comment on the quality of management or on their success in achieving the company's objectives.

4. The public sector auditor has more responsibility to report to the public than is the case with private sector auditors. This may be because 'the public' is seen as being the client of public sector auditors. In the private sector, shareholders may formally be the client, but reports on any matters of concern tend to be made to directors rather than to shareholders.

In a local authority, if the auditor discovers any matter giving rise to concern, s/he is required to consider whether it is in the public interest to report it to the council of the local authority or bring it to the attention of the public. Examples of cases which could call for reports include such things as fraud, weak financial controls and losses arising from waste. There are also public rights of access to information (with restrictions with regard to documents that contain personal details). Dates are advertised in the press showing where and when the accounts, documents, vouchers etc. will be deposited for seven days immediately before the audit starts so that persons interested may inspect them, take copies or send an expert to act as her/his agent. Once the audit is formally opened any local government elector for the area, or someone appointed by an elector, may question the auditor about the accounts and object to any item(s) contained in them; objections may be in respect of matters of legality, wilful misconduct, or otherwise in the public interest. If electors do not agree with auditors' decisions, they may require the auditors to give their reasons in writing and, if not satisfied, take the matter to court.

Equivalent rights do not exist with regard to the accounts of central government, other public bodies or companies. It is worth asking why such extensive rights are allowed in respect of local authorities, but not with other bodies. The differences may be attributed to historic democratic traditions in local authorities that do not exist to the same extent elsewhere. The additional accountability duties imposed by central government upon local authorities may also reflect the relative power positions: central government can assert its power over local authorities by requiring extensive disclosures.

5. In local authority audits there are more formal requirements to consider the interests of society and of different groups within it; this does not apply in private sector audits. For example, the Department of the Environment's code of practice requires auditors to check that proper accounting practices have been followed, and also to see whether different sections of the public have received unfair treatment in apportioning costs; and to check how the auditor can help to improve and maintain integrity in the conduct of public affairs – including whether the local authority has reached important financial decisions by considering irrelevancies or by omitting relevant factors. There are no such requirements in the private sector.

6. More emphasis is given in the public sector to monitoring the adequacy of internal audit arrangements. The Local Government Audit Code of Practice stipulates that external auditors must pay attention to the adequacy of internal audit arrangements.

7. In at least one respect, much of traditional public sector auditing is more objective or factual than is the case in the private sector; this is because the cash basis of accounting, rather than the accruals basis, has been more prevalent. Public sector auditors have therefore been less concerned with such difficult and controversial matters as expressing an opinion on profit, assets, depreciation, stock valuation and so on. But accruals basis accounting is gradually becoming more prevalent in the public sector which is becoming colonized by private sector accounting and auditing practices. The major exception to the idea that public sector auditing is more objective and factual is value for money auditing, where there is considerable scope for subjectivity; it has been introduced in most of the public sector but it is not a requirement in the private sector.

Some of these differences suggest that the expectations gap in the public sector is likely to be narrower than in the private sector. Public sector auditors are likely to be more independent, more likely to look for fraud and irregular practices, more likely to report in the public interest and more likely to check the competence of management, at least in relation to arrangements for avoiding waste and giving value for money. In other words, public sector auditing is more likely to serve the function that the public expect of it than is the case with private sector auditing. In some respects public sector auditing could be a model for the role in society that private sector auditing could play. Many of the differences between public sector and private sector auditing do appear to be diminishing, particularly in local authorities. But (with the exception of value for money auditing) it seems that local authorities are tending to move towards the private sector rather than the other way around. With regard to central government auditing, the National Audit Office appears to maintain a sturdy independence and, from the point of view of society, to be developing an interesting and challenging role in alliance with Parliament's Public Accounts Committee rather than with the accountancy profession.

THE CASE AGAINST AUDITING

It seems that the audit function, at least in the private sector, does not deliver what many expect of it. There is a substantial 'expectations gap' between public expectations of auditing and what the professional auditor delivers. Moreover, many of the basic concepts on which it is supposed to be based are doubtful. Lee (1982) outlines a number of postulates of auditing and goes on to suggest that auditing in practice is based on four concepts, as follows:

1. Auditor independence: the auditor should be in a position of complete independence from persons and situations which could cause his work and opinion to lack the objectivity and thus the credibility, which is so necessary to the credibility of the accounting information he is attesting to. Weaknesses in present arrangements with regard to independence were discussed on pp. 55–62.
2. Auditor responsibility: the company auditors can be held responsible, legally and ethically, for the conduct and quality of their work. The difficulty in holding auditors to account for their work was discussed on pp. 53–55.
3. Truth and fairness: that the profitability and financial position are truthfully and fairly described in accordance with generally accepted accounting practice. The limitations of this idea were discussed on pp. 50–53.
4. Audit evidence: that the auditor has collected sufficient competent evidence to support her/his opinion. Auditors appear to be reasonably careful to collect evidence that is adequate in some respects (as a defence in case of legal action for example). They are probably reasonably careful to collect evidence in support of any items in the final accounts that might subsequently be questioned. But if we do not know what is meant by a true and fair view, we cannot know what evidence is sufficient to support it!

With regard to the basic concepts of accounting it seems that auditing in practice falls short both of public expectations and of the profession's own aspirations.

Some critics appear to advocate the abolition of conventional auditing which they see as 'relatively worthless', arguing that 'the current structure is repetitious and outmoded, and that it represents from a national viewpoint a massive misdirection of scarce resources to have highly trained professional accountants checking the work of other highly trained accountants when that work has normally been checked internally by yet other highly trained accountants' (Briston and Perks, 1977).

They argued that the external audits for unlisted companies should be entirely voluntary. The argument for abolishing compulsory audits for small companies, perhaps to be replaced by 'reviews', continued through the 1980s and into the 1990s; but the accountancy profession still retains this business.

Briston and Perks accepted that the arguments for external audits for listed companies were more clear-cut, but argued that they are not as great as is often claimed. They suggested that the importance of shareholder protection had diminished with improvements in financial accounting and internal control; that manipulation of profit was still a problem, but that it was more likely to be exposed by subsequent company collapse than by the auditor; and that individual investors were less important than institutional shareholders, and institutional shareholders were less dependent on published financial statements as they could get information directly from the company.

Although this seriously questioned the value of auditing at the time, it was a call for major reform of audit rather than for its abolition. Less emphasis should be given to checking and re-checking and more emphasis to the audit of management and to internal audits; and external audits could be conducted on a random basis, perhaps by a state audit body.

There have been some changes in auditing practice in recent years, such as giving more emphasis to analytical review rather than to checking and rechecking. But such changes are probably more due to pressures to keep audit costs down, and to avoid scandals, than they are responses to public criticisms and expectations of what an audit should be.

Few critics of auditing have called for its complete abolition. Most call for reforms. But some recent critics have gone even further by suggesting that auditing may do more harm than good.

Tinker and Okcabol (1991) raise substantial questions about the ways in which the auditing function may be highjacked and used to support criminal activities.

It is commonly assumed that auditing and other accounting monitoring services are directed towards minimizing criminal activity, however, there is another alternative: accounting firms could assist clients in criminal acts. Indeed, we will see that, for many accounting firms, the provision of criminal support services may make sense, normatively and positively.

They provide four examples of 'criminal' activities supported by auditors:

1. By externalizing costs on to third parties, as with toxic dumping, and operating unsafe production facilities.
2. By internalizing (appropriating) revenue belonging to third parties, as in overbilling the government, selling dangerous products, 'capturing' employee pension fund excesses and illegally soliciting government contracts.
3. By increasing management's income and perquisite consumption while, at the same time, using 'discretionary' accounting practices to obfuscate the impact on shareholder wealth.
4. By increasing the value of management's shareholdings at the expense of 'external' shareholders by manipulating the stock price with 'timely' disclosure of financial and other (mis)information. For example, management may profit from their fiduciary position by engineering a 'bargain' in a leverage buyout or inflating the stock price prior to off-loading their holdings.

Few auditors would accept the suggestion that they actually condone and thereby encourage criminal activity. But it is at least arguable that, from a social point of view, conventional auditing can do more harm than good by offering reassurance that all is well when in fact much may be wrong with a company; and by adding legitimacy to the activities of companies and the accounts that they give of those activities.

SUMMARY AND CONCLUSIONS

This chapter has provided a critical account of auditing in society, particularly in relation to the auditing of companies. There is considerable scope for reform and improvement of these arrangements and a variety of suggestions has been explored. For example, the possibility of developing improvements based on the different traditions in the public sector should not be overlooked.

Although there may be substantial existing weaknesses, the practice of auditing does have positive benefits. It adds credibility to financial statements, provides some protection to investors, and credible financial information plays an important role in the operation of financial markets. Auditors do find frauds and errors and disclose them to management, and the existence of the external audit function also acts as a deterrent to such malpractice. Auditors also play a role in enforcing accounting standards and in checking that Companies Act accounting requirements are implemented. In defending the role of the auditor too much emphasis is sometimes given to the mystical or meaningless audit opinion, and perhaps not enough is given to the auditor's role in checking that proper accounting records have been kept and that the published financial statements are in agreement with them. Auditors can be influential in persuading companies to adopt best accounting practice, but even when a clean audit report has been given, things can still go wrong: companies can collapse and directors can turn out to be rogues. In any subsequent enquiry we may find that some of the assumptions in the published accounts are questionable, but we should at least be able to be confident that there are proper records and be able to trace where things have gone wrong and what has been distorted or misappropriated. In the absence of auditors and of proper accounting records, there would be no limits on the fictions that unprincipled directors could present as financial statements. Auditing should be seen as an essential part of the accountability process and a significant restriction on the freedom of action of those who control resources.

Auditing has a long history, much longer than the accountancy profession, and there is always likely to be a need for accounts to be verified by an independent person. This does not apply just to company accounts. We are likely to believe an account (or story, or version of events), only if either (1) we totally trust the person giving the account or (2) that account has been verified to our satisfaction. The idea that if a version of events – of any kind, and whoever presents it – may require verification by an independent person, is capable of much wider application and interpretation than is normally applied with regard to company auditing.

Auditing has a number of different potential beneficiaries, and each is likely to have different objectives and expectations from the audit. It is ostensibly conducted for the benefit of shareholders, but in practice it probably operates at least as much in the interest of the directors and the auditors themselves.

The potential benefits from auditing are not always achieved in practice. Many in society are likely to be disappointed by what they see as audit failures, especially where there is a major financial scandal, fraud or company failure. Such failures may be attributed to (a) the lack of competence by the auditors concerned; or (b) the critics having unrealistic expectations. The first of these explanations may seem to be more appropriate to some critics, or for some failures; for others, the second may seem more appropriate. The accountancy profession may attempt to educate other groups in society to understand and appreciate what the audit 'really' is, from the point of view of the profession. But, equally, others in society may seek to educate and change the accountancy profession, or perhaps the government, to assert their views about what an audit should be. Any significant alteration in the nature of auditing, or reduction in the expectations gap, is likely to require legislation and changes in the fundamental position of auditors.

FURTHER READING

Henley, D., Likierman, A., Perrin, J. R., Lapsey, I., Evans, M. and Whiteoak, J. (1992) *Public Sector Accounting and Financial Control*, 4th edn, Chapman & Hall.

Hopwood, A. and Tomkins, C. (1984) *Issues in Public Sector Accounting*, Philip Allan.

Humphrey, C., Moizer, P. and Turley, S. (1992) *The Audit Expectations Gap in the United Kingdom*, ICAEW.

Jones, R. and Pendlebury, M. (1992) *Public Sector Accounting*, Pitman.

Lee, T. A. (1972) *Company Auditing, Concepts and Practices*, 3rd edn 1986, Van Nostrand Reinhold.

Sherer, M. and Kent, D. (1983) *Auditing and Accountability*, Pitman.

Sherer, M. and Turley, S. (1991) *Current Issues in Auditing*, Paul Chapman.

Woolf, E. (1990) *Auditing Today*, Prentice Hall International.

ESSAYS AND DISCUSSION TOPICS

1. Why should the accounts of companies be audited?
2. Assume that you are a bank manager considering making a substantial loan to a relatively small company. You have the company's accounts for the past five years, all of which have an unqualified audit report. What information does such an audit report give you? What information would you like an audit report to give you? Could an audit report give you that information?
3. To what extent and in what ways could the Expectations Gap in auditing be reduced or eliminated?
4. In what ways, and for what reasons, does auditing in the public sector differ from auditing in the private sector?
5. Choose a type of 'account' other than financial statements (e.g. an election manifesto, police statement, television programme or economic forecast). Consider the desirability and practicability of establishing an independent audit of such an account.
6. Which groups in society are most likely to be dissatisfied with current auditing practice and why? Which groups in society are most likely to be satisfied with current auditing practice and why?
7. In what ways do you think that auditing is likely to change in the next ten years? What changes would you like to see? Give your reasons. What do you think are the main obstacles to change and pressures for change in auditing?

REFERENCES

Briston, R. J. and Perks R. W. (1977) The external auditor – his role and cost to society, *Accountancy*, Nov., 48–52.

Brown, R. (1905) *History of Accounting and Accountants*, Edinburgh, 1905.

Cadbury (Chairman) (1992) *Report of the Committee on the Financial Aspects of Corporate Governance*, Gee & Co., 1992

Chambers, R. J. (1965) Financial information and the securities market, *Abacus*, 1(1), 3–30.

Chatfield, M. (1977) A *History of Accounting Thought*, Robert E. Krieger, Huntington, New York, p. 111.

Cooper, E. [the youngest of the original Cooper Brothers from whom the practice of Coopers and Lybrand developed] (1921) Fifty-seven years in an accountant's office, *The Accountant*, 22 Oct.

Flint, D. (1988) *Philosophy and Principles of Auditing*, Macmillan.

Hansard (1977), 22 Mar., Col. 1082.

Humphrey, C., Moizer, P. and Turley S. (1992) *The Audit Expectations Gap in the United Kingdom*, ICAEW Research Board.

IIA (1981) *Standards for the Professional Practice of Internal Auditing*, Institute of Internal Auditors, quoted in A. D. Chambers (1981) *Internal Auditing*: Theory and Practice, Pitman.

Kitchen, J. (1982) Auditing: past development and current practice, in *Auditing Research: Issues and Opportunities* (eds A. G. Hopwood, M. Bromwich and J. Shaw), Pitman in association with Deloitte Haskins & Sells, London.

Lea, R. and Bagnall, S. (1992) 'So many owe so much to so few', *Accountancy Age*, 22 Oct.

Lee, T. A. (1972) *Company Auditing: Concepts and Practices*, 2nd edn 1982, Institute of Chartered Accountants of Scotland/Gee & Co.

Lyall, D. and Perks, R. W. (1976) Create a state auditing board?, *Accountancy*, June, 34–6.

Mills, P. A. (1990) Agency auditing and the unregulated environment: some further historical evidence, *Accounting, Auditing and Accountability*, 3(1).

Mitchell, A., Puxty, A., Sikka, P. and Willmott, H. (1991) Accounting for change: proposals for reform of auditing and accounting. Discussion Paper No. 7, Fabian Society, London.

Moizer, P. (1989) The image of auditors, in *Auditing and the Future*, Institutes of Chartered Accountants Scotland, and England and Wales, Edinburgh and London.

Moizer, P. (1985) Independence, *in Current Issues in Auditing* (eds D. Kent, M. Sherer and S. Turley), Harper & Row.

Russell, P. (1991) Department of Trade and Industry investigations, in *Current Issues in Auditing* (eds M. Sherer and S. Turley), 2nd edn.

Schandl, C. W. (1978) *Theory of Auditing*, Scholars Book Co., p. 194.

Sikka, P., Puxty, T., Willmott, H. and Cooper, C. (1992) *Eliminating the Expectations Gap*, Certified Accountants Educational Trust, London.

Tinker, T. and Okcabol, F. (1991) Fatal attractions in the agency relationship, *British Accounting Review*, **23**, 329–54.

Williams, D. W. (1985) Legal perspectives on auditors and auditing, *in Current Issues in Auditing* (eds D. Kent, M. Sherer and S. Turley), 1st edn, Harper & Row.

4 Corporate social reporting

INTRODUCTION

The previous two chapters were concerned with accountability and the role of the auditor. The approach concentrated on a traditional accountancy approach: that accountability is due mainly by directors to shareholders and perhaps also to creditors; it concentrated on accountability in financial terms and the role of accountants and auditors in this process. This chapter is concerned with a much wider view of accountability: the view that companies and other significant organizations are accountable to many different groups in society; and that they are accountable in respect of a wider range of issues in addition to financial position and performance.

Corporate social reporting (CSR) involves reporting by companies and other organizations about wider social and economic aspects of the organization's performance than profit and financial position alone. It is usually seen as reporting to a broader range of interest groups than shareholders and creditors, including employees and even society as a whole.

The term **social accounting** is sometimes used in relation to CSR but it can cause confusion as it may be used to mean very different things. It is sometimes used to mean national income accounting. Tinker and Okcabol (1991) use the terms social accounting and public interest accounting interchangeably. Indeed they argue that the two cannot be disassembled from accounting 'proper'. The extent to which accounting 'proper' is, or should be, in the public interest is a central theme of this book. The term **social audit** is also sometimes used in this context. It implies some sort of independent verification of the social accounting information that organizations produce.

This chapter begins with an overview of the development of CSR beginning in the 1970s and then examines some of the problems of CSR in practice. The following two sections deal with approaches to CSR that were prominent in the late 1970s: value added statements; and employment reports and reports to employees. The final two sections deal with approaches to CSR that had become prominent in the early 1990s: ethical investment and environmentalism.

THE DEVELOPMENT OF CORPORATE SOCIAL REPORTING

The involvement of accountants in the process of accountability was originally concerned mainly with the accountability of directors to shareholders and of companies to creditors. As companies came to be seen as increasingly powerful in society there were calls for companies to be made more accountable to a wider public. The 1967 Companies Act introduced a number of disclosure requirements that may be seen as being more to do with public accountability than accountability to shareholders, including the requirement to disclose charitable donations and donations to political parties.

The accountancy profession's *Corporate Report* (ASSC, 1975) may be seen as the first important step in the recognition by accountants of wider responsibilities to society. The authors took a very broad interpretation of the term 'accountability', as outlined in Chapter 2. With regard to corporate social reporting more generally they said that it was tempting to require entities to disclose information showing their impact on society, its amenities and the environment. But they regarded it as impractical at the time because of the absence of agreed measurement techniques. They used the term **social accounting** which they defined as 'the reporting of those costs and benefits, which may or may not be quantifiable in money terms, arising from economic activities and substantially borne or received by the community at large or particular groups not holding a direct relationship with the reporting entity'. They saw this as an area of growing concern to the accounting profession and recommended

> that further study be conducted into methods of social accounting, but that no obligation to report on social and environmental issues be imposed until acceptable, objective and verifiable measurement techniques have been developed which will reveal an unbiased view of both the positive and negative impact of economic activities.

They recognized that, for public relations purposes, companies would be likely to disclose any expenditure that could be identified as being primarily to protect the environment or to benefit society.

This conclusion may be seen as giving the green light to a great deal of public relations hype in annual reports. It also encouraged a great deal of research into methods of social reporting by academics who seemed to believe that it would be possible to develop **acceptable, objective and verifiable measurement techniques**. It may be, however, that in specifying this requirement the *Corporate Report* recognized that compulsory social reporting could be delayed indefinitely. Tinker *et al.* (1991) argued that

> Although there is no technical reason why measuring externalities is intrinsically more difficult than measuring costs such as pensions, depreciation, health care, deferred taxes and goodwill – all of which involve patterns of costs and benefits that are extremely uncertain, and may stretch far into the future–those opposing social costing cited measurement problems as the primary difficulty. Measurement became a smokescreen for their social objections.

By the standards of the 1980s *The Corporate Report* was a fairly radical document, but it was a reflection of the political climate of the 1970s, when it was produced. The profession might have been reluctant to become associated with a set of ideas if they had been markedly out of tune with the political climate of the time, or if such ideas had been the prerogative of one particular political party. But both the Conservative and the Labour parties advocated increased disclosures and wider views of accountability.

In 1973 Edward Heath's Conservative government published a White Paper on *Company Law Reform* (DTI, 1973) which called for the disclosure of more information by companies. Disclosure of information was seen as an essential part of the working of a free and fair economic system. Such openness was a means of securing responsible behaviour by companies (para. 10). The Government intended 'to require companies to report a much wider range of matters than they now have to do' (para. 11); and this was intended 'to give shareholders **and the public** the chance to judge companies' behaviour by **social** as well as financial criteria' (para. 12, emphasis added). Examples of possible disclosure requirements were given including the safety and health of the company's employees, the number of consumer complaints received and how they were dealt with and the conduct of industrial relations (para. 12). In addition the White Paper stated that 'A useful step forward would be to impose a duty on directors to report to the shareholders on specific parts of the company's response to the social environment.' Openness and disclosure were 'the best guarantee of fair dealing and the best antidote to mistrust' (para. 65). 'If shareholders, employees, creditors and the public generally are properly informed, innocent activity will be shown to be so and underhand activity will be inhibited.'

It is not surprising that advocates of a market economy are also advocates of increased disclosure of information that is required to make markets effective. But the White Paper's recommendations went beyond this. Information was to be disclosed in order to change companies' behaviour and to make them more socially responsible. It may have been seen as a way of changing what Heath called 'the unacceptable face of capitalism'.

The Labour party supported similar disclosures. In a 1974 green paper (Labour Party, 1974), for example, they proposed that a Companies Act should extend 'control in the public interest over the private sector by ... [*inter alia*] ... widening the scope of disclosure, in the public interest and in the interest of employees'. The Labour party's emphasis was slightly different from that of the Conservatives. Information for employees and their representatives was more important, and the idea of requiring information to 'control' private sector organizations may be seen as an alternative to public ownership.

It seemed that in the 1970s the Conservatives, the Labour party and the Accountancy profession were all pointing in the same direction. In addition many industrialists spoke up in favour of companies becoming more socially responsible (Perks and Gray, 1978). Few went as far as Friedman (1962) in declaring that

> few trends could so thoroughly undermine the very foundations of our free society as the acceptance by corporate officials of a social responsibility other than to make as much money for their stockholders as possible.

In addition there were a number of special interest groups that produced various kinds of 'social audit', including Social Audit Ltd, a group closely associated with the Consumers Association. They attempted to produce comprehensive, independent assessments of the activities of particular companies as they affected employees, consumers and the local community. They sought co-operation from the companies themselves, but perhaps because their reports looked more like critical exposés than objective assessments, such co-operation was not forthcoming. Other organizations such as Counter Information Services also produced critical assessments of companies' social performance. The 'social audit movement' comprises many different organizations with an interest in putting forward a critique of capitalism and attempting to force social issues on to the agenda in a predominantly market-based economy. The movement is discussed more fully in Geddes (1992).

But the consensus in favour of corporate social reporting in the 1970s was more apparent than real, and proved to be relatively short-lived. The accountancy profession's concern with such issues was immediately overtaken by their preoccupation with the problems of inflation and accounts. There were often very different and conflicting objectives. Many may be seen as 'defenders of capitalism' for whom the provision of information was a requirement of a free-market economy. In addition, many of this group thought that the provision of such information would serve to show companies in a favourable light – especially if the companies themselves decided what information should be disclosed.

Other advocates of CSR may be seen as critics of capitalism who saw the provision of information as a means of changing, or exposing, anti-social behaviour by companies. CSR could serve to discredit capitalism, especially if the information to be disclosed was controlled by those with this in mind.

Many who supported CSR were probably simply going along with the prevailing climate of the day, perhaps motivated in part by idealism. In addition the accountancy profession had an interest in maintaining its dominant position in the business of producing corporate reports, and so in taking on board likely changes in those reports.

The apparent 'constellation' in favour of CSR soon faded. Burchell *et al.* (1985) used the term 'constellation' to describe the combination of forces associated with the rise of the value added statement. A similar analysis can be applied to the rise of CSR. In 1979 the Wilson-Callaghan Labour government was replaced by the Thatcher Conservative government, with its commitment to an aggressive style of capitalism. When the book by Gray *et al.* on corporate social reporting was published in 1987 the authors stated that

> We write at a time when the omens for increased recognition of corporate
> social responsibilities and accountability through CSR could hardly look
> more unpromising.

Gray *et al.* advocated CSR as an attempt to capture the 'middle ground' between those who sought to defend and liberate capitalism, and those who sought to destroy it. Such an approach had its day in the 1970s. But, as Tinker *et al.* (1991) point out, the 'middle ground' is contested territory and is liable to move. They saw the decline in support for CSR as being the end of the 'Caring Society' period; this was followed by a 'Caring Market' period.

Interest in CSR continued throughout the 1980s, but this was a period of market-based studies. Stock market reactions to disclosure became the arbiter of corporate performance and of accounting policy. Studies of CSR concentrated on empirical questions such as:

1. Is there a relationship between social **performance** and social **disclosure**? The hypothesis was that companies with 'good' social performance (and there were various attempts at measuring this) were also the companies that tended to disclose most.
2. What is the relationship between **social disclosure** and **economic performance**? In other words, do the companies that disclose most also have the best performance?

There are of course enormous difficulties in creating measures of social performance, social disclosure and economic performance. But the impressive array of statistical techniques that was used appeared to add credibility to the conclusions of each of these studies. Unfortunately the many different studies came to many different conclusions; these are usefully summarized by Belkaoui and Karpik (1989). Overall they tell us more about the limitations of such studies than they do about what information companies should disclose, how they should behave socially or the effect on their economic performance of social activities and disclosures.

If it were conclusively shown that improved economic performance (if only in terms of higher share prices) is associated with high levels of social disclosures, and with 'good' social performance, then companies would have an incentive to improve their disclosures of socially relevant information and even their social behaviour. But studies so far are inconclusive.

By the 1990s two particular themes related to CSR had become prominent: (1) the ethical investment movement; and (2) the environmental movement. To some extent the ethical investment movement can be caricatured as idealists, particularly church groups, who did not want to soil their hands with investments that were associated with activities that they considered immoral, such as alcohol or nuclear weapons. But there were also those, such as Perks *et al.* (1992), who saw the potential power of ethical investment, particularly if large institutions such as pension funds could be persuaded to adopt ethical policies. Participants in a wide range of organizations might be able to establish ethical policies (such as not investing in companies with South African interests); if this were sufficiently widespread, the share price of companies shown to be unethical would suffer; and companies would have an incentive to be seen as ethical. But the extent to which major institutions pursue ethical investment is limited. And, as Perks *et al.* (1992) have shown, annual reports provide little information to assist those who want to make ethical investment decisions.

Environmental issues are of concern to ethical investors, and an important component of CSR more generally. Indeed, at the time of writing, the environment appears to be of concern to accountants and all political parties. Part 7 of this chapter discusses the involvement of accountants in this issue.

SOME PROBLEMS OF CORPORATE SOCIAL REPORTING

Corporate social reporting can take many different forms. Any decision to implement CSR, whether generally or in particular organizations, will require answers to a number of questions.

SHOULD IT BE DONE BY ACCOUNTANTS?

Accountants are well placed to produce any reports that are seen as an extension of conventional financial reporting. Accountants also have expertise in maintaining and controlling information systems required to produce particular data, and in verifying the information produced. But they have no particular expertise in assessing social or environmental impacts. And they may be wary of becoming involved in issues that appear to be political and controversial if this is likely to undermine their credibility in relation to conventional financial statements.

WHAT FORM SHOULD THE REPORTS TAKE?

Accountants have a natural tendency to think in quantitative terms and there have been a number of attempts to produce statements of social costs set against social benefits, to show some sort of overall social surplus or deficit created by a company. Techniques such as cost benefit analysis can be used, but there is inevitably a great deal of subjectivity in such assessments. A fuller discussion of these approaches may be found in Gray *et al.* (1987).

Although it is difficult to make an **overall** financial or quantitative assessment of a company's social performance, some particular aspects are relatively straightforward, and familiar territory for accountants. Employment reports (as shown on pp. 93–95), for example, include a good deal of reasonably objective quantitative information that is readily verifiable. Some suggestions for inclusion in CSRs, such as numbers of consumer complaints received, also seem designed to appeal to accountants. Much of the quantitative and financial information that it would be appropriate to include in CSRs, such as expenditure on community involvement or on environmental improvements, may be relatively easily manipulated and can be presented to enhance a company's image instead of being an objective assessment of social impact. Similar arguments may be used against other information included in company annual reports, but accountants and auditors, and the regulatory framework within which they operate, offer some reassurance regarding reliability and objectivity.

But, inevitably, many aspects of corporate social performance do not lend themselves to the sort of quantification with which accountants are familiar. Such reports often include a good deal of narrative that describes, often in glowing terms, the benefits that the company's activities have created for employees, consumers, the environment and the economy.

Most of the CSR literature assumes that corporate social reports consist of information included in a company's annual report and accounts. But there are other ways of reporting to society and to groups within society. Information can be included in regular newsletters to employees. Bankers, local authorities, customers and others may be in a position to demand specific information that they require. Particular documents, records and registers may be open to inspection by shareholders, public officials and even the general public. If there were general rights of access to an organization's records – freedom of information in practice – a wide range of interested parties could produce the kind of social reports that they consider appropriate.

SHOULD CSRS BE AUDITED?

There is not much point in corporate social reports being produced if no one believes what they say. The existence of an independent body of auditors who are qualified to verify the contents of such reports would add to their credibility. The normal auditing arrangements that apply to financial statements might be seen as being appropriate here, although there are doubts about auditors' independence, and whether they have the appropriate expertise to deal with many matters of social and environmental concern.

WHO PAYS?

The costs of producing and auditing conventional financial statements are at present met by the companies themselves. Similarly, most corporate social reporting to date has been financed by the company concerned. This, of course, casts doubt on the neutrality of such reports. Companies are unlikely to be willing to finance the production of additional reports unless these are thought to be to the company's advantage. If there is to be any consistent and comparable corporate social reporting legislation will be needed to enforce it.

Some attempts at producing CSRs (or 'social audits') have been financed by groups other than the company which is the subject of the report. In these circumstances there are difficulties in obtaining and verifying the information required, and the group producing the report usually has a particular axe to grind. Reports produced by companies may be seen as powerful in determining perceptions of the company and its activities.

Some groups in society take a different view of a company's social impacts from that which the company itself chooses to present. By publishing reports that present a different view they hope to change perceptions of the company's activities and hope that this will, in due course, lead to changes in company behaviour. If, for example, information is made public that shows that a company is producing excessive pollution, or operating dangerous working practices, then the company may be forced to become more socially responsible. Attempts to change corporate behaviour in this way has a number of limitations. It appears to assume that, on the basis of information disclosed, the best case will win. In many instances it is likely to be the most powerful party that wins. A company often has the resources to produce very credible information, supported by scientific and other 'experts', and presented by public relations professionals, to defend their position. It is not necessarily the 'best' case that wins; it may be the one presented by the most powerful group.

WHAT SHOULD BE DISCLOSED?

Corporate social reports can include a wide range of different information that may be relevent in assessing corporate performance. It may be presented either in narrative form or in quantitative terms, which involves significant measurement problems; or, more usually, it may be a combination of both.

The range of information that is disclosed voluntarily is very wide and Ernst and Ernst (1978) adopted the following classification which was subsequently followed by the ICAEW Survey (Skerratt and Tonkin, 1982).

1. **Environment** includes pollution control activities; prevention, or repair, of damage to the environment; and other environmental disclosures.
2. **Energy** includes conservation of energy policies; and energy efficiency of products.
3. **Fair business practice** includes policies and activities with respect to: racial minorities; young unemployed; women in employment; the disabled; employment overseas; and responsibility to suppliers.
4. **Human resources** includes policies and activities with respect to: health and safety; training; employee communication/participation; and treatment of pensioners.
5. **Community involvement** includes Community activities; health related activities; education and the arts; and other community involvement.
6. **Products** includes product safety; pollution from use; and other product related social information.
7. **Other social responsibility disclosures** includes general social policy statements; and availability of additional information.

The Ernst and Ernst survey showed that 446 of the 500 companies surveyed made social responsibility disclosures. The ICAEW Survey showed that 183 of the 300 companies surveyed made at least one disclosure in 1981–82 (compared with 134 in the previous year).

The extent of voluntary social disclosures is sometimes exaggerated. There is a tendency for official disclosure requirements to increase year by year, and many such requirements are not clear-cut. When a company is slightly ahead of additional disclosures becoming compulsory, or when it interprets a requirement in such a way as to disclose more than others, surveys often show that company as making additional voluntary social disclosures. And many of these 'disclosures' are no more than narrative statements on such things as training, health, or safety of products. Much of this is little more than publicity material and it is at first difficult to see why accountants involve themselves in such trivia.

Many advocates of CSR are interested in changing corporate social behaviour, particularly if they see it as being anti-social, or in revealing such behaviour. But they are likely to be disappointed because as long as such reporting 'remains within the control of the reporters (the pro-capitalist group) it will remain "safe" and its interesting and challenging consequences will be ignored' (Gray *et al.*, 1987).

Companies are, of course, free to include any information that they wish in their annual reports (in addition to that which is required by law). Advocates of CSR want to see more information disclosed. Different advocates of CSR are likely to have different pet concerns, and the range of possible disclosures is almost infinite. The important question is not, therefore, what should be disclosed, but **who should determine what should be disclosed**?

SHOULD CSR BE COMPULSORY?

Each company and each pressure group is likely to favour disclosures that they see as being in their particular interest. If there is to be credible, comprehensive and comparable CSR, it may have to be compulsory. Otherwise those with most power to produce such reports (mainly the companies) will tend to produce reports to suit themselves. National governments may be best placed to claim to be acting on behalf of society, but international bodies may be more effective in enforcing CSR.

The amount of disclosure required by Companies Acts tends to increase with each new act; the emphasis given to disclosures that are primarily social is fairly small, but increasing. There is also evidence that other compulsory disclosures in the future may derive from international organizations such as the European Community and the United Nations.

It can be argued that there is no need for CSR to be made compulsory. If investors were sufficiently concerned about corporate social activities and reporting, companies would feel the effects of that concern in share prices. If 'good' social behaviour and reporting is reflected in higher share prices, then the market would encourage companies in this direction, and the need for compulsion with CSR would not arise. The evidence on share price reactions is so far inconclusive.

WHAT IS THE PURPOSE OF CSR?

Perhaps the greatest obstacle to the development of a consistent and comparable system of corporate social reporting is the lack of agreement on the purpose(s) of such a system. Many different people advocate many different disclosures for different reasons. Their objectives may be to

1. reveal social benefits created by companies; and/or
2. expose social harm imposed by companies; and/or
3. change corporate behaviour.

Although many different groups may support some form of CSR, the approach of those who seek to defend capitalism is likely to be very different from the approach of those who seek to destroy it. Some seek to occupy the 'middle ground' between these extremes, and to 'improve' corporate social behaviour; they are likely to find themselves pulled in different directions.

Within the 'middle ground' different individuals argue for increased disclosures with regard to the many different issues that particularly concern them, such as safety of employees, levels of pollution, redundancies, women's pay, quality of products, energy efficiency and so on. As individuals we are all free to argue for whatever disclosures we wish. But what is the role of accountancy in this?

The accountancy profession might, one day, produce some form of Financial Reporting Standard dealing with disclosures of social and environmental matters. Their 1975 discussion document (ASSC, 1975) included fairly specific proposals for employment reports and value added statements. Any such recommendations would be the outcome of a political process in which the interests of the accountancy profession and their major clients dominate. It would not be realistic to expect the accountancy profession to meet the (disparate) needs of society, or to be the arbiter in determining what social information should be disclosed. These are essentially political questions, and the profession is likely to reflect the wishes of its major clients rather than those of an array of pressure groups. The profession is also likely to be concerned with presenting itself as objective and neutral, rather than taking sides in such controversial issues as those brought to the fore by CSR.

Insofar as it is possible to determine the information that society requires from companies, it is a responsibility of government rather than the accountancy profession. In a democracy governments are assumed to represent the people, or society. The accountancy profession's role in relation to corporate reports is usually seen in terms of verification and monitoring compliance with official requirements. This tends to be interpreted narrowly in relation to Companies Act disclosures. But society, through governments, imposes a range of obligations upon companies in relation to health and safety, pollution, employment policies and so on. Such obligations are likely to increase, and the availability of information on compliance with such requirements is also likely to increase. The role of the accountant in CSR should therefore be in terms of compliance with the law, more broadly interpreted than heretofore, as advocated by Gray and Perks (1982):

> any company's social report should be based on the extent to which the
> company has complied with current statutes and official recommendations

(for example, on pollution, health and safety at work and product safety). This makes it easier to define social responsibility.

Furthermore, the auditor's role might be seen more easily in such a context, as much of his training is geared to ensuring financial compliance-with-the law, and it would be a logical extension of this role to include statutes that deal with the social responsibilities of companies.

VALUE ADDED STATEMENTS

The development of the value added statement (or statement of added value – it means the same thing) was seen by some as 'a spontaneous thrust by major sections of British industry towards a significant form of social accounting' (Renshall *et al.*, 1979). This is rather an exaggerated claim, but it is one of a number of arguments that were put forward in the late 1970s in favour of value added statements being published.

The format of a value added statement is illustrated in Table 4.1 and it can be seen that it includes little, if any, more information than is required by

Table 4.1 A value added statement

	Year 1 £m	Year 2 £m
Henry Motor Company Value Added Statement for the year ended 31 December		
Turnover	5200	5900
Less bought in materials and services	3900	4200
VALUE ADDED	1300	1700
Distributed as follows		
To employees		
Wages salaries and related costs	750	770
To governments		
Tax on year's profit	100	180
To suppliers of capital		
Interest on borrowed money	90	80
Dividends	200	300
Retained for reinvestment		
Depreciation	140	200
Retained profit	20	170
	1300	1700

Companies Acts. The idea that a rearrangement of existing published information could be a significant form of social accounting is an interesting view of what some regard as social accounting! But it should not surprise us. The statement of source and application of funds, which for many years was required by SSAP 10, was regarded as an important statement by accountants, yet it contains little or no information that is not in any case disclosed in balance sheets and profit and loss accounts.

A value added statement was seen as being 'the simplest and most immediate way of putting profit into proper perspective *vis á vis* the whole enterprise as a collective effort by capital, management and employees' (ASSC, 1975, para. 6.7). Conventional financial statements were seen as giving too much emphasis to the shareholders, and the calculation of profit attributable to them. The value added statement presented the information as if the organization is a team effort to create added value, and the added value is then distributed among the members of the team. The idea was that the management of a company would sit down with representatives of the employees, and representatives of shareholders, and decide together how much of the value added that the team had created would be paid out as dividends, and how much was to be paid to the employees, and how much should be retained for reinvestment. This had some credibility at the time when incomes policies were the order of the day. The government might also have seen itself as part of that team, taking their share of added value in the form of taxation. But this notion of a team was something of a fiction, and the idea that bankers and other lenders were part of a team that shared out the added value was quite fictitious. They simply loaned money for a price, just as creditors supplied materials and services for a price.

Presenting the firm as a team that created and shared out value added was expected by some of its advocates to lead to 'some change in industrial outlook and attitudes so that employees will become more co-operative, will have enhanced motivation to work... and will put in more effort and perform better' (Morley, 1978). The form of the statement served to emphasize the relatively small proportion of value added that was paid out to shareholders, and the large proportion that was paid to employees. This would 'help combat the inaccurate belief of many workers that they are exploited and that their efforts unduly benefit and enrich the shareholder' (Morley, 1978).

The value added statement was also seen as directing attention to the share taken by the government in the form of taxation: 'it is clear from the Chairman's remarks in several corporate reports that a major motive for presenting an Value Added Statement had been to reveal the proportion of value added taken by Government' (Morley, 1978).

The value added statement was also seen as being useful in directing attention to the amount of funds generated internally to replace and expand fixed (and other) assets. This was done by adding together depreciation and retained profits, something that is not done in conventional financial accounts. Such presentation was intended to reveal trends in reinvestment, but it could be misleading. Any increase in retained profits and depreciation provisions is inevitably represented by an increase in net assets, but this could be in the form of reduced borrowing or increased liquid assets. Adding together the year's depreciation and retained profit does **not** therefore represent the amount of additional investment undertaken by the company. It does not even represent the amount of **potential** investment; there are many other ways of financing investment.

Value added was also seen as a useful indicator of a company's size and importance. It is, in some ways, a better indicator than conventional measures such as turnover, number of employees or amount of profit. It would, for example, give a better indicator of impact on a local economy than turnover, particularly where high turnover figures are inflated by inclusion of high taxes, or high value bought in components. Value added is also a more stable measure of size than profits: profits can fluctuate widely from year to year even though the firm stays much the same size.

The value added statement was also seen as having a role in introducing productivity schemes (Cox, 1979) whereby increases in incomes could be related to increases in 'value added', or 'wealth created', rather than, for example, profits. This was seen as being more acceptable to employees at the time. Relating wage and salary increases to value added may be a useful expedient, but it is doubtful if companies should be encouraged to maximize value added rather than profit, as Examples 4.1 and 4.2 illustrate.

Example 4.1

	£000
Sales	100
Less:	
Bought in materials	30
VALUE ADDED	70
To employees	70
To governmemt	30
To suppliers of capital	30
Retained for reinvestment	
Depreciation	30
Retained profit	(90)
	70

Does it mean anything to say that the above company has 'created' added value of £70 000 when it has paid out far more money that it has generated? It might be more meaningful to say that it has made a loss!

Example 4.2

A company has a choice of buying in a component for £5 per unit, or making it in-house. The direct manufacturing costs would be

Materials	£4
Labour	£12

If each component were then sold for £10, the bought in item would generate added value of £5; if it were manufactured in-house it would generate added value of £6. Attempts to maximize value added could therefore lead to a company paying £16 for a component that need cost only £5.

Companies that claim that they are in business to create added value could make some very strange decisions!

The advantages claimed for the publication of value added statements were somewhat exaggerated. Such statements are really no more than a cosmetic rearrangement of information that is published in any case.

Those who opposed the publication of value added statements, or who saw little point in it, eventually triumphed. Any suggested additional statements in annual reports usually come up against the standard arguments;

- it would increase the cost of producing annual reports;
- it would delay the production of annual reports;
- the provision of additional information would confuse and overload readers;
- disclosing additional information may damage a company's competitiveness (although, in fact, a value added statement need not disclose any additional information);
- different companies would disclose the information in different ways; the lack of standardization would be misleading.

The lack of standardization is a serious obstacle for value added statements. In Britain 'gross added value' is usually used, where depreciation is treated as part of added value, not as part of the cost of bought in materials and services (to be deducted from sales). But 'net added value' is sometimes used where depreciation is treated as being (an allocation of) bought in goods, and so deducted from sales. The merits of each approach can be argued at length, but in the absence of standardization there will be different interpretations of what 'added value' means. There are also different views on whether VAT and Customs and Excise Duties should be included in turnover, and so be part of value added which is distributed to the government, or whether they should be excluded. In some cases companies have changed their policy from one year to another. There are also differences concerning the treatment of items such as national insurance contributions and income tax deducted from employees' remuneration; sometimes they are shown as being distributed to employees, and sometimes to the government.

Value added statements became popular fairly quickly in the late 1970s. The ICAEW's Annual Survey of Published Accounts showed that only 5 per cent of their 300 companies published such statements in 1975, but by 1980 it had increased to 30 per cent. But interest waned rapidly in the 1980s and few companies now produce them.

It is interesting to question why the value added statement developed and flowered, and then died, in such a short period. It could be interpreted as an indication that accounting practice is subject to short-term changes of fashion, and other examples can be cited of accounting practices that are introduced with much flag-waving enthusiasm, only to fade away and die within a few years (e.g. different forms of inflation adjusted accounts). But changes in accounting practice are related to other changes in society.

Burchell *et al.* (1985) provided a history of the value added statement. They associate its emergence with the existence of an 'accounting constellation'. At the time the language of efficiency and productivity was intertwined with concern about industrial democracy and participation. They drew attention to three important aspects of the constellation:

1. the specification of standards for financial reporting (although there was no proposed standard for value added statements);
2. macroeconomic management, involving incomes policies related to productivity, a situation where productivity schemes based on value added were viewed more favourably than those which emphasized profitability; and
3. a climate of industrial relations that favoured industrial democracy and disclosure of information to employees.

The decline of the value added statement is associated with this 'constellation' being eclipsed by a newly elected Conservative government in 1979 that favoured different policies based on market forces, monetarism and the emphasis of managerial prerogatives rather than industrial democracy.

EMPLOYMENT AND EMPLOYEES

Employment practices and reporting to employees are important issues in CSR.
   In examining these areas it is important to distinguish between

1. employment reports; and
2. reporting to employees.

Employment reports are reports to shareholders and others **about** employment, giving data about employees and employment costs.

Reporting to employees is concerned with producing reports about the company's financial performance, and indeed all or any aspects of a company's performance **specifically for employees.**

The final part of this section refers to **human resource accounting**.

EMPLOYMENT REPORTS

The Corporate Report recommended that full employment reports should be published and provided an illustration of such a report that included the following data.

1. **Numbers employed**, showing totals and numbers of males and females in full-time, part-time and temporary employment. The number of permanent employees at the beginning of the year would be reconciled with the number at the end of the year by showing the number of recruitments and the number of 'separations', with redundancies shown separately.
2. **Location of employment** showing the numbers employed in each of the company's main UK units and in each major unit or country of employment overseas.
3. **Age distribution of employees**, showing, separately for the UK and overseas, the numbers of employees under 20 years old, and numbers in their 20s, 30s, 40s, 50s and over 60.
4. **Hours worked during the year showing** (separately for home and overseas) the total paid at normal rates, the total paid at overtime rates, paid and unpaid lost hours showing whether the hours were lost because of sick leave, industrial accidents, lay-offs, or internal or external industrial disputes; also the average required and actual working hours per week and the average paid holiday hours per annum.
5. **Employee costs** showing the total (separately for home and overseas) of wage and salary costs and of fringe benefits.
6. **Pension:** details of pension scheme including employers' and employees' contributions, the numbers of employees included and pension benefits.

Most of the above information should be reasonably easily available; it can readily be expressed in quantitative terms – something with which accountants are familiar; and it can be verified. Employment reports are therefore a way in which accountant can employ techniques with which they are familiar, express concern with matters other than profit and be involved in corporate social reporting.

The provision of such a statement might serve a number of purposes. It is likely to be of interest to employees but is probably most helpful to investors and analysts attempting to predict future employment costs. In practice the amount of information disclosed about employees varies considerably. In the years immediately after the publication of *The Corporate Report* a significant minority of companies included a specific employment report as part of their published annual report and accounts. This practice rapidly faded and few companies now produce anything like a formal employment report. However, the amount of information regarding employees has increased since the publication of *The Corporate Report*, mainly in response to increased official disclosure requirements.

The Companies Act (1985) requires that the following information is disclosed:

- total wages and salaries payable to employees (including directors with a contract of service) for the year;
- total social security and other pension costs;
- number of employees;
- total directors' remuneration (excluding social security costs, but including the estimated value of benefits in kind);
- remuneration of chairman and of highest paid director; number of directors receiving emoluments in each band of £5000 (£0–£5000; £5001–£10 000; £10 001–£15 000 and so on).

Companies with more than 250 employees are also required (7th Sch., para. 9) to disclose their policy on employment and training of disabled persons including consideration of applications, and continuing employment of and providing training for employees who become disabled. Although there are requirements that companies above a particular size should employ a proportion of disabled people,[1] there is no requirement to disclose the numbers actually employed. The inclusion of such information in annual reports, to be verified by external auditors, would be a straightforward way of involving accountants in social reporting and auditing; it could also be an effective way of encouraging compliance with a social requirement that has been determined by government.

Companies with more than 250 employees are also required (7th Sch., para. 11 [3]) to give information about employee involvement. In particular they are required to describe action taken: to provide information systematically to employees on matters of concern to them as employees; to have regular consultation with employees; to involve employees, for example through a share scheme; and in 'achieving a common awareness on the part of all employees of the financial and economic factors affecting the performance of the company'.

There are also provisions in the 1985 Companies Act (7th Sch., para. 10) for the Secretary of State to make regulations requiring certain classes of company to include in their directors' report information about the arrangements in force for securing the health, safety and welfare at work of employees.

The Act also requires that number of employees by category should be disclosed, but it is left to directors to decide what categories should be used, having regard to the way in which the company's activities are organized. Some companies choose categories by geographical location, sex, part-time or full-time,

---

[1] The Disabled Persons (Employment) Acts of 1944 and 1958 required firms employing more than 20 people to ensure that 3 per cent of their labour force consists of registered disabled persons. There is a lack of strong enforcement mechanisms for this provision, and the Secretary of State now has power to vary the required proportion.

hourly, weekly or monthly paid, or by function (e.g. production, administration, sales). Others choose not to identify separate categories.

In addition, *SSAP 24* requires that companies should disclose certain information about their pension schemes. This includes information such as whether the schemes are based on defined contributions or defined benefits, the accounting policies used, details of any deficiencies and the most recent actuarial valuation. These seem like technical accountancy matters concerned with the measurement of income and of balance sheet items. But since the Maxwell scandal there are greater concerns in society regarding the investment and safety of pension funds assets and how they are managed. Issues of accountability, reporting and audit of pension funds have not yet received the attention that they deserve.

Many companies publish rather more than the minimum information that would be required to ensure compliance with the Companies Act, but few publish a specific employment report. It would be fair to say, however, that corporate social reporting, albeit with statutory backing, has probably made more progress with the sort of information that would be included in an employment report than in any other area.

REPORTING TO EMPLOYEES

Most companies provide some sort of information to employees, typically in the form of newsletters or on notice boards. Many also make copies of their annual report and accounts available to employees. But when we talk about reporting to employees in an accounting context, or of 'employee reporting', we mean the provision of specially designed statements for employees. These are usually much simplified versions of the annual report and accounts, often similar to the 'Annual Review' that many companies now offer shareholders in place of the full annual report and accounts.

Surveys (e.g. Tonkin and Skerratt, 1991) suggest that the main reasons why companies produce employee reports are to involve employees more in the affairs of the company and to encourage a sense of responsibility. The reports themselves include a variety of simplified and diagrammatic presentations of financial information including pie charts, bar charts, graphs, pictorial representation and even value added statements.

It is doubtful if these statements are of much use to employees. They provide management with an opportunity to present a particular version of events to employees, but employees are often not in a position to understand or question that version. Indeed, any such attempt is likely to require a full annual report and accounts. Such information may be of use in a relatively small company where most employees are in much the same position as each other. In major quoted companies, however, the financial position and performance of a company over-all may be of little interest to workers threatened with redundancy, or bargaining for wage increases in a particular location. Employees have to depend on management for more specific ('disaggregated') information in such cases, although the basis for such information may be very questionable, for example as shown by Bery *et al.* (1985).

HUMAN RESOURCE ACCOUNTING

The subject of human resource (or human asset) accounting is sometimes seen as 'putting people on the balance sheet'. At first this might seem an unlikely proposition – how can we put a value on people? But accountants have started to attribute values to brand names and to show these as balance sheet assets; and football clubs do buy players and have to account for this.

Academic interest in human resource accounting has continued since the seminal work of Likert (1967) (for example Flamholtz, 1989), and it has often been seen as a financial reporting issue. But the advocates of HRA are more concerned with the value and management of people as organizational resources. At the time of writing there has been no significant inclusion of 'human assets' in corporate reports, and it does not appear to be a developing aspect of CSR.

ETHICAL INVESTMENT

Concern with 'ethical investment' came to prominence in the UK in the 1980s, prompted particularly by the concern of churches and other organizations with funds to invest who did not want to invest in companies engaged in activities to which their organizations were particularly opposed. The organization Ethical Investment Research Services (EIRIS) was established in 1983 to advise such investors on which companies they should avoid investing in. The first ethical investment trust was established in 1984 and by 1989 there were 17 ethical funds.

> The number of ethical investment vehicles is increasing ... organisations, including some local authority pension funds are endeavouring to invest in an ethical manner. There has also been a spawning of related ethical products such as ethical pension funds, ethical Personal Equity Plans (PEPs) and ethical PEP mortgages. (Perks *et al.*, 1992)

Dunham (1990) claimed that in 1990 about £6 billion of investors' funds in the UK were invested on ethical principles.

What different investors and trusts regard as un/ethical varies considerably. A study of 14 investment trusts (Perks *et al.*, 1992) showed that there were nine main activities which they sought to avoid, to varying extents. These activities, and the number of trusts seeking to avoid involvement in them were as follows:

Activity	Number of Trusts
Tobacco	11
Armaments	10
Alcohol	9
Gambling	8
South Africa	8
Animal experiments	4
Nuclear power	3
Drugs	1
Political donations	1

Ethical investment trusts are also concerned to encourage investment in companies with positive records in such areas as concern for employees, positive employment policies and creating benefits to society, particularly in relation to the environment. These various social concerns are often hard to define and the extent of particular trusts' commitment to them varies. But ethical investors appear to be an increasingly important group, with particular information needs. As corporate reports are usually portrayed as presenting information that is useful in making investment decisions, it might be reasonable to expect some form of corporate social report to supply the appropriate information.

An investigation by Perks *et al.* (1992) established the investment policies of the main investment trusts, particularly in relation to environmental issues; identified the companies that were most frequently invested in for environmental reasons; and examined the published annual reports and accounts of those companies. Although it has been established (Harte *et al.*, 1991) that annual reports are 'often' or 'always' used by ethical trusts in making investment decisions, Perks *et al.* found that the reports concerned provided virtually no information to indicate whether or not the companies complied with the ethical environmental criteria with which the investors were concerned.

Ethical investors need the sort of information for making investment decisions that it is usually said that Corporate Social Reports should contain. But, in practice, CSR has not progressed sufficiently to meet the information needs of ethical investors.

ENVIRONMENTALISM

By the early 1990s the environment was the predominant concern of those interested in the (anti-) social activities of companies and who wanted to enforce public accountability for such activities.

It seemed to many that current economic development and policies were not sustainable and that major environmental crises were on the way. The main pressures, which were said to be increasing exponentially, included such things as the rate of ozone depletion, desertification, deforestation, incidence of acid rain, depletion of fishing stocks, erosion of soil, rates of usage of non-renewable resources, rates of species extinction and so on.

Accountants have to some extent been involved in environmental issues at least since the publication of *The Corporate Report* (1975). In relation to environmental issues it recognized that companies might wish to disclose expenditure undertaken to protect the environment for public relations purposes. Even Gray *et al.*'s (1987) major work on corporate social reporting included only passing references to environmental issues. The Institute of Chartered Accountants of Scotland's major work on corporate reporting (*Making Corporate Reports Valuable*, 1988) made no references to the environment.

Other organizations can claim to have a more long standing interest in environmental issue. The British Institute of Management, for example, produced a checklist of management's responsibilities in relation to the environment in 1979. An important international development was the development of the 'Valdez' Principles, adopted by the European INAISE (International Association of Investors in the Social Economy), for organizations

> which invest in undertakings of an ethical, ecological, cultural and self-managing nature, including women's undertakings, undertakings of ethnic minorities, in undertakings whose aims are concerned with people with disabilities, healthier living, peace and the Third World, and in undertakings in the social economy generally.

These Principles were named after the Alaskan oil spillage from the *Exxon Valdez*, and the United States Social Investment Forum fostered the idea of getting companies to adhere to these principles which are, in effect, a charter for corporate social responsibility (Miller, 1992):

1. **Protection of the Biosphere**
   We will minimise and strive to eliminate the release of pollutant that may cause environmental damage to the air, water, earth or its inhabitants. We will safeguard habitats in rivers, lakes, wetlands, coastal zones and oceans and will minimise contributing to the greenhouse effect, depletion of the ozone layer, acid rain, or smog.

2. **Sustainable Use of Natural Resources**
   We will make sustainable use of renewable natural resources such as water, soils and forests. We will conserve non-renewable natural resources through efficient use and careful planning. We will protect wildlife habitat, open spaces and wilderness while preserving biodiversity.

3. **Reduction and Disposal of Waste**
   We will minimise the creation of waste, especially hazardous waste and wherever possible recycle materials. We will dispose of waste through safe and responsible methods.

4. **Wise Use of Energy**

   We will make every effort to use environmentally safe and sustainable energy sources to meet our needs. We will invest in improved energy efficiency and conservation in our operations. We will maximise the energy efficiency of products we produce or sell.

5. **Risk Reduction**

   We will minimise the environmental, health and safety risks to our employees and the communities in which we operate by employing safe technologies and operating procedures, and by being constantly prepared for emergencies.

6. **Marketing Safe Products and Services**

   We will sell products and services that minimise adverse environmental impacts and that are safe as consumers commonly use them. We will inform consumers of the environmental impacts of our products and services.

7. **Damage Compensation**

   We will take responsibility for any harm caused to the environment by making every effort to fully restore the environment, and to compensate those persons who are adversely affected .

8. **Disclosure**

   We will disclose to our employees and to the public incidents relating to our operations that cause environmental harm or pose health or safety hazards. We will disclose potential environmental, health or safety hazards posed by our operations, and we will not take any action against employees who report any condition that creates a danger to the environment or poses health and safety hazards.

9. **Environmental Directors and Managers**

   At least one member of the Board of Directors will be a person qualified to represent environmental interests. We will commit management resources to implement these Principles, including the funding of an office of vice president for environmental affairs or equivalent executive position, reporting directly to the CEO, to monitor and report on our implementation efforts.

10. **Assessment and Annual Audit**

    We will conduct and make public an annual self-evaluation of our progress in implementing these Principles and in complying with all applicable laws and regulations throughout our worldwide operations. We will work towards the timely creation of independent environmental audit procedures which we will complete annually and make available to the public.

Two major reports further increased the importance attached to environmental issues: the Brundtland Report (1987) and the Pearce Report (1989). The Pearce Report was commissioned by the Government to identify how economic and industrial policies could be developed which reflect the full cost of using environmental resources which are usually seen as being 'free'. It recommended that economic policies should be integrated with environmental objectives and that the 'polluter pays' principle should be adopted. It emphasized the role of financial quantification and market-based incentives – this appeared to lead to a role for accountants. The Pearce Report was endorsed by Chris Patten, then Secretary of State for the Environment.

Both Brundtland and Pearce adopted the concept of **sustainable development**, the idea that the environmental impact of growth is managed in such a way that future generations are able to sustain living standards and make further progress. A distinction can be made between:

1. man-made and natural capital that is renewable, sustainable, or substitutable, e.g. machines, roads and most farm animals; and
2. critical natural capital, e.g. the ozone layer, or rare species, which are difficult to renew.

As capital maintenance is central to profit measurement, ecologist-accountants might argue that measures of profit are misleading if they make no allowance for maintaining critical natural capital. This is part of a general criticism of accountancy in relation to CSR: it considers only costs and benefits with a direct financial impact on the entity concerned. Externalities, such as pollution or desertification, are ignored. Companies might be happy to report expenditure that they have incurred to improve the environment (and/or to avoid penalties for non-compliance with pollution controls). They might be less inclined to report on, and to try to attribute a value to, the damage that they do to the environment.

Accountancy is also implicated in the environmental crisis in advocating investment appraisal techniques that emphasize the short term rather than the long term, particularly in relation to electricity generation. Energy from renewable resources, such as wind, wave, tide and water, tend to have heavy capital expenditure and are seen to be economic only over a very long period. Accountants' methods, particularly where high discount rates are used in discounted cash flow calculations, tend to favour the quick and dirty types of power generation.

The Environmental Protection Act 1990 implemented the principle that the polluter should pay. Companies had to pay for regulatory bodies which were set up to control and inspect emissions, with fines for those exceeding defined levels. Companies were expected to minimize waste production using the Best Available Technology Not Entailing Excessive Cost (BATNEEC) principle. There was also a commitment to giving public access to information about polluting industries through registers to be kept by enforcing authorities. Such registers, if they are properly kept, and if the information in them is verifiable and accessible, could well be a more effective form of public accountability than an annual report that is overwhelmingly influenced by the interests of management.

In 1990 the Government also produced a large, glossy White Paper (DOE, 1990) on environmental issues, but many found it disappointing and largely lacking in positive commitments. It may be that the European Community will be more influential in enforcing environmental improvements. A draft directive has called for compulsory environmental auditing for particular types of companies.

By 1990 accountants were becoming seriously interested in environmental matters. The Chartered Association of Certified Accountants produced a major report, *The Greening of Accountancy: The Profession after Pearce* (Gray, 1990), which suggested that the Pearce Report would require a voluntary response from organizations and made some specific suggestions for new environmental accounting systems. In 1992 the first major book on the subject was produced, Dave Owen's *Green Reporting: Accountancy and the Challenge of the Nineties* (Owen, 1992). He suggested that environmental issues might be becoming big business for the accountancy profession:

> environmental consultancy is taking off in a big way and indeed is bidding fair to replace value for money and efficiency studies as the growth area of the 1990's.

There was a danger that accountants might miss the boat in what was emerging as a major concern of the 1990s:

> Clearly for accounting to maintain its prominent position within ... public policy and corporate decision-making arenas, the profession must grasp the nettle of green reporting sooner rather than later. (Owen, 1992)

In practice most of the major international accounting firms now offer services in relation to environmental issues including briefings on regulatory requirements, compliance reviews, waste and loss audits, planning an environmental strategy and environmenal auditing.

But what can accountants actually **do** in relation to environmental concerns? The answers of those who want to save the world from environmental disaster might be slightly different from the answers of those who see environmentalism as a current concern from which they might be well placed to earn fees or advance their careers. Both would probably see that accountants have particular skills and techniques to offer that could be useful in relation to environmental concerns.

Accountants are not necessarily well placed to determine what environmental policies should be adopted, but they might play a role in assessing which environmental impacts can be defined, quantified and reported. Environmental policies may be established by national governments or by international agreement; or companies may adopt their own policies, perhaps based on the Valdez Principles, or one of the various check lists that are being produced. Once the policies are clear, accountants are well placed to establish the systems and controls required to capture the necessary data, reporting for example on the costs of pollution controls, environmental improvements; setting environmental budgets and reporting on their implementation in practice; and attempting to measure and value environmental damage inflicted.

Accountants can also play an important role in auditing. Energy audits and waste audits can be expected to lead to valuable savings for a company, as well as reducing environmental damage. Auditors are also used to reporting on compliance with official requirements, traditionally those established by Companies Acts, although this role has been extended to include value for money auditing. Environmental audits, which assess the extent to which an organization implements the environmental policies that it has adopted, are bound to rely on techniques familiar to accountants.

Environmental issues can also, of course, be an important element of corporate social reports, where the accountant also has an established role to play. The report itself may be seen as the end product of an accounting system that records and classifies data, based on a system with in-built controls, and using data that is verified by independent auditors if the report is to have credibility.

SUMMARY AND CONCLUSIONS

Conventional financial accounts focus on the calculation of profit, the shareholders' interest in the organization and the maintenance of capital. Various strands of corporate social reporting have emphasized the importance of employees and the environment. Future developments will, no doubt, concentrate elsewhere.

It would be a crude generalization to characterize the 1960s as the decade of consumerism; the 1970s as the decade when employees were to the fore; the 1980s as the decade of aggressive free market capitalism; and the 1990s as the decade of environmentalism. Nevertheless it is fair to say that predominant concerns in society change from time to time in ways such as this, and to some extent accountancy mirrors these changes.

Accountants have, so far, given relatively little consideration to consumers. They were mentioned by *The Corporate Report* as being users with information needs, and some approaches to **value for money auditing** and the publication of **performance indicators** have suggested that data such as the number of complaints received is relevant. Such matters were given renewed prominence by John Major's 'Citizens' Charter'.

It is difficult to predict how the emphasis of accounting in relation to social issues will change and develop. Various aspects of the environment, such as energy and conservation, may remain centre stage for some time to come. But other concerns may come to the fore, such as the international economy, the Third World, total quality management and relationships with suppliers. Slightly wilder speculation may lead to the interests of a company's bankers or auditors coming to predominate. The interests and influence of government are likely to remain powerful, whether as economic planners or as representatives of the public in particular ways (such as concern for employees or the environment) or simply as tax gatherers. Concerns of the European Community are likely to be at least as important as those of national governments, and international agencies, such as the United Nations, may become an important influence on accountancy and annual reporting in relation to issues such as control of multinational companies.

It is reasonable to predict that accountancy and published annual reports will continue to reflect the interests of those who have most influence over them. At present the directors of a company are among the most powerful influences. Some information about the directors has to be disclosed by law, mainly as a protection to shareholders, creditors and others. Annual reports increasingly include public relations type information which appears to be intended to reflect the directors' good management. It may be that the value of the human assets employed by the company itself, particularly the directors, will be included in future corporate reports.

FURTHER READING

Cannon, T. (1992) *Corporate Responsibility*, Pitman.

Gray, R., Owen, D. and Maunders, K. (1987) *Corporate Social Reporting, Accounting and Accountability*, Prentice Hall.

Lehman, C.R. (ed.) (19??) *Advances in Public Interest Accounting* (journal), especially Vol. 4, JAI Press Inc., Grenwich, Connecticut 06836.

Owen, D. (ed.) (1992) *Green Reporting: Accountancy and the Challenge of the Nineties*, Chapman & Hall, London.

ESSAY AND DISCUSSION TOPICS

1. Who are the main potential users of annual reports besides creditors and shareholders? What are their main information needs likely to be?
2. To what extent do companies disclose socially relevant information in their annual reports on a voluntary basis? Select a company's annual report and try to identify what information is disclosed that is not officially required.
3. Whose interests are served by company annual reports and accounts at present? In what ways and to what extent has this changed over the last 15, 30, 45 years? How is it likely to change in the future?
4. What information (if any) are consumers likely to seek in a company annual report and accounts?
5. What information is a potential student likely to want to know about a university before deciding whether or not to go there? Is that information included in the university's annual report and accounts?
6. When applying for a job do you study your potential employer's annual report and accounts? Why/why not? What information would you like to find there? Is it likely to be provided?

7. Discuss the potential power of (a) environmentalists, (b) ethical investors, (c) employees and (d) consumers to change corporate reports in their own interest.
8. Discuss the potential role of accountancy in implementing a 'Citizens' Charter' in respect of a major organization of your choice.
9. What does the rise and fall of the value added statement tell us about the nature of accountancy and the ways in which accountancy changes from time to time?
10. Distinguish between employment reports and reporting to employees. Why would companies produce such reports?
11. In what ways could accounting contribute to preserving the environment?

REFERENCES

Accounting Standards Steering Committee (ASSC) (1975) *The Corporate Report.*

✗ Belkaoui, A. and Karpik, P. G. (1989) Determinants of the corporate decision to disclose social information, *Accounting, Auditing and Accountability Journal,* **2**, 36–51.

Berry, A. J., Capps, T., Cooper, D., Ferguson, P., Hopper, T. and Lowe, E. A. (1985) Commentary: NCB Accounts – a mine of misinformation? *Accountancy*, Jan. 11–12.

Brundtland, G. H./United Nations World Commission on Environment and Development (1987) *Our Common Future*, Oxford University Press.

Burchell, S., Clubb, C. and Hopwood, A. G. (1985) Accounting in its social context: towards a history of value added in the United Kingdom, *Accounting Organizations and Society*, **10**(4), 381–483.

Cox, B. (1979) *Value Added: An Appreciation for the Accountant Concerned with Industry*, CIMA, London.

Department of the Environment (DOE) (1990), *This Common Inheritance*, HMSO, London.

Department of Trade and Industry (DTI) (1973) *Company Law Reform*, Cmnd 5391, HMSO, London.

Dunham, R. (1990) Ethical funds, no bar to profit, *Accountancy*, June, 111.

Ernst & Ernst (1978) *Social Responsibility Disclosure: 1978 Survey*, Ernst & Ernst, Cleveland, Ohio.

Flamholtz, E. G. (1989) Human resource accounting: an overview, in *Behavioural Accounting* (eds G. Siegel and H. Ramananskas-Marconi), Cincinnati SouthWestern Publishing.

Friedman, M. (1962) *Capitalism and Freedom*, University of Chicago, p. 133.

Geddes, M. (1992) The social audit movement, in *Green Reporting, The Challenge of the Nineties* (ed. D. Owen), Chapman & Hall.

Gray, R. H. and Perks, R. W. (1982) *Accountancy*, Apr., 102.

Gray, R., Owen, D. and Maunders, K. (1987) *Corporate Social Reporting, Accounting and Accountability*, Prentice Hall.

Gray, R. H. (1990) *The Greening of Accountancy: The Profession after Pearce*, The Chartered Association of Certified Accountants, London.

Harte, G., Lewis, L. and Owen, D. (1991) Ethical investment and the corporate reporting function, *Critical Perspectives in Accounting*, **2**(3), Sept., 227–54.

Labour Party (1974) *The Community and the Company*, London, May.

Likert, R. (1967) *The Human Organisation*, McGraw-Hill, New York.

Miller, A. (1992) Green investment, in Owen (1992), op. cit.

Morley, M. F. (1978) *The Value Added Statement: A Review of Its Use in Corporate Reports*, Institute of Chartered Accountants of Scotland, Gee & Co., London.

Owen, D. (1992) *Green Reporting: Accountancy and the Challenge of the Nineties*, Chapman & Hall, London.

Pearce, D., Markandya, A. and Barbier, E. B. (1989) *Blueprint for a Green Economy*, Earthscan Publications, London.

Perks, R. W. and Gray, R. H. (1978) Corporate social reporting – an analysis of objective, *British Accounting Review*, **10**(2), 43–59.

Perks, R. W., Rawlinson, D. and Ingram, L. (1992) An exploration of ethical investment in the UK, *British Accounting Review*, **24**, 43–65.

Renshall, M., Allan, R. and Nicholson, K. (1979) *Added Value in External Financial Reporting: A Study of its Aims and Uses in the Context of General Purpose Financial Reports*, ICAEW, London.

Skerratt, L. C. L. and Tonkin, D. J. (1982) *Financial Reporting 1982–83: A Survey of Published Accounts*, Institute of Chartered Accountants in England and Wales.

Tinker, T., Lehman, C. and Neimark, M. (1991) Falling down the hole in the middle of the road: political quietism in corporate social reporting, *Accounting, Auditing and Accountability Journal*, **4**(2).

Tinker, T. and Okcabol, F. (1991) Fatal attractions in the agency relationship, *British Accounting Review*, **23**, 329–54.

Tonkin, D. J. and Skerratt, L. C. L. (1991) *Financial Reporting 1990–91, A Survey of UK Reporting Practice*, ICAEW, London, pp. 113–33.

5 Beyond profit

INTRODUCTION

This chapter begins by explaining why and how accountancy emphasizes profit as the principal measure of performance, and summarizes some of the limitations of profit as a performance indicator. The chapter then outlines other measures of performance, particularly in relation to economy, efficiency and effectiveness. Some of the characteristics of the public sector are then examined to show why there is a case for value for money (VFM) auditing, and the use of performance indicators, in the public sector. From a social point of view there is a case for wider views of performance being examined in all organizations; VFM auditing has become a requirement in most of the public sector and not in the private sector. The way in which VFM audits are conducted is then briefly described. Indicators of performance other than profitability can be used in many different ways in many different organizations and the chapter discusses their use in nationalized industries and in higher education. VFM audits and the use of performance indicators are then critically appraised, emphasizing the problems and difficulties in practice. The chapter concludes by drawing attention to how the use of other performance indicators, beyond profit, is influenced by the relative power positions of the parties involved.

IMPORTANCE AND PROBLEMS OF PROFIT

Profit figures are seductive. They appear to tell us what we want to know. We tend to assume that a profitable organization is efficient and effective, whereas an unprofitable one must be inefficient and ineffective; a profitable organization will survive and prosper, whereas an unprofitable one will fail; a profitable organization will attract investment and so, in the national interest, investment resources will go to the most efficient and effective organizations; unprofitable organizations will find it difficult to attract additional resources, which is just as well because they would not use them efficiently and effectively; and we can have faith in profit figures because there are well established procedures for measuring and reporting profit, supported by accounting standards and independently audited.

Unfortunately what happens in practice does not live up to these expectations and there are at least three good reasons why society should not take profit figures too seriously:

1. it is not clear how 'profit' should be defined and measured;
2. profit does not necessarily indicate what we expect it to; and
3. profit is of questionable relevance in assessing the performance of many organizations.

1. Definition and measurement

The lack of clarity in the definition and measurement of profit is clear from the plethora of constantly changing accounting standards, the popularity of 'creative accounting' (Jameson, 1988; Griffiths, 1987) and the concern of analysts with the 'quality' of earnings because they cannot take profit figures at face value. Acres of academic analysis of the theory and measurement of business income have failed to produce even an agreed definition of profit. It is easy to come up with such things as income less expenses, but then we have trouble with defining 'income' and 'expenses'. Alternatively we can define profit as an increase in net assets after deducting new capital introduced and adding back any dividends that have been paid out; but then we do not have agreed definitions of 'assets' and 'liabilities'. These issues may seem straightforward enough at first sight, but detailed examination of the problems of definition and measurement in areas such as goodwill, stocks, off balance sheet finance, leased assets and the effects of inflation on accounts, and the accountancy profession's attempts to deal with them, indicate how far we are from resolving the problems of profit definition and measurement. The accountancy profession's attempts to deal with these problems are examined in Chapter 6. Chapter 7 then examines the intractability of developing a conceptual framework on which to base accounting standards – the fundamental problems in defining profit and establishing rules for measuring it.

2. Expectations of profit

The problem that profit frequently does not provide the information that we want from it has long been known, but it has probably not been recognized sufficiently widely. It may be seen as an 'expectations gap' every bit as serious as the expectations gap in auditing. At the very earliest stages of developing guidance on how to deal with the effects of inflation on accounts the ICAEW (1952, para. 28) stated that

> results shown by accounts prepared on the basis of historical cost are not a measure of increase or decrease in wealth in terms of purchasing power; nor do the results necessarily represent the amount which can prudently be regarded as available for distribution ... similarly the results shown by such accounts are not necessarily suitable for purposes such as price fixing, wage negotiations and taxation ...

Such warnings of what such profit figures should **not** be used for begs the question: what can they be used for? In spite of their reservations about historic cost accounting, the ICAEW went on to recommend that it should continue to be the basis for preparing annual accounts. Forty years later the position was much the same, except that, in the intervening period, the accountancy profession has turned itself inside out and stood on its head during the inflation accounting debate; and the expectations of users of accounts are now much higher.

Profit figures can only be a surrogate for the information that we would really like. We want to know what future dividends will be and whether previous dividends were justified. We want to be able to forecast future share prices and to know if the company is about to go into liquidation or receivership. We want to know if it is well managed and if the company is generating more resources than it is using. We want to know if it is efficient and effective. And we expect a single profit figure, perhaps expressed in relation to capital employed, to give us all this information.

The owners of companies may be less interested in the amount of profit that the company makes than they are in the direct cash benefits to themselves in the form of dividends and the share price, particularly future dividends and any increases in the share price. As it is not possible to know what future cash flows will be generated by particular shares, investors have to make do with whatever surrogates are available. Profit figures are perhaps the most accessible and widely used proxies for the cash flow information that rational investors (assuming that there are such people) really want to know. There are debates about the success of profit as a predictor of future cash flows. It may be that other information, past cash flows for example, is a more accurate predictor. There are also debates about what information shareholders really want: different shareholders are likely to have different interests. In Chapter 4 it was suggested that various users of accounts might want a range of different information besides profit, including, for example, information about employment and employees and about the environment. From time to time academic accountants and the accountancy profession show signs of enthusiasm about the topics of the day, such as value added statements or inflation accounting. But the basic core of financial accounting in companies has remained unchanged: it concerns the reporting of profit.

3. Relevance of profit

In the public sector and in many not-for-profit organizations (such as charities, clubs or trade unions) profit figures are of little relevance – unless the organization is about to be privatized or converted to a plc. These organizations are usually funded on a cash basis and there is no need for accruals based profit figures as a guide to investors. There are no dividends and so profit calculation is not required to guide dividend decisions. Public sector organizations are unlikely to go bankrupt and so profit figures are not required as an indicator of financial viability. And profit is not an objective of these organizations: they are there to provide a service to society or to some part of society and they are given funds for this purpose. If such an organization underspends its funds or makes a profit, the government or other funding body might reasonably ask why the organization was accumulating funds instead of spending them on the intended purpose – improving the service to the public for example. The organization might respond that it needs to accumulate funds for future improvements and perhaps for capital expenditure. Once an organization starts to build up 'its own' funds, its managers are taking a degree of control away from the funding body. In the public sector restrictions on carrying forward underspent funds, and the provision of separate funding for capital expenditure, have helped to maintain central control. But many organizations (such as universities and local authorities) have succeeded in building up substantial funds (or 'balances') of 'their own'. It may be that public sector organizations will become increasingly capitalistic in the sense that public funding for capital expenditure will be restricted and they will be encouraged to use savings in revenue expenditure (or 'profits') to finance capital expenditure. But, hopefully, making profits will not become a more important objective than providing health care, education,improving human happiness and fulfilment, or whatever the organization is set up to do. Profit is an inappropriate indicator of performance in many organizations, particularly in the public sector. There is a need for other indicators of performance.

PERFORMANCE INDICATORS

A performance indicator is a piece of quantitative data collected at regular intervals to indicate the performance of a particular aspect of an organization or part of an organization. It may be financial or non financial, and is usually dependent on two pieces of data where either

1. one is divided by the other, e.g. cost per unit produced or number of students per member of staff; or
2. one is expressed as a percentage of the other, e.g. percentage of units that are defective, or wages and salary cost as a percentage of income generated.

The production of performance indicators can serve a number of useful functions.

1. It is part of the accountability process whereby particular aspects of an organization's performance are monitored by the public or by an official body acting on behalf of the public.
2. They can provide information to enable consumers to make informed choices, for example about which education institution to attend or which area to live in.
3. It is a tool of management to monitor, compare and improve aspects of performance.
4. The requirement to produce performance indicators may assist in defining the objectives of organizations and particular activities conducted within them.
5. They provide information to enable managers, funding bodies, users of services and others to investigate aspects of performance that appear to be unusually good or bad.
6. They can provide a basis for governments and funding bodies to identify where changes in funding levels are most appropriate and to implement policies intended to encourage, or to discourage, particular aspects of performance.

Indicators can be selected to indicate many different aspects of performance. Efficiency and effectiveness are the most widely attempted, but, in assessing the performance of a service activity, Sorensen and Grove (1977) have suggested seven properties of service functions for which performance indicators can be produced. These are as follows.

1. **Efficiency**, which compares resource inputs with the outputs produced. This tells us how much it costs per service hour provided, per client served, per mile travelled or whatever.
2. **Effectiveness**, which compares what an organization achieves with what it intends to achieve. It assesses success in achieving goals. Examples of such measures might be number of patients cured, number of road accidents per thousand vehicle miles, or actual outcome as a percentage of planned

outcome (e.g. we reached 95 per cent of our target in providing nursery education or in our planned reduction of the housing waiting list).

3. **Availability**, which tells us the amount and type of service provided. This may simply list what is available.

4. **Awareness**, which tells us the extent to which potential users of a service know of the existence, the range of services available, and the conditions upon which they are available. Measures would be the percentage of users aware of particular services, and of how users came to know about particular services.

5. **Accessibility**, which indicates if a service can be obtained by appropriate groups and the ease of reaching that service. Appropriate measures include average travel time of users, availability of public transport, availability of ramps and sloping kerbs for wheelchairs.

6. **Extensiveness**, which compares the quantity of services rendered to the backdrop of the problem. Examples would include percentage of children under five attending nursery school, or percentage of houses with mains electricity, water and drainage.

7. **Appropriateness**, which indicates whether the correct type and amount of service is provided for the problems presented. Examples include any mismatch between diagnosis and service provided.

This list suggests a broad array of information that would be appropriate in assessing the performance of services, but some of these do not lend themselves to 'indicators' in the sense that is usually meant. With 'availability', for example, a list of services that is available does not look much like a performance indicator. A performance indicator might express the number of services offered by a particular unit as a percentage of the total number of services that such units could offer. For example, one school might offer 25 per cent of all possible GCSE subjects; another might offer 10 per cent.

The above list does not specifically mention **quality** as an indicator, although this is an obvious concern of users of a service. But **effectiveness** and **appropriateness** might both be seen as indicating aspects of quality. From the point of view of a user, a high-quality service is one that is effective in achieving what is expected of it; extensiveness, availability and accessibility might also be seen as indicators of quality.

ECONOMY, EFFICIENCY AND EFFECTIVENESS

In developing performance indicators most emphasis has been given to the three 'E's': economy, efficiency and effectiveness, especially the second of these.

Economy is concerned with obtaining a given quantity and quality of resources at least cost. An economical organization will use a low-paid accounts clerk rather than a more highly paid, qualified accountant for routine tasks. An organization that is overstaffed, or that uses equipment and other resources that are of a higher quality and a higher price than is necessary, is said to be uneconomical. An uneconomical organization might use an expensive limousine when a smaller, cheaper car would be quite adequate. It is sometimes, however, a false economy simply to use the cheapest resource available if there are a lot of breakdowns for example, or if the resource concerned fails to deliver what is required of it. It is tempting to say that being economical means doing things cheaply: it is then relatively straightforward for accountants and auditors to assess which organizations appear to be most 'economical'. The difficulty is to establish what quality and quantity of a resource are really required.

Efficiency is concerned with the costs of providing whatever the organization provides. It is measured by expressing outputs (e.g. number of dustbins emptied, graduates produced or operations completed) with inputs (resources consumed or costs). This is readily expressed in indicators such as cost per dustbin emptied, or cost per graduate produced or operation completed. An efficient organization is one that has a low cost per unit of output. It sometimes seems that the most obvious way of increasing an organization's apparent efficiency is to reduce costs, but without reducing the level of output. But efficiency can be increased in any of the following ways:

1. by increasing both inputs and outputs, provided outputs increase more than inputs; the potential for economies of scale suggests that this may be an attractive option.
2. by increasing outputs without increasing inputs;
3. by reducing inputs without reducing outputs;
4. by reducing both inputs and outputs, provided inputs are reduced more than outputs.

Pressures on funding in the public sector often mean that a reduction in costs is necessary and the aim is to do this with little or no reduction in service or other outputs.

Where the output is clear, for example tonnes of coal produced, it is straightforward to express costs, in varying degree of detail, in relation to output to give a measure of efficiency. In a service organization measures of output may be less clear and it may be desirable to relate costs to units of output rather than to units of work done. Examples of measures of work done would be miles travelled (British Rail or National Bus), number of students or hours taught (e.g. schools or universities), number of clients seen (e.g. social work or health service). An organization does not become more efficient by reducing the cost per mile travelled if the service is not used; or by reducing the cost per teaching hour if class sizes are reduced; or by reducing the cost per client or patient if fewer clients are helped or a fewer patients are cured. An output measure that encompasses both work done and the client or customer's use of that work may be more appropriate in some areas; an example of this is 'passenger miles' in transport; and in education combining students and hours to give 'student hours'; the cost per 'student hour' may be a better output measure than using hours or student numbers alone. A further stage in sophistication might be to relate costs to successful outcomes, e.g. cost per graduate or cost per graduate who obtains employment or cost per graduate who obtains 'suitable' employment. But as measures of efficiency become more sophisticated, they begin to look more like measures of effectiveness.

In some areas it is difficult to derive meaningful output measures and unsophisticated approaches to measuring efficiency are sometimes used, such as treating income generated, or sales, as the output, and then relating costs to income in an attempt to measure 'efficiency'. This can be more like using profitability as an indicator.

Effectiveness is concerned with achieving objectives. An effective organization is one that succeeds in doing or producing what it intends to do; the more successful it is in producing outputs that actully satisfy its goals, the more effective it is said to be. Attempts to measure effectiveness depend on measurements of outputs achieved and of objectives intended: effectiveness is seen as the relationship between the two. An effective unit is one where the outputs produced fulfil its objectives. An organization might be very efficient, but if the outputs produced do not achieve the intended goals, then the unit is ineffective. There could be a very efficient school dinners operation, for example, that was able to produce a very large number of meals at a very reasonable cost per meal; but if most of the schoolchildren would not eat the meals, the unit would (presumably!) not be meeting its objective and so would not be effective. The real objective of providing school meals is probably more to do with the nutrition and health of the children rather than the number of pupils participating; but this is more difficult to measure. One of the problems in the public sector is that it is often very difficult to establish precisely what the objectives of a particular activity are. Objectives may relate to providing a good quality service to as many potential users as possible; or perhaps keeping costs down by providing the minimum possible service; or carefully targeting the service to those in most need. If there are clear objectives that do not contradict each other and that do not change frequently, performance indicators can be developed to indicate some aspects of effectiveness.

The three E's are key ingredients of any performance appraisal system. In the public sector the emphasis, particularly during the 1980s, was on achieving 'value for money', which was interpreted as meaning economy, efficiency and effectiveness. It was assumed that the public sector, left to its own devices, would not adequately achieve the virtuous three E's and so VFM auditing was needed to encourage and monitor progress in this direction.

CHARACTERISTICS OF THE PUBLIC SECTOR

In the private sector, where profitability is both a primary motivating force and the key performance indicator, there is less pressure for value for money auditing than in the public sector. If a company is profitable, there may seem to be no need to question its effectiveness, efficiency or economy. But it would be naive to assume that private sector organizations are successful at the three E's, and, particularly in the near monopoly positions of privatized public utilities, there are often good reasons for considering other aspects of performance in the public interest. Citizens' charters consider some aspects of performance other than profitability, and the monitoring of these charters may become of increasing interest to accountants.

Effectiveness is about achieving goals: if profits are the primary objective of a company, we can assume that a profitable company is an effective one. Efficiency is about the relationship between inputs and outputs: if sales are the outputs of a company, and costs are its inputs, then maximizing the difference between sales and costs, or maximizing profits, means maximizing efficiency. Similarly, pressures to earn profits are also pressures to operate economically: to obtain the appropriate quality and quantity of resources at minimum cost. In order to operate profitably, companies must operate economically, efficiently and effectively.

Even highly profitable companies can sometimes be wasteful, inefficient and unsuccessful in achieving some of their goals and it is always possible for a company to be **more** profitable and more successful in achieving the three E's. But the need for such improvements is usually seen as a matter between shareholders and directors, rather than a matter of public concern. As long as companies survive and appear to be doing nothing illegal, society often seems content to leave them alone. It is true that there is increasing concern in society about issues of corporate governance and the possible abuse of their position by directors who seem to run their companies like personal empires. But with regard to any inefficiencies, it is often assumed that these are matters that 'the market' will take care of: when the share price of inefficient companies falls, they become prey to aggressive takeovers, and the 'guilty', inefficient directors are pushed out of office.

But the public sector is a very different matter. Central government and local government spend a substantial proportion of the national income and there are inexorable pressures to increase public expenditure. But it all has to be financed from the taxes paid by the public and there are also pressures to keep taxation down. On the one hand society wants more and better services: there is always a case for increased expenditure on health, education, transport, housing, social services and so on. But on the other hand these services have to be financed from taxation, and most members of society appear to be against tax increases – unless someone else is paying them! It seems that voters are not much more likely to vote for their taxes to be increased than turkeys are likely to vote for an early

Christmas! The Labour party has advocated paying for better services with additional revenues from economic growth; but this is not credible at time of zero or negative growth. For some in the Conservative party, advocating reductions both in taxation and in public services is ideologically sound. But the more pragmatic solution to this dilemma – improving public services without increasing taxation – is that the public sector should be more accountable, better managed and give better value for money. Value for money auditing is seen as playing a key role in achieving this and it has been strongly promoted by central government.

Accountability in the public sector is ultimately to the public or society. But, in practice, governments act on behalf, or in the name, of the public. The various parts of the public sector are accountable, directly or indirectly, to central government for their performance and use of public funds. In local government, elected councillors may act on behalf of the public: local authorities are accountable to local electors via locally elected councillors. But, powerful central government, which finances a substantial part of local authority expenditure, has asserted its power over local authorities and forced them to be increasingly accountable to central government.

Accountability is required by central government from most parts of the public sector in prescribed formats, with increasing emphasis on performance indicators (In Chapter 2 we noted that, in an accountability relationship, it is usually the most powerful party that determines the form of the account that is provided.) The sanction, if central government is not happy with the accounts provided, is that central government can reduce the funds supplied to the part of the public sector concerned. VFM auditing is intended to check that mechanisms are in place to monitor and evaluate performance and to implement improvements in performance where the need to do so is identified.

It is the responsibility of management of the organization, not the auditors, to ensure that value for money is achieved but there are concerns about the quality and success of managers in the public sector. VFM auditors can play a role in improving management and in reassuring the public that any shortcomings in public sector management and performance are identified and overcome. Public sector management is less obviously successful than management in the private sector. This is partly because it is doing a different job and success is more difficult to demonstrate.

There are, no doubt, examples of the 'deplorable state of affairs' that Anthony (1971) reported on, where the absence of competition insulates and protects management; councils and governing bodies are weak and do not enforce good management; traditions are lax; the pay and quality of management is low; and frequent political interventions and decisions militate against consistent implementation of management plans.

But the quality and success of management in the public sector is often much greater than at first appears. Where there is a straightforward measure of success, such as profit, success is easy to demonstrate. Where there are many different objectives, some of which are in conflict with others, a successful manager may be one who achieves a reasonable balance, but still gets complaints from different sides. Given the lack of single, clear, agreed objectives, political influences are to be expected and it is in the nature of democratically established organizations that there is no single master to be served. Greenough (1991) has drawn attention to the fact that in public sector organizations such as local authorities 'the locus of decision-making is not always clear'. Sometimes the council makes only broad policy decisions, leaving all detail of operations to officers. In other authorities the council involves itself in much more detail. He has also pointed out that 'The operational style of most local authorities is more participative than in the private sector.' This can lead to considerable delays. Public sector organizations espouse such notions as serving the public or serving society, but there is no single view of the public interest, and the public servant must be constantly weighing the needs of one section of the public against another.

Where performance falls short of the ideal it is also more difficult to hide this fact in the public sector for several reasons. In the public sector it is usually services rather than products that are supplied. Where goods are being produced it may be generally accepted that a proportion will be defective and that only those that are 'perfect' will be sold. It is also straightforward to maintain production in periods of slack demand and build up stocks so that customers can be satisfied at times of peak demand. With services it is not possible to stockpile and it is more difficult to vary the level of provision to meet public demand. It is inevitable that there will sometimes be queues, waiting lists, delays and lack of availability: it would be uneconomic to have over-provision to meet any demand at a moment's notice. And it is also inevitable that the service provided will sometimes not be up to scratch, but, unlike in a manufacturing environment, it is not possible to discard or ignore defective services that are provided. Indeed, such services are often very much in the public eye and complaints may receive more attention than is the case with manufactured items; it is much easier to replace a defective consumer good than to replace a defective education or failed health treatment. And when services fall short in the public sector it is more likely that politicians (who are responsible for public services) and the media will make an issue of it.

There are legitimate concerns about the quality of public services and if those who operate them are to be publicly accountable it is quite proper that they should be subject to some sort of monitoring of quality of service provided, and of its economy, efficiency and effectiveness.

In competitive environments outside the public sector there is less concern with public accountability for the quality of goods and services provided. If consumers do not like what one business supplies they can go elsewhere and businesses that fail to satisfy customers do not survive. In the public sector there is the fear that organizations which perform very poorly can still survive. As there are concerns about the performance of management and the use of resources in the public sector, and in order to meet the demands of public accountability, auditors can play a useful role in providing reassurance that there is systematic monitoring of management's success in delivering 'value for money'.

It is difficult to assess whether bad management and such things as waste, extravagance, empire building, poor service and resistance to change are any more widespread than in the private sector. But these things are likely to be more obvious and more a matter of public concern. In the absence of external monitoring there are less pressures to be seen to 'perform'. Many characteristics of the public sector, together with concerns about the quality of management, together with the need for public accountability and reassurance, point to the need for some form of value for money auditing.

VALUE FOR MONEY AUDITING

In addition to the traditional financial audit, which is concerned with matters such as accuracy, regularity and propriety, the public sector auditor is also concerned with value for money. This is usually interpreted as achieving economy, efficiency and effectiveness. Originally such concerns related primarily to economy, and Henley (1989) relates how the Comptroller and Auditor General was in conflict with the army in 1888 over whether the auditors had the right to investigate the economy of contracts for the supply of ribbon; the auditors emerged as the winners, with the support of the House of Commons Public Accounts Committee. Subsequently more work was done on the elimination of waste and extravagance, and increasing attention was paid to productivity and efficiency. Concern with effectiveness is more recent, and there are still problems with this. It is not the auditor's job to become involved in political issues, or to question policy objectives, but it is difficult to assess effectiveness without becoming involved in clarifying policy objectives. Where policy objectives are not clear, and the auditor seeks to highlight particular aspects of effectiveness, it can easily appear that the auditor is influencing policy objectives.

In central government the establishment of the National Audit Office in 1983 gave a statutory basis for, and additional prominence to, value for money, although it had long been a matter of concern to the Exchequer and Audit Department that preceded the NAO; their reports had, over the years, provided valuable evidence for the Public Accounts Committee's investigations. Concern with value for money auditing in local authority audits can be traced back to the Department of the Environment's guidelines in 1973 which stated that auditors should be concerned with issues of substance arising from the accounts such as the possibility of loss due to waste, extravagance, inefficient financial administration, poor value for money, mistake or other cause. Prior to the establishment of the Audit Commission the District Audit Service typically devoted up to 20 per cent of its resources to value for money work as opposed to traditional legality and regularity auditing. This increased significantly following the Local Government Finance Act 1982 which widened the local authority auditor's remit in relation to value for money, particularly with regard to management issues and checking that local authorities have made proper arrangements for securing value for money and the Commission now recommends that 40–50 per cent of audit work should deal with value for money.

It is, of course, the job of the management of any organization, not its auditors, to achieve value for money. The auditor is concerned:

1. to ensure that the organization as a whole is giving attention to value for money and has arrangements in place to monitor the achievement of the three E's, and to take action where there is unsatisfactory performance; and
2. to investigate particular areas of an organization in detail to see if value for money is being achieved there.

The auditor is likely to seek answers to questions such as:

1. Are policy objectives clearly established?
2. Does management have procedures in place to establish the extent to which policy objectives are achieved, making use of performance indicators that deal with effectiveness?
3. Are the costs properly collected and classified to indicate the costs of particular activities?
4. Are those costs related to measures of output to indicate efficiency?
5. Are comparisons made between the organization's own performance indicators and indicators in other comparable organizations to identify where performance appears to be out of line?
6. Where unsatisfactory performance is indicated, are actions taken to improve the performance, explain peculiarities, variances, differences and, where appropriate, to reconsider policy objectives?

In detailed examinations of particular areas the VFM auditors are likely to make their own comparisons with other organizations and make suggestions as to where and how performance might be improved.

NATIONALIZED INDUSTRIES

Performance indicators have a longer history in nationalized industries. Governments have continuing problems in controlling nationalized industries, mainly because they have multiple, changing and conflicting objectives. At different times and to varying extents, nationalized industries have been expected to make a profit, defined in terms of return on capital employed; keep within set external financing limits; provide particular services to the public, some of which are known to be uneconomic; and serve the needs of particular macroeconomic policies such as restrictions on increases in prices and wages, boosting investment and employment, and restricting imports.

The case for publishing performance indicators for nationalized industries rests on the inadequacy of profit figures in a number of respects. Most nationalized industries were virtually monopolies and could, if uncontrolled, be very profitable simply by charging high prices. Protection of the public suggests the need for controls over such behaviour, in relation to efficiency and quality of service for example, and appropriate performance indicators might indicate the extent to which the industries were exploiting their monopoly position to the disadvantage of the public. Similar arguments might be applied in private sector organizations, especially where there is a monopoly or near monopoly position. Performance indicators could also indicate the extent of success in meeting the various (non-profit) objectives imposed upon industries, such as success in controlling price increases, and the extent and quality of service. Performance indicators could also serve to explain changes in profitability. The losses incurred by some nationalized industries has been a matter of continuing public concern, and a full set of performance indicators might indicate to what extent and in what ways the various industries were meeting public expectations other than in terms of profits.

The 1967 White Paper on Nationalised Industries (HMSO, 1967) stated that

> The Government departments directly concerned will continue to develop, in consultation with the industries, indicators of performance which will provide regular and systematic information about each industry's success in controlling its costs, increasing efficiency, and economizing in the use of manpower and capital resources.

The 1978 White Paper stated that

> The Government has ... asked each industry, in consultation with its sponsoring department, to select a number of key performance indicators, including valid international comparisons, and to publish them prominently in their annual reports. They should be supported by an explanation of why they had been chosen and of significant trends ... There will probably be some indicators common to most including, for example, labour productivity and standards of service where these are readily measurable. The Government has asked each industry to start publication of historic performance series ... preferably in their next report and accounts.

Nationalized industry accounts have generally tended to publish extensive statistical data, some of which would require little or no adaptation to be seen as performance indicators. Indicators of labour productivity can be based on a quantitative (usually non-financial) measure of output in relation to number of employees or labour costs. Examples include: therms sold per employee, and salary and wages costs in pence per therm (British Gas); vehicle miles per employee (National Bus); sales (in £) per employee, sales per £ of labour costs, revenue per £1000 of paybill costs (British Rail); tonnes output per manshift, tonnes output per man year (National Coal Board); number of employees per unit of electricity supplied/sold (Electricity Council); revenue tonne kilometres per employee (British Airways). Indicators of quality are more difficult to calculate, and are less commonly presented. Examples include: % passenger trains arriving on time or less than 5 minutes late; % of timetabled passenger trains cancelled; % of first-class letters delivered on the day following posting.

A significant change between the 1967 and the 1978 White Papers was that in the first it was to be the government departments that developed the performance indicators; in the second it was to be the industries themselves. The fact that the second required that they should be published in annual reports for all to see may be seen as an important element of accountability to the public. However, in handing over to the industries themselves the right to determine what indicators should be selected, and how they should be calculated and presented, the government was handing over a significant power.

In practice the performance indicators published by nationalized industries was less than satisfactory, and did not live up to the expectations of the White Paper. Likierman (1979) drew attention to a lack of compliance in a number of respects: four industries published no performance indicators at all; many were not published 'prominently in their annual reports' as the White Paper had recommended; very few provided an explanation of why particular indicators had been chosen; only four provided international comparisons; some provided a 'historic performance series' for only two years; standards of service indicators were generally notable by their absence; and it was not clear whether figures had been selected primarily as measures of performance or for public relations purposes. It might be expected that there would be difficulties in producing the suggested information immediately after the publication of the 1978 White Paper, but a similar analysis in respect of the 1981 published accounts of the nationalized industries showed very little improvement (Perks and Glendinning, 1981).

The nationalized industries could, of course, trot out the usual arguments against publishing more information: it would damage their competitive position, it would cost too much to produce, it would delay the production of their annual report, there would be too much information and it would overload the reader, the figures are difficult to calculate and might be misunderstood or give the wrong impression. But it can also be seen as another example of how the senior management of an organization can, in some respects, take over and colonize the accountability process, use it for their own ends and screen themselves from effective controls.

HIGHER EDUCATION

Performance indicators in higher education came to prominence with the publication of the Jarratt Report (1985) which recommended that universities should have stronger management and planning structures, work to clear objectives, give value for money and develop reliable and consistent performance indicators.

A distinction was drawn between 'internal', 'external' and 'operating' indicators. Internal indicators reflect either inputs to the institution (e.g. attractiveness of courses, attraction of research funds), or evaluations internal to the institution (e.g. award of degrees, teaching quality). External indicators reflect evaluations of the institution's performance in the market place, such as the employment of its graduates or the publication of its research. Operating indicators include productivity ratios, such as unit costs, and reflect variables such as the availability of library and computing support facilities, and staff workloads.

The Government's Green Paper (DES, 1985) stated the purpose of performance investigation was to provide 'some concrete information on the extent to which the benefits expected from education expenditure are actually secured, and to facilitate comparisons in terms of effectiveness and efficiency as between various parts of the system, and as between different points in time'. It stated that performance indicators should be related to stated objectives; be specific, quantifiable and standardized; be as simple as possible and consistent with their purpose; be acceptable and credible in the sense of being free from systematic bias; and useful and capable of acting as signposts to areas where questions concerning operations can and should be asked.

The Government's interests and priorities in performance, and the development of appropriate indicators, were explained in some detail in the 1987 Higher Education White Paper. The relevant parts are quoted below.

> The productivity of higher education as a whole has increased greatly since 1979 ... Average unit costs are estimated to have fallen in real terms ... by 5% in universities, by 15% in polytechnics ... (para. 3.3)

> Academic standards and the quality of teaching in higher education need to be judged by reference mainly to students' achievements. The numbers and class distribution of degrees awarded provide some measure as, conversely, do non-completion rates. The subsequent employment patterns of students provide some indication of the value of higher education courses to working life. Evaluation of institutional performance also requires students' achievements to be set alongside their entry standards ... the essential data on performance in each institution should be published so that its record can be evaluated by the funding agencies, governing bodies, students and employers. (para. 3.15)

> The CVCP and the UGC have also adopted proposals ... for the regular publication from 1987 of a range of efficiency and effectiveness measures covering all universities. Initially, efficiency indicators will included student: staff ratios (SSRs) and a range of unit costs broken down by the main categories of expenditure. Effectiveness indicators will include income from research grants and contracts, the numbers of research and sponsored students, submission rates for research degrees, the first occupation of

graduates and the institutions's contribution to postgraduate and professional training. (para. 3.27)

In the polytechnics and colleges sector in England and Wales, unit costs and SSRs are now accepted indicators of the intensity of resource use. The NAB has accepted an average SSR target of 12:1; this underlies its advice to the Secretary of State for Education and Science and the Government's decisions on the overall funding and planning of the sector. The Polytechnic Finance Officers Group, in conjunction with the Committee of Directors of Polytechnics (CDP), also publishes a range of expenditure data by institution. The Government is discussing with interested parties the possibility of publishing information about the first destination of students by institution, and has encouraged pilot work towards the wider use of data about students who do not complete their courses. (para. 3.30)

The 1987 White Paper seemed to be based on the assumption that higher education is relatively inefficient and wasteful. This use of language is one of the ways in which power is exercised. The Government appeared to be more concerned with making higher education more closely controlled by central government than it was with wider public accountability. With universities it stated that the objectives of reconstituting the funding body (with a Universities Funding Council to replace the University Grants Committee) were 'to clarify responsibilities, **improve financial accountability** and to **increase effectiveness**' (emphasis added). Similar statements were made regarding polytechnics, which were taken out of local authority control. 'Polytechnics and colleges are at present almost wholly dependent on public funds ... Institutions receiving public funds are accountable for the uses to which the funds are put and for the effectiveness and efficiency with which they are employed. One of the objectives of the proposed contracting arrangements between the polytechnics and the Polytechnics and Colleges Funding Council (PCFC) was to 'sharpen accountability for the use of the public funds which will continue to be required'.

The White Paper favoured the use of performance indicators and increased public accountability. But the emphasis was more on polytechnics as institutions being held accountable to central government and less on the polytechnics (or those who controlled them – directors, governors, funding bodies) being held accountable to the public. The White Paper did recommend that 'the essential data on performance in each institution should be published so that its record can be evaluated by the funding agencies, governing bodies'. But, in practice, the emphasis has been less on provision of comparable and consistent performance indicators to the public and more on the provision of detailed information to the funding bodies. Annual reports of higher education institutions are becoming more like public relations documents than sources of performance data.

The first statement by the Committee of Vice Chancellors and Principals/ University Grants Committee (CVCP/UGC) working group adopted a similar approach, and included a number of aspects of performance that were even more difficult to measure (e.g. peer review; editorship of journals). When it came to publishing indicators that really could be measured, the approach became much more narrow and limited. Nearly all of the 39 indicators suggested were merely analyses of costs, usually expressed per Full Time Equivalent (FTE) student; the only exceptions were numbers of postgraduate students, and occupations of students after 6 months.

Those who have most influence in determining what performance indicators should be published and deemed to be of significance are likely to have an important influence on perceptions of higher education and how it develops. The debate on performance indicators may be seen as a struggle for power between different groups with different interests. The government was interested in reducing unit costs, producing substantially more graduates with only modest increases in costs, and perhaps in improving the employability of graduates. The universities were interested in maintaining their independence, and their unit of resource (trying to ensure that funding increased in proportion to student numbers), and perhaps in emphasizing their distinction from polytechnics, particularly in research, in part as a justification for their higher unit costs. It is not therefore surprising that polytechnics muscled into the debate to try to influence it to their advantage.

The Committee of Directors of Polytechnics adopted six primary indicators in 1987. These were:

1. revenue cost per student;
2. the value added to student attainment;
3. ratio of external research income to research expenditure; this was intended to indicate external recognition of the value of research activity: the higher the proportion of research expenditure that is externally funded, the greater the external recognition of the research.
4. capital investment per student;
5. proportion of activity that is specifically regional;
6. income generation and consultancy.

Most of these indicators were likely to show the polytechnics in a more favourable light than universities. Funding for polytechnics was at a lower level than for universities: both the first and the fourth indicators would show polytechnics as being 'better' (i.e. cheaper) from the government's point of view than universities. The second indicator, value added, expressed students' entry qualifications in relation to their exit qualifications. Students with poorer A-levels, who obtained a given class of degree would thus have gained more 'added value' than students with better A-levels. The implication is that those courses and institutions with the lowest entry levels, usually those that are least popular with applicants, create the most added value. This seems to be an ingenious way of demonstrating that the best shall be worst, and the worst shall be best! The use of this indicator might encourage institutions to take more non-standard entrants (e.g. mature students without acceptable A-levels). It might also encourage them to close down their most successful courses where pressure of demand had led them to restrict student numbers by requiring high A-level scores.

The third indicator was also carefully selected. It appears to show that polytechnics did better research than universities, in that it was more likely to be externally sponsored. But universities did far more research than polytechnics, and were funded by the UGC to do research. They were therefore less dependent on external funding. As polytechnics had few resources of their own to fund research, they were more dependent on external funding. The fact that a bigger proportion of research in polytechnics was externally funded tells us nothing about the amount of research that was carried out, and little or nothing about its quality. It is another ingenious way of selecting a performance indicator to give a very different impression from that which would otherwise emerge.

The fifth indicator was intended to show the extent to which institutions fulfilled a particular objective, namely serving their local regions. A convenient indicator of this is the proportion of part-time students, as they would usually live locally. The fact that polytechnics tend to have more part-time students than universities was thus taken to indicate that they were better at serving their local regions.

The point of all this is not that polytechnics were 'wrong', but that there are no 'right' indicators. The selection of any indicator, and the determination of how it is measured is a political process that reflects the interests and the relative power positions of the parties involved. Now that the binary line between polytechnics and universities has been removed, and both are funded by the same council, there will still be struggles between different institutions to encourage the adoption of funding models that suits particular cases; but such struggles will be less obvious than when polytechnics and universities were in more open competition with each other.

Even something that at first sight seems very straightforward, the number of students in an institution, is dependent on political negotiation. For most purposes simply adding together student numbers, whether they are full-time, or part-time, day-release or evening-only, does not give appropriate information. Student numbers are therefore usually expressed in terms of 'FTEs' (full-time equivalent student numbers). This requires various fractions to be used to convert part-time students into FTEs; a part-time student typically counts as somewhere between 0.2 and 0.75 of an FTE; as the funding of institutions is usually dependent on student FTEs, it is a matter of great concern what fraction is used for a particular category of student, and, from time to time, funding bodies can, and do, change the rules for calculating FTEs in order to encourage or discourage particular categories of students and courses.

There is a temptation to use 'quick and dirty' performance indicators rather than develop a whole range to incorporate the many different aspects of performance that the various interested parties might consider to be important. But we should avoid being too simplistic. In 1990 two different listings were published which ranked universities on two different bases. In terms of research performance Oxford and Cambridge came out top; in terms of 'popularity' (measured as number of applicants) they came out bottom! By contrast, the university that was ranked top in popularity (i.e. the one that had most applicants) came out almost bottom in terms of research. What does this indicate? The contrast was striking, and suggests the hypotheses that poor research ranking was associated with popularity, and that high research ranking was associated with unpopularity; but the rest of the data did not bear this out. It shows only that performance indicators need to be interpreted with care, and that they usually need to be supported by additional information.

PROBLEMS OF PERFORMANCE INDICATORS AND VFM AUDITING

Although it is important that the performance of organizations should be measured in terms other than profit, and VFM auditing has undoubtedly stimulated the development of such measures, there are serious problems with this approach. This means that VFM auditing in practice may be less acceptable or successful than its advocates would wish.

1. Definition and measurement of outputs and objectives

In the first place there are problems of definition and measurement of outputs and of objectives. As effectiveness, by definition, relates outputs to objective, it is not possible to have measures of effectiveness without measures both of objectives and of outputs. In many parts of the public sector, managers have no clearly defined objectives. It would suit the VFM auditor if such objectives were clearly established so that s/he could then assess the extent to which these objectives have been achieved. But such an approach is rather naive and simplistic. In public sector organizations there are often multiple objectives, some of which are ill-defined, and relate to coping with future crises and avoiding subsequent political difficulties that are hard to predict. A particular unit may be trying at the same time to encourage the public to make more use of the service provided, to reduce operating costs, to improve the quality of the service, to campaign for more resources for the service, and to target the use of the service to particular groups. Greater success in achieving some of these may be associated with reduced success in others. There is rarely a single, overall measure of effectiveness and it is may be quite meaningless to talk about greater effectiveness generally, as opposed to greater effectiveness in particular ways. It is usually possible to define some objectives that are quantifiable, thus enabling VFM auditors to get on with their business, but it is likely to be only an incomplete, partial, selected aspect of achievement that is thus highlighted, and many of the objectives that are perhaps more important (such as contributing to individual happiness and fulfilment) are excluded from measurement and so, perhaps, from consideration.

The problems of defining and measuring outputs in service-orientated not-for-profit organizations are well established (Wilson, 1978). Some measures of output may be readily available, such as sales revenue, or number of clients/students/patients. But sales revenues may be unavailable, or inappropriate in public sector activities; and there is the danger that other 'output' measures are more like measures of work done, or inputs, than they are measures of outputs. Examples of such measures are number of hours of service provided, number of clients/students/patients seen. The objectives of most organizations are presumably to provide a worthwhile service in the hours worked and to the clients seen. It is the service provided, rather than the work done, that is the output. Inappropriate measures of output lead to inappropriate and misleading attempts to measure effectiveness. Effectiveness means that the client gets what is intended and measures should relate to **successful** outcomes. But it may be very difficult to determine what is success. For example, there might be two units dealing with infertility problems, with effectiveness measured as the percentage of couples that become parents within two years. If Unit A reports 75 per cent success, but Unit B reports only 60 per cent success, then Unit appears to be more effective than Unit B. But if most of Unit A's 'failures' go away depressed and suicidal, whereas, after almost all of Unit B's 'failures' go away much better adjusted and happy than they were previously, which unit is more effective? The answer depends on who is doing the measuring and what they are trying to show.

2. Overemphasis on easily measured costs

The difficulties in defining and measuring outputs and objectives lead to more emphasis being given to costs that are relatively easy to measure rather than to other aspects of performance. In the public sector this often emphasizes short-term cash costs to the public purse or to the entity concerned. Longer-term costs, such as the use of fixed assets, are often excluded, although this is changing as increasing emphasis is given to utilization of fixed assets, and capital charges are developed. 'Externalities', or costs to society that are not borne by the entity concerned, are also often excluded. A public sector unit may be seen as being efficient or effective if it succeeds in reducing its own costs or in increasing its throughput of clients, by passing the problem to some other part of society, perhaps elsewhere in the public sector where even greater costs might be incurred subsequently.

The fact that costs to the entity are one of the most easily measured aspects of performance means that most attention tends to be given to costs, and to cost reductions. Notions of quality, and improvements in effectiveness, are too difficult to measure. It is easier to have a 'quick and dirty' cost-cutting exercise. It seems clear that in conducting VFM audits far more attention has been given to measures of efficiency than to measures of effectiveness. Indeed, in assessing the success of the Audit Commission Greenough (1991), perhaps unwittingly, seems to make it clear that the main concern is with cost cutting rather than with other improvements in performance. He states that

> It is in the area of VFM auditing that the Commission's work is most appreciated. The suspicious and defensive approach initially adopted by many local authorities has now disappeared and considerable savings are being achieved. There is also considerable evidence that these savings are being achieved at an earlier stage.

He then mentions that 5800 projects had identified 'opportunities' for savings of £992 million of which 40 per cent had been achieved. He does not comment on the implication that 'savings' are the only things to be assessed. Were there any projects that suggested that a 10 per cent increase in costs could produce a 20 per cent increase in outputs (and/ or a better quality of service). Or did most 'opportunities' for cost reduction also have adverse implications for effectiveness and quality of service?

Overemphasis on 'efficiency' and cost-cutting is likely to be at the expense of effectiveness, and quality of service. But it can also be argued that emphasis on short term performance, so common in the private sector, is inappropriate in the public sector where longer term considerations of the public interest should predominate. It is often sensible to deal with problems before they show up in the statistics, even if this means incurring additional expenses that make short-term performance look worse. An organization that is highly economical, efficient and effective in the short term may have little or no capacity to adapt and no high calibre staff to identify and plan for future problems. Organizations may give value for money in the short term, but become increasingly fossilized and irrelevant after a number of years.

Taking a longer term view of the public interest would depend on the professional judgement and integrity of professional teachers, doctors, social workers and so on. But 'managerialist' approaches to performance measurement tend to reduce managers' freedom to determine priorities for themselves and, instead encourage conformity with centrally imposed, short-term performance criteria. Pollitt (1986) referring to these managerialist approaches states that

> **overconcentration** on these aspects tends to exclude a whole series of issues that should be integral to the concept of a public service ... for example public participation, equity, a concern with quality, an emphasis on social impact, and a respect for persons.

Improvements in value for money and reductions in public expenditure can bring benefits, but not without costs, particularly the costs that are most difficult to measure.

3. Behavioural implications

One of the objectives of developing performance indicators is to improve performance. It is intended that those who are responsible for a service should take heed of the performance indicators that are used, and improve their performance accordingly. 'Reactivity', or the tendency for measurement to have an impact on that which is measured, is to be expected. But it will not necessarily lead to the desired results. Those whose performance is being assessed are likely to change in ways that lead to better scores, even if this means doing something different from what is really intended. If we measure the performance of social workers in terms of the number of clients that they see and the cost per client, some might concentrate on improving their 'scores', rather than successfully tackling their clients' problems. The 'professionalism' of individual employees and their freedom to determine how their job should be done can be undermined by the need to improve their scores in a game, the rules of which may seem irrelevant to the objectives of the organization. It sometimes appears that the only things that count are the things that can be counted. Pressures for an organization to be seen as successful can lead to employees concentrating only on the tasks that directly improve their scores at the expense of helping people and regardless of externalities and longer term effects that will not immediately show up in performance indicators.

Where particular indicators of effectiveness are accepted an organization may be tempted to take on only those cases where there is a good prospect of success. 'Good' universities tend to take only 'good' students, and so tend to produce 'good' graduates. If schools choose to improve their performance indicators by taking only 'good' pupils they might be failing society, if society's objective is to provide a good quality education for all. If doctors and hospitals chose to help only those patients who were most likely to recover, seriously ill patients might find it difficult to obtain suitable treatment and the health service would be failing society, while individual units within it demonstrate their own 'good' performance. If the police force is mainly concerned with indicators such as the proportion of crime cleared up, we may find the figures distorted by exclusion of some crimes from the statistics, inclusion of crimes where the culprit is already known, and suspects being 'persuaded' to confess to crimes that they did not commit. In short, over-emphasis on assessing people and organizations on the basis of a limited range of performance indicators can lead to silly games being played with the figures, inappropriate priorities and decidedly anti-social activities.

Where the government of other funding body determines levels of funding in relation to particular aspects of performance, then the organizations concerned are likely to try to arrange their activities so as to maximize the levels of funding received (although this might not make economic sense where the costs of doing so are greater than the additional funding that would be received). The balance and nature of activities that would maximize funding is likely to be much the same for any unit within a given group of organizations (e.g. universities, hospitals, schools). A significant problem in this scenario (although some might regard it as an advantage), is that all of the different organizations might be encouraged to act in much the same way; the imposition of one central view of what performance is appropriate diminishes the freedom of individual hospitals, universities and so on to determine their own priorities and to devote resources to developments that might prove to be giant leaps forward for society in the longer term, but which have adverse effects on performance indicators in the short term. If the use of a narrow range of performance indicators reduces the richness and variety of institutions and activities in society, then society is likely to be the loser in many ways.

Managers within a public sector organization who are of a managerialist disposition are likely to want to play the government's managerialist games: maximizing income by delivering the performance that is expected. Where government expectations are stable and predictable, such an approach makes some sense. But government policies and priorities can change with disconcerting frequency. Just when managers think that they have managed to prioritize appropriately, there is a new minister or a new priority, and their plans may have to be changed again.

Even if government priorities are clear and stable, there is no necessary and predictable relationship between funding levels and performance achievements. It does not always make sense for the poorer performers to have their inadequate resources further reduced: they may be given additional support so that they can improve their performance. Similarly it does not necessarily make sense to reward the best performers by giving them additional resources when they are doing very well on existing resource levels.

Where there is a predictable relationship between resources and performance, managers will be tempted to play silly games to maximize resources; where the relationship is unpredictable or opaque, managers may appear even more silly as they twist and turn, like in a game of blind man's-buff, to try to meet requirements at which they can only guess. An example of this is the University Funding Council's attempts to relate funding of research to measures of research performance in individual universities and departments. No one knew what counted, how it would be counted, or what the funding consequences would be. Each time the UFC put forward proposals as to how the exercises would be conducted, they were different from previous proposals. By the time any institution had implemented changes to its research programmes intended to improve performance indicators, the proposals had been amended, often making these changes inappropriate. The only certainty was that no one would know the relationship between performance and funding until **after** the funding had been decided. Research strategies that were rational in relation to UFC funding were not therefore possible. It is not surprising that at least one university decided not to play such a silly game, and to opt out of the whole exercise. In many cases it seems likely that the amounts of funding received by particular universities or departments would be way below the research costs incurred.

Given that governments and their priorities are subject to change, it is likely that from some perspectives (future historians for example) the 'best' managers will prove to be those who are able to ignore the effects of short-term performance indicators and do what they believe to be right, or in the public interest, or in the interest of their clients, region, or group that they believe they should serve. This is likely to reflect many different interpretations of what various public sector organizations are supposed to be doing. Some balance is required between variety and diversity on the one hand, and standardization in accordance with current government priorities on the other.

4. Surreptitious political agenda

Improved performance, better value for money, and greater economy, efficiency and effectiveness do not sound like the dogma of a particular political party, and are likely to command widespread support in society. Many accountants appear to accept that value for money auditing is not, or ought not to be, part of a political agenda. Holtham and Stewart (1981) state that

> We argue, however, that the process of search for value for money is politically neutral, even though what is decided in that process will not be.

Glynn (1985) supports this:

> The auditor is not concerned with policy, which is the responsibility of elected politicians and public servants who administer their directions. The auditor is concerned with investigating the outcomes of policy and whether such effects correspond with the intentions of the policy. **This is an apolitical monitoring process** (emphasis added).

But emphasis on performance indicators and value for money auditing might hide a more significant political agenda which includes the assertion and enhancement of the power of central government, reducing public expenditure, and commercializing and/or privatizing most of the public sector. Those who require an organization of group to produce performance indicators are asserting, and perhaps enhancing, their power over that organization. Pollitt (1986) states that

> Performance indicators hold out to senior management the promise of improved control of lower levels in the hierarchy. It may be particularly

attractive to Whitehall in those frequent situations where a central department finances services delivered by local government, health authorities or some other decentralized agency.

Senior management might use the requirement to produce performance indicators as a way of exerting their power and priorities over junior managers; similarly, central government and Whitehall might use this approach to assert their power and priorities over local authorities, nationalized industries, higher education, the health service and so on. To some extent these organizations can resist, and publish and give prominence, credibility and legitimacy to different aspects of performance from those that the government wished to prioritize. But once the government decides to relate the funding of these organizations to particular performance indicators, those aspects of performance are likely to predominate.

As we have seen, the difficulties of defining and measuring objectives and outputs has led to emphasis on efficiency measures; and economy and efficiency are convenient justifications for cost reduction. For those whose political ideology involves reducing public expenditure, VFM helps to make it appear more politically neutral and acceptable; increases in effectiveness can still be discussed and promised for the future, while increased economy and efficiency are actively implemented in the short term.

It is not realistic to expect VFM auditing to be politically neutral. Although VFM auditors are usually specifically excluded from questioning the merits of policy objectives, this can be very difficult in practice. The boundary between what is the legitimate concern of the VFM auditors, and what is 'policy' can never be clear-cut. Almost anything that is criticized as being 'inefficient', or 'ineffective' can also be defended as being the result of a policy decision. If, for example, a VFM auditor was concerned about the sale of some government owned assets (such as the Rover Group) because only one potential purchaser was considered, then the Department concerned need say only that it was 'a matter of policy' to consider only one purchaser (to avoid uncertainty in the industry concerned for example), and the matter appears to be excluded from the VFM auditor's remit. The point is that 'policy' is not really a separate matter, and VFM auditors cannot be completely neutral and avoid involvement in policy issues.

The Conservative government's political agenda for the public sector included the privatization of most nationalized industries and the increasing introduction of private sector management techniques and commercial objectives (often in preparation for privatization). The commercial ethos was introduced widely, with an emphasis on different schools, hospitals, universities and so on competing with each other rather than co-operating with each other. Notions of 'public service' and ill-defined 'public interest' were overtaken by managerialism, commercialism and competition, all in the name of economy, efficiency and effectiveness.

If the political agenda and surreptitious changes to the public sector were clearly spelled out there might be more substantial and effective opposition to them. But it is difficult to oppose economy, efficiency and effectiveness, and the idea that the public sector should give value for money. Jowett and Rothwell (1988) note that there have been some difficulties in implementing these ideas in the public sector because of 'unexpected sensitivities' and 'the seemingly irreconcilable conflict between those who insist that value for money (i.e. economy and efficiency) is incompatible with effectiveness, and the government, who by contrast maintain that economy and efficiency are essential pre-requisites for an effective service'. They are however convinced that 'attitudes and managerial techniques must change, but ... Rome was not built in a day ... similarly ... a new, vigorous, **commercially minded** and effective public sector will not overnight rise phoenix like out of the dying embers of the inefficient 1945 model' (emphasis added).

Concentration on performance indicators and value for money has masked major changes in the public sector that are more politically controversial.

5. Need more indicators

Most of the problems and criticisms of VFM stem from the limitations and biases of the performance indicators that have been developed and used so far, and the fact that notions such as effectiveness and quality do not receive sufficient prominence. The obvious answer to this problem is that a wider range of performance indicators should be developed and used.

Similarly it may be accepted that too much aggregation and averaging takes place: Muddletown may have a 'good' hospital, local authority or university on average, but this does not mean that every part of it is good. Sometimes an exceptionally good performance in one area can disguise an unacceptably awful performance in another area while, as a whole the organization appears to be satisfactory. The answer to this problem is, again, that more detailed performance indicators should be developed and used.

There is also the danger that too simplistic interpretations of a narrow range of performance indicators can lead to distorted and misleading interpretations. The example of universities that were 'best' under one criterion, but 'worst' under another are an extreme example. In many areas where there appears to be poor performance, more detailed explanations may show that, given the particular difficulties that apply, the performance is a lot better than at first appears. Again, the solution is to produce more performance indicators.

But producing more and more performance indicators will only lead to more problems that may need to be investigated. Each piece of data that appears to explain abnormal performance is likely to require further explanation with further data; this could go on almost indefinitely resulting in an excess of little used data. In relation to American experience Pollitt (1986) states that

> despite the efficiency rhetoric, those performance indicators that are established frequently fall into disuse. More than 3,000 performance

indicators have grown out of the 1973 Federal Government Productivity Measurement Programme, 'yet they suffer from a general lack of use' (here Pollitt quotes from Mayston, 1985).

It is not possible to produce performance indicators that will answer all questions, and it is likely that those who use performance indicators will concentrate on the small number that suit their purposes.

6. General problems with quantification

Finally, it should be acknowledged that some aspects of performance, and perhaps some of the most important things in life, do not lend themselves to quantification. Performance indicators might be like swimsuits: what they reveal is interesting, but what they conceal is vital!

SUMMARY AND CONCLUSIONS

The idea of performance is not, of course, a neutral, unchanging concept. Its 'definition is, to a large extent, dependent upon the perspective of the interested party – whether that be the government, public sector employees, consumers etc.' (Jowett and Rothwell, 1988). Much of the discussion of performance indicators and value for money is about different groups in society trying to give priority to their own views of what aspects of performance are most important.

Those who hope that numerical indicators will provide answers to difficult political questions must proceed with caution. Central government has used VFM and performance indicators to gain acceptance for a political ideology that favours reductions in public expenditure. The debate on developing the 'best' indicators of performance is not conducted on equal terms: different groups will argue for different indicators, but the most powerful groups will gain acceptance and credibility for the indicators that suit their purpose. We should not be seduced into thinking that there are fair and objective measures of economy, efficiency and effectiveness any more than we should be seduced into thinking that profit figures tell us what we really want to know.

FURTHER READING

Cave, M. (1988) *The Use of Performance Indicators in Higher Education: a Critical Analysis of Developing Practice*, Jessica Kingsley Publishers.
Glynn, J. J. (1985) *Value for Money Auditing in the Public Sector*, ICAEW/ Prentice Hall.

Henley, D., Likierman, A., Perrin, J. R., Lapsley, I., Evans, M. and Whiteoak, J. (1992) *Public Sector Accounting and Financial Control*, 4th edn, Chapman & Hall.

Jowett, P. and Rothwell, M. (1988) *Performance Indicators in the Public Sector*, Macmillan.

Pendlebury, M. (ed.) (1989) *Management Accounting in the Public Sector*, Heinemann.

Price Waterhouse (1990) *Value for Money Auditing*, Gee & Co.

Tomkins, C. (1987) *Achieving Economy, Efficiency and Effectiveness in the Public Sector*, ICAS/Kogan Page.

ESSAY AND DISCUSSION TOPICS

1. Why is VFM auditing advocated mainly in relation to the public sector?
2. What performance indicators would you like to see used in relation to:

    (a) British Gas;
    (b) Water Authorities;
    (c) British Rail;
    (d) another organization of your choosing?

3. Suggest how economy, efficiency and effectiveness can be measured in each of the following areas:

    (a) a local authority housing department;
    (b) a hospice;
    (c) a university department of accountancy.

4. In relation to a particular educational institution with which you are familiar (e.g. the university where you are studying), suggest performance indicators that would show it in the most favourable light.
5. With reference to a Social Services Department, examine the different interests of the following groups in relation to performance: central government; the local authority treasurer; a social worker considering applying for employment in that local authority; an orphan; a family living on state benefits where one parent is in prison; a senior manager of the department who is seeking promotion; taxpayers.

REFERENCES

Anthony, R. N. (1971) Can non-profit organizations be well managed?, *Vital Speeches of the Day*, 18 Feb., quoted in Glynn, J. J. (1985) *Value for Money Auditing in the Public Sector*, Prentice Hall/ICAEW.

Department of Education and Science (DES) (1985) *The Development of Higher Education into the 1990's*, Green Paper, Cmnd 9524, HMSO.

Department of Education and Science (DES) (1987) *Higher Education: Meeting the Challenge*, White Paper Cmnd 114m HMSO.

Glynn, J. J. (1985) *Value for Money Auditing in the Public Sector*, Prentice Hall/ICAEW.

Greenough, J. (1991) The Audit Commission, in *Current Issues in Auditing* (eds M. Sherer and S. Turley), Paul Chapman.

Griffiths, I. (1987) *Creative Accounting*, Unwin.

Henley, D. (1989) External audit, in *Public Sector Accounting and Financial Control* (eds D. Henley, C. Holtham, A. Likierman and J. Perrin), Van Nostrand Reinhold.

HMSO (1967) *Nationalised Industries: A Review of Economic and Financial Objectives*, Cmnd 3437.

HMSO (1978) *The Nationalised Industries*, Cmnd 7131.

Holtham, C. and Stewart, J. (1981) *Value for Money: A Framework for Action*, Institute of Local Government Studies, University of Birmingham.

ICAEW (1952) *Accounting in Relation to Changes in the Purchasing Power of Money, Recommendation on Accounting Principles*, N 15, May, Institute of Chartered Accountants in England and Wales.

Jameson, M. (1988) *A Practical Guide to Creative Accounting*, Kogan Page.

Jarratt Report (1985) *Report of the Steering Committee for Efficiency Studies in Universities*, Committee of Vice Chancellors and Principals.

Jowett, P. and Rothwell, M. *Performance Indicators in the Public Sector*, Macmillan.

Likierman, A. (1979) Performance indicators for state industries, *Accountancy*, Oct., 91.

Mayston, D. J. (1985) Non-profit performance indicators in the public sector, *Financial Accountability and Management*, **1**(2), Summer, 51–74.

Perks, R. W. and Glendinning, R. (1981) Performance indicators applied to the nationalised industries, and little progress seen in published performance indicators, *Management Accounting*, Oct. and Dec.

Pollitt, C. (1986) Beyond the managerial model: the case for broadening performance assessment in government and the public services, *Financial Accountability and Management*, **2**(3), 155–70.

Sorenson, J. E. and Grove, H. D. (1977) Cost-outcome and cost-effectiveness analysis: emerging nonprofit performance evaluation techniques, *The Accounting Review*, July.

Wilson, R. M. S. (1978) Management control of non-profit organisations: the problem of specifying outputs, *AUTA Review*, **10**(1).

6 Accounting standards

INTRODUCTION

The first part of this chapter outlines what is meant by accounting standards, and the background to the setting up of the Accounting Standards Committee (ASC). The second section outlines the history of the ASC, and the various reviews of, and changes to, its operations, culminating in its abolition. The factors that contributed to its apparent failure are then examined. The changes brought about by the Accounting Standards Board, which replaced the Accounting Standards

Committee, are then outlined. The case for not having mandatory accounting standards is examined. The final section concludes that there is a need for accounting standards in society and suggests some ways of making the setting and enforcement of standards more effective.

THE ORIGINS OF ACCOUNTING STANDARDS

WHAT ARE ACCOUNTING STANDARDS?

All companies and most organizations in society are required to produce annual reports and accounts. The 'rules' for these documents are established by legislation for the particular kinds of organization (e.g. Companies Acts, Building Society Acts) and to some extent modified by the accountancy profession's accounting standards. The main responsibility for producing such accounts lies with the directors of companies and other organizations, and they have considerable discretion in such productions. Accounting standards may be seen as the accountancy profession's rules, which supplement Companies Act requirements, that are intended to restrict directors' freedom of manoeuvre and to ensure that the financial statements are presented on a more comparable, consistent and 'standard' basis. The case for having accounting standards is summarized on pp. 151 *et seq.*

The word 'standard' should be interpreted with care. In this context it should be seen as a level of attainment or a measure of what is adequate for some purpose. Although it may imply 'standardization', or even 'uniformity', the British accountancy profession prefers some flexibility and opposes the idea of a comprehensive code of rigid rules. Accounting standards are intended to narrow, but not eliminate, the areas of difference and variety in accounting practice, and to improve 'comparability' and to contribute to the 'harmonization' of accounting standards with other countries.

Accounting standards recommend how particular items should be treated in the published accounts of companies and other organizations. They may deal with any or all of the following:

1. **Definition of terms** Most standards include definitions of particular terms that they use.
2. **Measurement** Some standards prescribe particular ways of measuring items such as income, expenditure, assets and liabilities. A standard with a requirement to depreciate freehold property, or to write off research expenditure, is prescribing a measurement rule.
3. **Presentation** A standard may prescribe that information should be presented in a particular way, such as a particular layout for a balance sheet or a cash flow statement. Often, illustrations of presentation are provided, although these are not necessarily prescribed as standard practice.

4. **Disclosure of data** Some statements require that a particular piece of information should be disclosed, such as the total amount of deferred taxation for which provision has not been made.
5. **Disclosure of accounting policies** Sometimes, rather than specifying that a particular accounting policy should be adopted, standards require only that there should be disclosure of the policy that has been adopted. SSAP 2 is an example of such a standard. Where particular issues have been difficult to resolve, some standards have accepted different treatments provided the policy that has been adopted is disclosed. For such standards to be effective, there is a need for agreement on terminology used, so that if, for example, a company states that accounts are prepared on an **accruals** or on a **current cost** basis, these terms are defined in an accounting standard.
6. **Conceptually based** Such a standard would lay down broad principles from which detailed rules can be derived. Attempts to deal with off balance sheet financing (ED 42 and 49) specifically opt for a general approach based on the essential characteristics of assets and liabilities rather than attempting to specify detailed rules for every possible case, or leaving companies to deal with each case on an ad hoc basis.

Many of these matters are dealt with by the Companies Acts, particularly the 1985 and 1989 Companies Acts. There are minor differences between requirements specified by legislation, and requirements specified by accounting standards. Accounting standards, for example, usually include more detailed explanation and illustration than is contained in comparable parts of the Companies Acts. But the major differences is that Companies Acts are established by the state, on behalf of society, with the power of the law, including the courts, and with penalties for infringement. Accounting standards are set by private sector bodies, largely dominated by the accountancy profession, with enforcement mechanisms dependent mainly on persuasion.

BACKGROUND TO THE ACCOUNTING STANDARDS COMMITTEE

The Institute of Chartered Accountants in England and Wales issued a *Statement of Intent* in December 1969 and formed the Accounting Standards Steering Committee in January 1970. This is often seen as the beginning of the accounting standards programme in Britain.

However, the accountancy profession had for many years produced guidance on how annual accounts should be produced. The ICAEW's first two *Recommendations on Accounting Principles* were published in 1942, and, as shown in Appendix I, additional *Recommendations* continued to be published regularly until 1969 immediately before the Accounting Standards Steering Committee was established. It is worth noting that many of the problems of the 1940s and 1950s (such as depreciation and valuation of stocks) are the subject of more recent statements and revised statements, and include problems that remain unresolved today. Similarly, for example, the 1980 SSAP 17 Accounting for post balance sheet events had been foreshadowed by the 1957 N17 which also dealt with events occurring after the balance sheet date. During the period that the Accounting Standards Committee operated, most of the old problems re-emerged, sometimes with more satisfactory solutions; and a number of new problems were tackled.

The events leading to the establishment of the Accounting Standards Committee have been fully related elsewhere, for example by Stamp and Marley (1970). It was largely in response to a number of scandals and severe criticisms of the accountancy profession, particularly the GEC–AEI takeover and the affairs of Pergamon Press.

The directors of AEI, in defending themselves against a takeover by GEC, produced a profits forecast in October 1987 that showed a profit of £10 million for 1967. Their reporting accountants stated that this forecast had been 'prepared on a fair and reasonable basis and in a manner consistent with the principles followed in preparing recent published annual accounts'. As nearly ten months of the year had already elapsed it seemed reasonable to conclude that such a forecast should have been reasonably accurate. But the directors of AEI did not retain the confidence of their shareholders, and GEC's takeover succeeded. In July 1968 GEC published AEI's 'actual' profits for 1967, which could be compared with the £10 million that had been forecast. It turned out to be a loss of £4.5 million! The difference between forecast and 'actual' amounted to £14.5 million of which £5 million was attributed 'to matters substantially of fact', and £9.5 million 'to matters substantially of judgement'.

The problems of Pergamon Press were also much publicized. During a takeover battle in 1969, when Leasco Data Processing Equipment Corporation was bidding to take over Pergamon Press Ltd, it was alleged that the profits figures in the published and audited accounts of Pergamon were exaggerated. A subsequent Department of Trade and Industry enquiry into the affair gave examples of accounting practices that many would regard as unusual, or even unacceptable, and labelled Robert Maxwell as being an unsuitable person to be trusted with the stewardship of a public company. But there was apparently nothing to prevent the directors of companies from publishing accounts that showed their own interpretation of financial position and performance.

The affairs of Pergamon Press Ltd, and of the GEC takeover of AEI, were symptomatic of a lack of confidence in the published accounts of companies, in auditors and in the accountancy profession more generally. It seemed that there were no clear accounting principles; that company data could be manipulated to produce widely different profit or loss and balance sheet figures; and that company auditors were willing to accept very different interpretations. The ICAEW's attempts at regularizing accounting practices through its series of *Recommendations* had failed, and it became clear that if they did not put something better in its place the task might be taken on by the Board of Trade.

THE ACCOUNTING STANDARDS COMMITTEE

ESTABLISHMENT

In December 1969 the ICAEW published a *Statement of Intent on Accounting Standards*. The intention was to 'advance accounting standards along the following lines:

1. narrowing the areas of difference and variety in accounting practice;
2. recommending disclosure of accounting bases that have been used in respect of items which depend substantially on judgement, or on the estimated outcome of future events;
3. disclosing departures from established definitive standards;
4. having wider exposure of new draft standards to provide an opportunity for appropriate representative bodies to express their views; and
5. continuing a programme for encouraging improved accounting standards in legal and regulatory measures.'

More specifically it was stated that 'The Council will continue its programme of suggesting appropriate improvements in accounting standards established by legislation, of which the proposals on "Companies Legislation in the 1970's" submitted to the President of the Board of Trade in March this year are an example'.[1]

It seemed to be recognized that effective accounting standards depended on legislation, but the accountancy profession soon became very protective of accounting standards and successfully argued that responsibility for them should remain in the private sector and not be taken over by government.

With regard to enforcement it was stated that 'The Council will do all in its power to assist and support members in the observance of established standards. To this end, it intends to strengthen its machinery for investigating and pointing the lessons of lapses from standards.' This recognized the importance of enforcement, but seemed also to accept the limitations of the Institute's powers: they could do little more than investigate lapses and 'point the lessons'.

[1] *Accountancy*, Jan. 1970, 2–4.

The Institute also used the word 'uniformity'. The aim of the first part of its Five Point Plan was 'The encouragement of increased uniformity of accounting practice'. They stated that 'this is entirely to be welcomed', but only to a limited extent! They went on to say that 'some pruning of permissible practices is both possible and desirable ... But ... rigid uniformity is impracticable'. This relatively modest aim and the avoidance of 'standardization' may in part have been a recognition that they would be unable to enforce anything that took away the freedom of individual accountants to decide for themselves what accounting treatment they considered to be appropriate in the circumstances.

The ICAEW formed the Accounting Standards Steering Committee in January 1970 comprising 11 members, with Ronald Leach as Chairman. In the following years its composition was changed several times and extended to include representatives of the other main professional accountancy bodies; and it was renamed the 'Accounting Standards Committee'. But it continued to be dominated by the ICAEW.

ENFORCEMENT

Enforcement of accounting standards continued to be a problem.

The ASC's *Explanatory Foreword* states that the Councils of the six CCAB professional bodies expect members who assume responsibilities in respect of financial accounts to observe accounting standards, and that they may enquire into any apparent failures by members to do so, or to disclose departures therefrom. This approach has a number of weaknesses. It is largely voluntary and relies on persuasion. The implied threat of disciplinary action against members has amounted to little in practice. And the *Explanatory Foreword* itself contains escape clauses. Where members are directors or other officers they are expected only to

> use their best endeavours to ensure that standards are observed or, if they are
> not observed, that significant departures from them are disclosed and
> explained in the accounts. The effect of such departures should, if material,
> be disclosed unless this would be impracticable or misleading in the context
> of giving a true and fair view.

Members of professional bodies who acted as auditors were also expected to state the extent of their concurrence with departures from standards.

Members had to do no more than 'use their best endeavours'. Departures were acceptable and they needed to be 'disclosed and explained' only if they were 'significant'. In practice a brief statement that some method other than that prescribed in a SSAP was preferable in the particular circumstances, or in the interest of giving a true and fair view, was adequate. The recommendation to disclose the financial effects of departures from standards applied only if the amounts were 'material', and could be avoided if it was 'impracticable', or 'misleading in the context of giving a true and fair view'.

If accounting standards are not followed, but the financial effects of non-compliance are disclosed, there is no significant loss of information to users. There is much to be said for this approach. Accounting standards could be very strict; companies could present their accounts in whatever way they judged to be 'true and fair'; and there would always be sufficient information for users of accounts to interpret them in accordance with standard practice. But this was not the position with the ASC. They rejected this 'benchmark' philosophy on the grounds that users would not want to have to adjust accounts themselves in order to achieve comparability.

Lafferty (1981) stated that 'It took almost a decade of standard setting before people came to realize that all this amounted to very little other than pious hope. In reality, no enforcement mechanism existed.' He predicted that Britain would

> muddle through with the present system of setting and pretending to enforce accounting standards for another decade of two. Within a year or so the present ASC will be reformed to include some outsiders, and a supervisory panel will be established to look into cases of non-compliance with standards. Inevitably the Stock Exchange will play an important role in the new set-up. Before the system ever gets going, it seems safe to predict that it will achieve very little.

> Eventually the failure of total self-regulation in British accounting will become so self-evident that political intervention will become inevitable. At that time, round about the year 2000, a statutory enforcement body will be established to act in the 'public interest'.

At the time of writing, 11 years after Lafferty wrote this, his predictions sill seem realistic.

In the USA all companies above a certain size[2] are required to file their accounts with the **Securities and Exchange Commission** (SEC) which has the responsibility and authority to prescribe accounting standards and rules for those companies' reports. The SEC also defines what is meant by 'independence' for auditors and disciplines those who violate these conditions. It has five full-time commissioners appointed by the President, and a large body of full-time professional and other staff. In practice the SEC has delegated much of its power over standard-setting to the accountancy profession (the FASB). The American approach has advantages over that which applies in the British Isles where accounting standard setting and enforcement are entirely in the private sector.

In practice SSAPs were often not clear-cut and a number of different approaches could satisfy their requirements. Definitions (such as the difference

---

[2] 500 shareholders and $1 million assets.

between an exceptional item and an extraordinary item) often leave considerable scope for interpretation and manipulation. In some instances the Accounting Standards Committee tried to establish clear rules at the exposure draft stage, but were persuaded to back off.[3] On other occasions they have attempted to establish clear-cut rules, but these have been openly flouted.[4]

It is difficult to see how accounting standards can be enforced without legal backing. The extent to which such standards have legal authority is not clear. The overriding principle is that published accounts should show a **true and fair** view; but in determining what constitutes such a view, courts are likely to find statements of standard accounting practice to be persuasive.

There are arguments against having effective enforcement mechanisms. These concern cost, the interests of the regulators and the question of whether accountants and businesses really want them.

In the USA the SEC may be seen as a substantial and costly bureaucracy. Benston (1981) argues that such regulatory commissions are staffed by people who (like others) tend to maximize their own welfare. They are likely to prefer administratively efficient regulations with written rules that protect the commission from public criticism and which at least give the appearance of avoiding crises. They do not benefit from saving resources by avoiding or withdrawing unnecessary regulations. The effect is that

> companies and public accountants are faced with the expense of learning and following these regulations, while it is doubtful that users have achieved much in the way of benefits.

To Watts and Zimmerman (1986) the value of regulation is an empirical question, and they are concerned with the failure of regulatory authorities to assess the costs and benefits of regulation.

The extent to which accountants and businesses really want effective enforcement mechanisms is difficult to gauge. On the one hand they want a degree of freedom to choose and adapt accounting principles to suit particular circumstances; but on the other they must recognize that if such freedom goes too far the statements that they produce, and the accounting profession itself, lose credibility. There has to be an appearance of enforcement, but there are also pressures to combine this with a degree of laxity, or turning of blind eyes, that is usually called 'flexibility'.

---

[3] ED 14, issued in January 1975, proposed that all research and development expenditure should be written off in the year in which it was incurred. ED 17, issued in April 1976, allowed development expenditure to be capitalized in some circumstances. The ASC's attempt to impose the deferral method for deferred taxation (ED 11 1973), gave way to SSAP 11 (1976) which allowed either the deferral or the liability method. But this was seen as being too rigid (as it applied to **all** timing differences) and was replaced by the more flexible ED 19 (1977), then SSAP 15.

[4] Depreciation of freehold property, for example.

REVIEWS AND CHANGES

The Accounting Standards Steering Committee originally included only ICAEW members, but this was soon extended. In April 1970 three members from the Institute of Chartered Accountants of Scotland and one from the Irish Institute joined the ASSC. Following the failure of the six main professional accountancy bodies to merge (in June 1970) the ACCA and the ICWA joined the ASSC in September 1971.

In February 1976 the committee was reconstituted as the Accounting Standards Committee (ASC) with 23 members including 12 from the ICAEW, 3 from ICAS and 2 each from ICAI, ACCA, ACMA and then also from CIPFA. The ASC became a joint committee of the six 'governing bodies' which made up the Consultative Committee of Accountancy Bodies (CCAB). Additional emphasis was given to earlier and wider consultation in developing accounting standards.

In 1978 the ASC set up a group to review the accounting standard setting process in the light of experience since 1969. A consultative document was issued; 132 written submissions were received and public hearings were held in London, Glasgow and Dublin. The ASC published their conclusions and recommendations in January 1981 in the Watts Report (Watts, 1981) They considered that accounting standards should continue to be set in the private sector, rather than by government; that the standard setting body should consist primarily of accountants, but with some recognition of the needs of users of accounts and of the wider public interest; that the six main accountancy bodies should retain the constitutional power to issue standards produced by the ASC; and that there should be wider and earlier consultation. The Council of the Stock Exchange and the accountancy profession should establish a joint panel to review non-compliance. More resources and staffing should be devoted to accounting standards.

The ASC considered other approaches to enforcement. They noted that in Canada standards are set in the private sector, but that compliance is required by law, and the courts could be used for enforcement. But they considered that the UK and Irish legislatures could not be expected to delegate law-making in this way to a private sector body. They also rejected the American approach in which the Securities and Exchange Commission refuses to accept the registration of financial statements bearing a qualified audit report. The possibility of a withdrawal of a company's stock exchange listing was also rejected. They proposed instead a 'supervisory body' which they saw as being 'more in keeping' with British practice. In any case it is difficult to see how refusing to accept a set of accounts, or withdrawing a stock market listing, helps investors in a situation where directors refuse to accept accounting standards.

The ASC's proposal was for a joint panel of the Council of the Stock Exchange and the CCAB to review cases of apparent departures from accounting standards. One of the main weaknesses of such approaches to enforcement is that they apply only to listed companies.

Many of the Watts Report recommendations for change and improvement were adopted. Membership of the ASC was revised; wider and earlier consultation was established with discussion papers being published prior to the exposure draft stage; and the *Explanatory Foreword* was revised following the recommendation that 'a material departure from standard should be permitted only in those exceptional circumstance where to adhere would fail to give "a true and fair view"'. The revised *Explanatory Foreword* stated that 'A justifiable reason may therefore exist why an accounting standard may not be applicable in a given situation, namely when application would conflict with the giving of a true and fair view. In such cases, modified or alternative treatments will require to be adopted.'

In 1982 the ASC was again reconstituted and its membership was presented as being

Members in practice	7
Members in private and public	
Industry and commerce	5
User members	5
Members from non-trading	
Public sector	2
Academic member	1
	20

But the change was more apparent than real. Of the twenty members half were members of the ICAEW and (as several members belonged to more than one professional body) each of the other five bodies could claim at least as many members as previously. Only two of the twenty members (one from the Society of Investment Analysts and one from Barclays Bank) were not members of professional accountancy bodies.

Other recommendations were not implemented and were taken up by the Dearing Committee. These included the establishment of a supervisory body to monitor implementation of standards; applying some standards only to large companies; and the need for additional resources and a full-time chairman. The ASC commissioned research into the possibility of developing an agreed conceptual framework; this led to the Macve Report, and the question was taken up again by the Dearing Committee.

In 1983 another working party report *Review of the Standard Setting Process* (the Mckinnon Report) was produced to follow up some of the recommendations of the Watts Report, to speed up the standard setting process and to consider new forms of statement. It recommended some changes in procedures, and the production of **Statements of Recommended Practice** (SORPs) for matters that

are not of fundamental importance or which are applicable only in specific industries or types of organization.

Finally, the Dearing Report (The Making of Accounting Standards) was to be the final review of the Accounting Standards Committee.

FAILURE AND ABOLITION

After twenty years of work there was at least as much criticism of the accountancy profession, auditors and accounting standards as when the ASSC began. Books on 'creative accounting' were on the best-seller lists; there were spectacular financial collapses; dubious accounting practices designed to exaggerate profitability and growth had become well-known; there was no effective enforcement mechanism for accounting standards; many standards permitted more than one treatment in circumstances that were not clearly specified; many standards had been found inadequate and had been revised, but further problems led to the need for further reviews and revisions. And the second Maxwell scandal was about to break: it seemed to show that nothing had been learned from the first scandal, except by Robert Maxwell himself who ran rings around any attempts by accountants, auditors and others to control him.

It is worth pointing out that the ICAEW's attempts at producing Recommendations on Accounting Principles (1942–69) collapsed and were superseded by the Accounting Standards (Steering) Committee in much the same way as the ASC collapsed and was superseded by the Accounting Standards Board. Whether the ASB's attempts to promulgate accounting standards will last any longer than its predecessors remains to be seen.

The failure of the ASC is evidenced by the fact that it was abolished and superseded by the ASB. Its membership, remit and operations were subject to regular review and change. The shambles over failed attempts to deal with the effects of inflation on financial accounts was the most dramatic, but many other statements that were produced failed to achieve what was required of them and had to be reviewed or had been amended or withdrawn.

In defence of the ASC we can point out some limited success. It is fairly clear that there were some increases in disclosure and some reduction in the variety of different practices adopted. But there was also evidence of companies adopting parts of standards that flattered their performance more readily than they adopted other parts (Perks and Radcliffe, 1982). It must also be recognized that some of the improvements in financial reporting during the lifetime of the ASC were attributable to the introduction of fairly extensive additional Companies Act requirements. The Committee might claim some success in increasing awareness of the problems of financial accounting, and the fact that a variety of different treatments of particular items was possible, and in making a major contribution to a substantial increase in the standard of debate about financial accounting.

This, no doubt, encouraged some to adopt better practices; but it also served to open the eyes of others to the possibilities of more creative practices.

But why did the ASC fail? Much of the explanation lies in the lack of an effective enforcement mechanism. Accountants and auditors knew that they could bypass accounting standards with impunity. The lack of such a mechanism meant that the ASC frequently shied away from promulgating standards that would obviously be flouted. The standard producing process was dependent on political consensus and compromise, and many standards are fairly permissive. Rather than risk a confrontation that they could not win, the ASC frequently backed down and allowed a variety of treatments to continue. This was evident on a number of occasions when the discussion documents and exposure drafts published by the ASC were more prescriptive or extensive in their recommended disclosures than the accounting standards that emerge after political lobbying (Hope and Gray, 1982; Nobes, 1991).

But the lack of success was also because what seemed to be expected of them was not achievable. If there were such a thing as proper and correct financial accounting, then there would be some possibility of enforcing it. Chapter 7 explores the feasibility of producing an appropriate framework as a basis for this. But, at present, there appears to be no basis for 'proper' accounting, other than following the relevant legislation. The accounting profession and its committees do not have the power to legislate, and the following of accounting standards is largely on a voluntary basis. The changes and developments in the accounting standard setting process, including the establishment of the Accounting Standards Board, may be viewed as attempts to get out of this dilemma; as a way of adding legitimacy to the standards and enforcing them, and so allowing the standard setters to face up to issues and produce clear-cut standards.

THE ACCOUNTING STANDARDS BOARD

THE DEARING REPORT

The CCAB established a Review Committee, chaired by Sir Ronald Dearing, in November 1987 to carry out a wide-ranging review of the accounting standard setting process. Their report, *The Making of Accounting Standards* (September 1988), recommended:

1. further work on a conceptual framework; and that even in the absence of such a framework there should be statements showing principles underlying particular standards, and why alternatives had been rejected;
2. emphasis should be on quality, timeliness, reducing permitted options and promoting compliance, and not on producing a large volume of standards;
3. further exemptions for small companies from particular standards;

4. standards should be equally applicable in the public sector, with the appropriate Secretary of State being responsible for compliance;
5. standards should not be incorporated into law as this would be too legalistic and would hinder fast responses to new developments.

Although the report resisted the incorporation of accounting standards into law they recommended that standards should be made more effective in a number of ways as follows.

- Directors of large companies should state whether their accounts have complied with standards and explain reasons for any departures.
- Certain authorized bodies and the Secretary of State should be able to apply to courts for an order to require a revision of accounts that do not give a true and fair view.
- There should be a presumption that standards have the support of the courts; the burden of proof that departures give a true and fair view should fall on those responsible for such departures.

The new institutional arrangements proposed were as follows:

1. A **Financial Reporting Council** should be established representing a wide constituency of interests, with the chairman appointed jointly by the Secretary of State for Trade and Industry and the Governor of the Bank of England. It should guide the accounting standard setting body on its work programme and matters of public concern; ensure that it is properly financed; and promote good accounting practice. It should have about 20 members, with the British and Irish governments invited to nominate members or observers, and meet three or four times per annum.
2. An **Accounting Standards Board** should take over from the ASC. It should have a full-time chairman, and technical director, and no more than nine members, and be able to issue standards on its own authority (with a two-thirds majority) instead of with the approval of each of the six professional bodies. It should also be able to publish authoritative but non-mandatory guidance on emerging issues.
3. A **Review Panel** should be established with the objective of achieving 'good financial reporting'. It would investigate any identified or alleged material departures from standards and state what revisions or additional information should be provided to users to give a true and fair view. This was intended to meet the criticism that accounting standards lacked effective enforcement mechanisms.
4. An adequate secretariat with about ten professional staff should be established. Total annual costs would increase from £440 000 per annum for the ASC to about £1.5 million. This could be met partly from a levy on companies filing their annual reports; sales of ASB publications; and a contribution from the Stock Exchange from listing fees.

IMPLEMENTATION

There was at first some difficulty in establishing acceptable financial arrangements, but most of the Dearing Committee recommendations were implemented in 1990. Sir Ronald Dearing was appointed as Chairman of the Financial Reporting Council with three deputies.[5] Professor David Tweedie was appointed as Chairman of the Accounting Standards Board which replaced the ASC and Simon Tuckey, QC was appointed as Chairman of the Review Panel; the deputy chairman was Michael Renshall, who had been chairman of the ASC.

The main differences between current arrangements and those that applied under the ASC are as follows:

1. According to its Chairman (Dearing, 1990) it 'radically widens the field' of those involved in the standard setting process. The Financial Reporting Council, which represents preparers, users and auditors, has about 25 members, plus observers, including the accountancy profession, the financial community and the world of business, management and administration generally. The way in which this change was presented echoes that following the reconstitution of the ASC in 1982, when it was deemed to be more widely representative although it continued to be overwhelmingly dominated by professional accountants.
2. The ASB will issue accounting standards on its own authority; the approval of the individual professional bodies will no longer be required.
3. The Review Panel is undertaking a new function – examining departures from standards. The Companies Act 1989 (Sch. 4, para. 36A) requires published accounts to state whether they comply with SSAPs and to explain material departures. If directors fail to provide explanations of any non-compliance, the auditors are required to draw attention to this. The Review Panel can examine such departures, and others be referred to it. The Secretary of State or the Review Panel can refer departures to the courts, and, if the court finds that accounts do not comply with the overriding requirement to show a true and fair view, the court may order the directors of the company to circulate a revized set of accounts to all who were likely to have relied on the original set. The courts can also require the directors concerned to pay part or all of the costs.

   Any proceedings would be in the civil, not the criminal courts, and the Review Panel is likely to rely on persuasion in the first instance rather than legal action. There appear to be no particular penalties for auditors who have not qualified accounts that are subsequently found not to show a true and fair view. The Chairman of the FRC states that in such circumstances they might

---

[5] Philip Couse, Chairman of the CCAB. Andrew Hugh Smith, Chairman of the International Stock Exchange. Sir Trevor Holdsworth, President of the CBI.

'find themselves in an uncomfortable position' (Dearing, 1990). This sounds no more fierce than the original *Explanatory Foreword*'s threat that professional accountancy bodies, through their disciplinary committees 'may enquire into apparent failures by members ... to observe accounting standards or to disclose departures therefrom'.

4. Substantial additional resources are provided.

FINANCIAL REPORTING STANDARDS

To begin with the Accounting Standards Board simply adopted the SSAPs that existed at the time, but rapidly began to produce its own Financial Reporting Exposure Drafts (endearingly called FRED 1, FRED 2 and so on), and Financial Reporting Standards (FRS 1, FRS 2 etc.). The Board certainly began boldly. FRS 1 (*Cash Flow Statements*) abolished the requirement to publish statements of source and application of funds and replaced them with Cash Flow Statements. FRS 2 (*Accounting for Subsidiary Undertakings*) does little more than bring SSAP 14 into line with the 1989 Companies Act, particularly in relation to the definition of subsidiaries to be included in group accounts. But FRS 3 (*Reporting Financial Performance*) is more radical: it abolishes the emphasis on a single profit figure as we know it by introducing a new statement of gains and losses.

In addition to the new FREDs and FRS's the ASB has produced a number of exposure drafts of Chapters of Statements of Principles. These start with a Foreword to Accounting Standards, and then proceed to deal with the objectives of financial statements and the qualitative characteristics of financial information. They are the latest attempt at producing a conceptual framework. They have also produced regular Urgent Issues Task Force (UITF) abstracts which provide guidance, based on 'consensus' on urgent issues that have not been made clear by standards.

The Financial Reporting Review Panel has already dealt with one well-publicized case in respect of Trafalgar House. The company reported profits of £79 million for the year to September 1991, but after adjustments agreed with the FRRP this will become a loss of £44 million. The company had written down the value of properties which were held as current assets, but had avoided passing the loss through the profit and loss account by reclassifying them as fixed assets before revaluing them. There were also questions about the company's treatment of corporation tax. Trafalgar resisted restating its accounts because they believed that there was nothing wrong with the treatments adopted. But the Review Panel were prepared to take legal action, and in the face of this, Trafalgar agreed to restate its 1991 figures in the 1992 published accounts.

The Trafalgar House dispute demonstrated the teeth of the Review Panel. It was clear that they were prepared to take legal action, and their credibility remained intact. It will continue to do so as long as they are prepared to tackle issues in this way, and as long as they continue to win. But sooner or later there are bound to be cases when they back down, or which they choose to ignore, or when they lose a case in the courts, and their effectiveness will then be called into question.

Whether the new accounting standards regime will be any more successful than the ASC remains to be seen, and Lafferty's predictions (p. 142) may still apply. The new regime does not have clear legal rights to enforce accounting standards. They rely on persuading courts that not to follow accounting standards would mean that the accounts do not show a true and fair view. According to a leader in *Accountancy*[6]

> if a number of reputable companies and their auditors concur in the view that a particular departure from a standard is consistent with giving a true and fair view ... then it is possible that the court will not condemn them. It may instead conclude that there is more than one generally accepted accounting practice ...
>
> If there is no consensus on particular accounting issues, legal enforcement of the resulting standards may not be feasible ...
>
> If no such consensus emerges, the new regime's enforcement powers may soon need to be strengthened.

It seems that there is still no effective enforcement mechanism. The different treatments that could be defended as presenting 'a true and fair view', and so which bypass the requirements of accounting standards, are so wide as to make accounting standards seem superfluous, other than as a cosmetic public relations exercise.

DO WE NEED ACCOUNTING STANDARDS?

THE NEED FOR STANDARDS

At first sight it may seem obvious that we need accounting standards. The published financial statements of different companies, and of particular companies from one year to the next, should be produced on a comparable basis if they are to be useful. If the accounting principles and policies adopted by different companies vary too widely then our attempts to assess financial position or performance could become almost meaningless. There is also a need for standardized terminology for the language of accountancy to be comprehensible and useful. In a market economy accounting information is a public good that is required if the forces of supply and demand are to operate effectively. The credibility of financial statements is enhanced if they are seen to comply with a fine looking set of accounting standards.

[6] *Accountancy*, Apr. 1990, 1.

The accountancy profession is also interested in avoiding the sort of scandals, abuses, disclosures of creative accounting and financial collapses that lead to a loss of confidence in accountancy and auditing. It is natural that the professional accountancy bodies should wish to defend its own members and their activities.

SOCIETY'S INTEREST

Financial reporting is not just a matter for the accountancy profession and there are others in society with an interest in accounting standards. Those who are concerned about honesty and integrity in business life would presumably also want to see company reports properly produced in accordance with official requirements. And if accounting standards influence decisions on investment, prices, closures, job losses, or the distribution of income and wealth, then they are of importance to society.

If published financial statements influence the distribution of wealth and resources in society, and have an effect on where most new investment takes place, then accounting standards can be influential, and so are important from this point of view. Whether or not accounting standards have an effect on share prices is discussed on pp. 155 *et seq.*

It could be argued that those who make decisions on such matters are influenced more by market forces and by underlying 'economic reality' than by the particular gloss created by published financial statements. It may also be that decision-making is not as rational as is usually presented, and that accounting information is often part of the process of justifying decisions rather than the basis for making them. It would however be too extreme to suggest that accounting standards have no effects in society.

The accountancy profession's attempts to implement current cost accounting failed partly because they would have reduced reported profits. This in turn might have led to reduced dividends, price increases to make up for reduced profits, pressure to keep wages down, difficulties in raising funds for investment and a change in patterns of investment in the economy. This is of course speculation, and it may be that those who prevented the imposition of CCA were merely wanting to avoid complexities and more work. It seems likely, however, that many feared the consequences of reductions in reported profits. And there is evidence that companies are more keen to adopt accounting standards that increase reported profits than standards that reduce them (Perks and Radcliffe, 1982).

In public utilities it appears that the accountancy profession influenced government decisions that CCA should be adopted and, as such utilities are regulated in relation to current cost accounts, accounting policies are bound to affect behaviour. Griffiths (1987), for example, stated that in 1983–84 the difference between the electricity industry's historic cost profit and current cost profit was equivalent to £20 per person per annum. It is reasonable to conclude that the adoption of current cost accounting may have resulted in higher electricity prices than would have been the case with historic cost accounting.

Many decisions in society are justified on the basis of accounts and whether or not they show adequate profits. The choice of a particular accounting policy (which can affect the amounts shown for, *inter alia*, depreciation, stocks, deferred tax) can affect the profit figure shown, and, in turn, the decision made. Accounting standards can, therefore, affect bank lending decisions, and so, in turn, the profits, losses and lending policies of banks; decisions by suppliers on whether or not to deal with particular customers on a credit basis, and so, in turn, influence which suppliers get into financial difficulties; which companies become listed on stock markets and who invests in them, and the extent to which they gain or lose in turn; which companies take over which other companies; and they may also influence share prices, though this is more likely in unlisted companies than in listed companies where the efficient markets hypothesis is assumed to apply.

There is a fairly powerful case for having accounting standards, but who should produce and enforce them? It has been mainly the responsibility of the accountancy profession for many years, and this of course, has the danger that it might be undertaken more for the benefit of the profession than for others in society. The possibility of the government taking over responsibility has always been in the background, and successive companies acts have specified accounting rules, policies, disclosure and presentation requirements in increasing detail, often at the behest of the European Community. There is a case for accounting standards being a matter for governments, rather than the accountancy profession, on behalf of a wide range of different interests in society. But there is also a case for not having accounting standards at all.

ABOLISH MANDATORY STANDARDS?

In this 1978–81 consultation exercise the ASC found that a small number of those making submissions (Professor McCosh, for example) argued that accounting standards are unnecessary on the grounds that the 'Efficient Market Hypothesis' (EMH) shows that share prices will automatically adjust to appropriate values whatever accounting principles are used. This implies that the emphasis should be on disclosure of information, rather that on prescribing measurement rules or the format for such disclosures. Unfortunately the ASC has not been particularly successful in requiring additional disclosures. Indeed, Stamp (1981) proposed that the ASC should attempt to require disclosure of cost of sales figures (which was not then required by law) to demonstrate that the ASC needed more teeth to enforce standards. Another weakness of the argument is that it applies only to listed companies whereas accounting standards are intended to apply to most organizations, including many that are large and important, although they are not listed.

Some, such as Benston (1981), argue that mandatory accounting standards are neither necessary nor desirable but are in favour of voluntary accounting standards. Benston's case begins with a recognition of the stewardship role of accounting and auditing. Those who control a company may direct company resources to their own ends, rather than for the benefit of investors. But investors are aware of this possibility, and accounting and auditing serve to provide assurance outsiders about management's actual intentions. He states that public accountants may be relied upon by investors to conduct honest and effective audits and to render adequate reports of their findings. He argues that this is the case because the costs of not fulfilling this requirement would be excessive. There is the cost of loss of reputation; of being seen to fail in protecting the interests of investors against the interests of directors and those who produce the financial statements. There could also be the cost of law suits. And there is the more important consequent cost of losing other clients as a result.

Benston's argument rests on the assumption that auditors are clearly on the side of the shareholders rather than the directors. This assumption is examined in Chapter 3. It does not deal with the situation where directors, auditors and shareholders might all be on the same side. If a company could succeed in exaggerating profits it might be that directors, auditors and shareholders would all be happy with higher directors' and auditors' fees and with dividends and share prices that were higher than would otherwise be justified. Benston would argue that investors would attach lower valuations to the reports of auditors who indulged in such practices. On the other hand they might never know, and might even prefer auditors that helped companies to flatter their results. When a company is riding high on the back of exaggerated profit figures, existing shareholders may not thank auditors for bursting the bubble.

Favourable earnings reports tend to be welcomed by investors and others with an interest in the company, and auditors' reputations are unlikely to suffer as long as favourable impressions can be maintained. There is always the possibility that lenders and potential shareholders will be misled by such practices and, as a result, they may be dissatisfied with the auditors. The auditors could be sued, but this is unusual, and generally unlikely to succeed. The reputation of the auditors may also suffer to such an extent that they lose business through putting their names to dubious practices. On the other hand they could also lose business if they try too hard to prevent directors from presenting a company's financial position and performance in the way that the directors prefer. Benston's reliance on it being in the auditors' interest to maintain reputable accountancy standards is probably not an adequate safeguard, either for investors or for society more generally.

Benston would probably not accept that producing financial reports in accordance with standards has value **to society**; he sees them as being principally for investors and creditors. 'The general public is (by definition) diffuse and only indirectly and indifferently interested in financial statements until a perceived scandal occurs or if it appears that an enterprise is operating contrary to the public interest.' He was concerned with who would bear the costs of mandatory accounting standards and who would benefit from them. He argued that mandatory standards were likely to be of more benefit to smaller firms of accountants, who were less able than the large firms to rely on their own reputations; but an accounting standards regime would impose cost disproportionately on smaller firms, and this could encourage their displacement by larger firms.

Academics such as Benston, or Watts and Zimmerman (1986), would not accept that a dubious increases in reported profits lead to higher share prices and increases in shareholder wealth. The EMH suggests that investors see through changes in accounting policies and that share prices reflect all available information.

The extent to which accounting standards influence share prices is not clear. Before the EMH became the accepted wisdom in many financial and academic circles it was usually assumed that the stock market can be misled by changes in accounting policies; and that if new accounting standards led to different accounting policies, and so to different reported profit and balance sheet figures, then stock market prices would change accordingly. But positive accounting researchers such as Watts and Zimmerman (1986, p. 108) see this 'mechanistic hypothesis' as contradicting the EMH. The EMH implies that the stock market reacts in an unbiased fashion to all information; presenting information differently would not therefore affect share prices.

It certainly seems likely that the stock market 'sees through' many attempts at creative accounting. Accounting adjustments are often only a matter of timing, and a loss-making business is unlikely to be able to hide its losses for very long. If closing stocks and profits are overstated in one year, profits will be reduced accordingly in the following year. Over the lifetime of a fixed asset the difference between the price paid for it and the price at which it is sold will have to be charged against profits; but careful choice of depreciation policies will affect reported profits in any particular year. In assessing the effects of accounting policies on society both **timing** and **impressions** matter.

Any decision (such as the closure of a pit or factory, an investment or a takeover) are made at a particular time. If investing in a company looks particularly promising when the investment decision is made, it is no consolation to the investor that, in the long run, manipulations of accounting policies, and poor financial performance, will be revealed.

Watts and Zimmerman[7] argue that the efficient market hypothesis invalidates many of the traditional arguments in favour of corporate disclosure regulation. They present the traditional arguments in favour of accounting standards in the following terms:

---

[7] Watts and Zimmerman, 1986, p. 158, based on Leftwich, R. (1980) Market failure fallacies and accounting information, *Journal of Accounting and Economics*, 2 Dec., 193–211.

1. In the absence of accounting standards, investors would not be able to distinguish between efficient and less efficient firms, with the effect that share prices would be distorted, and resources are misallocated.
2. Managers have a monopoly control of the information about a company's financial position and performance that is available to investors, and so they are able to manipulate stock prices to their own advantage, unless there is regulation to prevent them from doing so.
3. Naive investors may be misled and lose money as a result of investment decisions based on accounting information if they do not have the expertise to compare one company's results with other companies' results. Accounting standards are assumed to facilitate such comparisons.
4. Accounting numbers are meaningless in that they are based on a diversity of different procedures and bases of valuation. To the extent that stock market prices reflect 'earnings' they cannot identify which companies are more efficient than others.

Watts and Zimmerman contend that these traditional arguments do not apply in an efficient market. Management has no monopoly of information and managers cannot systematically mislead an efficient stock market. Naive investors are **price protected** – i.e. share prices are fair in the sense that on average they earn a normal rate of return. Share prices do not react mechanistically to earnings figures because 'sophisticated' investors interpret accounting procedures and share prices react accordingly. And even if accounting numbers are meaningless and based on a diversity of procedures, 'in an efficient market managers cannot use diverse procedures to mislead investors systematically. Investors are price protected'.

There are, however, a number of problems with this approach.

Although Watts and Zimmerman may be correct in stating that individual investors are price protected in the sense that 'on average' share prices are 'fair', this is likely to be of little consolation to individual investors for their specific losses, and it does not prevent scandals. If a company collapses shortly after publishing set of accounts that appears to show a healthy financial position, the finger of blame inevitably points at the accountancy profession.

It seems clear that the stock market does react to information that is disclosed. But it also seems reasonable to assume that it does not react to information that is not disclosed. In so far as directors can determine what is and what is not disclosed they can, therefore, influence stock prices. And, in so far as accounting standards influence what is and what is not disclosed, they too can influence stock prices and/or restrict the freedom of management to influence stock prices. It seem, then, that accounting standards **do** matter and **do** have real effects.

Watts and Zimmerman also argue that, even if the traditional arguments were valid, the imposition of government regulation would not necessarily improve the markets' ability to allocate capital efficiently. They say that the issue is an empirical one, depending on relative costs and benefits of private production of information and governmentally regulated production of information. Whether such costs and benefits can be measured and compared is questionable. But we should be wary of arguments that imply that the sole or main function of accounting standards is to improve the allocative efficiency of stock markets. Within the assumptions of Watts and Zimmerman it may not be possible for accounting standards to improve market efficiency (in the sense of what information is reflected by share prices). But it does not necessarily follow that an efficient stock market leads to efficient allocations of resources in society, or to maximizing social welfare (unless these terms are carefully defined so that the idea of allocative efficiency, like the Efficient Market Hypothesis, becomes somewhat tautological). Accounting standards are also applicable in a wide range of organizations, other than listed companies, which represent the majority of the country's economy.

SUMMARY AND CONCLUSIONS

The accountancy profession has given a high profile to the production of accounting standards at least since 1969, although the previous recommendations on principles go back as far as 1942. But there have been regular and recurring problems. There have never been effective enforcement mechanisms; standards have tended to be flexible and permissive; and there seems to be no limit to the various ways around them that have been found.

It seems that published financial statements do have some real effects in society, and society has an interest in effective accounting standards. Much of the case against mandatory accounting standards rests on the stock market reaction to information, regardless of the ways in which that information is disclosed. The strongest case for accounting standards is therefore in their requiring the disclosure of information. While they may be persuasive with regard to some disclosures, to be effective any disclosure requirement needs the backing of the law.

The profession's involvement in accounting standards does much to create the impression of activity, expertise, complication, difficulty; and it suggests that there is a need for accountants, auditors, companies and other organizations to comply with a detailed and comprehensive set of complex requirements. But it does little to force determined, recalcitrant directors to disclose any more information than the law requires.

Accounting standards may be assessed in terms of their actual or potential contributing to economic efficiency. But the objectives of many of those who advocate an accounting standard setting process are likely to be more political than economic. The accountancy profession is keen (a) to retain accounting standard setting in the private sector and (b) to avoid major scandals. One way of avoiding scandals would be to have a set of clear-cut measurement and disclosure requirements so that producing published accounts would become a mechanistic exercise, applying the rules rather than exercising professional judgement. On some occasion blindly applying the rules might not result in a 'true and fair view' in the eyes of some, but there is nothing to prevent a company from disclosing additional information to 'correct' any 'misleading' impressions. An accounting standards system based on simple, clear-cut rules might be cheaper to administer than the present system, and writers such as Watts and Zimmerman could not object to such simplification if they believe that it is not possible to mislead the market.

An example of a simple, clear-cut rule would be regarding profits/losses on disposals of fixed assets. One can agonize for ever whether, in a particular case. such a profit or loss should be regarded as **ordinary**, **exceptional**, or **extraordinary**, and no SSAP can produce definitions of these terms that remove the need for subjective judgement in application. A simple, clear-cut rule would be to require all such profits/losses to be disclosed.

Although such a simplified, straightforward approach might remove the cause of many accounting scandals (where published accounts are alleged to have been misleading) it has little appeal to the accountancy profession. It would require additional disclosures, and the accountancy profession has no power to enforce such disclosure. It would also reduce the role of financial accounting to mere application of rules and form-filling, with no requirement to exercise professional judgement as to what constitutes a 'true and fair' view in particular circumstances. In this situation there would be less need for highly qualified and expensive chartered accountants. A straightforward and effective system could lead to a substantial reduction in the remuneration of chartered accountants.

Professional accountants need uncertainty, lack of clarity, professional judgement and general mystification to maintain their distinction from ordinary people. But if it were generally realized that accounting principles have more to do with ritual and magic than with clarity or consistency, there would be a general loss of confidence in the accountancy profession and the financial statements that it produces. Scandals which threaten the reputation of accountancy recur regularly, and the accountancy profession regularly revises its system for developing and implementing accounting standards, only to have to do the same again a few years later. With any specific accounting problem the profession can always create the impression that it is being tackled and will be solved. There is usually a working party, or a research report commissioned, or an exposure draft being revised, or a new standard to be produced shortly. The problem is not, of course, finally 'solved', but the standard setters can go through the motions again on the grounds that the previous proposed solution was not quite right. It is all rather like a rain dance: if it does not produce rain, the same ritual is carried out again once the failure has become apparent. An important difference is that sooner or later it will rain, and the whole procedure will seem to have been vindicated. But the problems of accountancy standards will not be solved by the accountancy profession. Perhaps accountants are like witch doctors or magicians. Some believe that their magic will work. Others are more concerned to use ritual, mystification and magic to maintain their position in society.

APPENDIX A ICAEW RECOMMENDATION ACCOUNTING PRINCIPLES

1942	N1 Tax Reserve Certificates
	N2 War Damage Contributions, Premiums and Claims
1943	N3 The Treatment of Taxation in Accounts
	N4 The Treatment in Accounts of Income Tax Deductible from Dividends Payable and Annual Charges
	N5 The Inclusion in Accounts of Proposed Profit Appropriations
	N6 Reserves and Provisions
1944	N7 Disclosure of the Financial Position and Results of Subsidiary Companies in the Accounts of Holding Companies
	N8 Form of Balance Sheet and Profit and Loss Account
1945	N9 Depreciation of Fixed Assets
	N10 Valuation of Stock-in-Trade
1946	N11 Excess Profits Tax Post-War Refunds
1949	N12 Rising Price Levels in Relation to Accounts
	N13 Accountants' Reports for Prospectuses: Fixed Assets and Depreciation
	N14 The Form and Content of Estates of Deceased Persons and Similar Trusts
1952	N15 Accounting in Relation to Changes in the Purchasing Power of Money
1953	N16 Accountants' Reports for Prospectuses: Adjustments and Other Matters
1957	N17 Events Occurring After the Balance Sheet Date
1958	N18 Presentation of Balance Sheet and Profit and Loss Account
	N19 Treatment of Income Tax in Accounts of Companies and Treatment of Investments in the Balance Sheets of Trading Companies
	N20 Treatment of Investments in the Balance Sheets of Trading Companies
1960	N21 Retirement Benefits
	N22 Treatment of Stock-in-Trade and Work in Progress in Financial Statements
1964	N23 Hire Purchase, Credit Sale and Rental Purchase Transactions
1967	N24 The Accounting Treatment of Investment Grants
1968	N25 The Accounting Treatment of Major Changes in the Sterling Parity of Overseas Currencies
	N26 Land Commission Act 1967: Accounting Implications
	N27 The Treatment of Taxation in the Accounts of Companies
1968	N28 The Accounts of Investment Trust Companies
1969	N29 Trust Accounts

APPENDIX B STATEMENTS OF STANDARD ACCOUNTING PRACTICE

	Issued	*Revised or added to*
Explanatory foreword	May 75	Aug. 86
1. Accounting for associated companies	Jan. 71	Apr. 82
2. Disclosure of accounting policies	Nov. 71	
3. Earnings per share	Feb. 72	Aug. 74
4. The accounting treatment of government grants	Apr. 74	July 90
5. Accounting for value added tax	Apr. 74	
6. Extraordinary items and prior year adjustments	Apr. 74	Aug. 86
8. The treatment of taxation under the imputation system	Aug. 74	Dec. 77
9. Stocks and work in progress	May 75	Sep. 88
10. Statements of source and application of funds	July 75	June 78
12. Accounting for depreciation	Dec. 77	Jan. 87
13. Accounting for research and development	Dec. 77	Jan. 89
14. Group accounts	Sep. 78	
15. Accounting for deferred tax	Oct. 78	May 85
17. Accounting for post balance sheet events	Aug. 80	
18. Accounting for contingencies	Aug. 80	
19. Accounting for investment properties	Nov. 81	
20. Foreign currency translation	Apr. 83	
21. Accounting for leases and hire purchase contracts	Aug. 84	
22. Accounting for goodwill	Dec. 84	July 89
23. Accounting for acquisitions and mergers	Apr. 85	
24. Accounting for pension costs	May 88	
25. Segmental reporting	June 90	

APPENDIX C FINANCIAL REPORTING STANDARDS

	Issued
1. Cash Flow Statements	Sep. 91
2. Accounting for Subsidiary Undertakings	July 92
3. Reporting Financial Performance	Oct. 92

FURTHER READING

Beaver, W. H. (1989) *Financial Reporting: An Accounting Revolution*, Prentice Hall.

Blake, J. (1991) *Accounting Standards*, Pitman.

Bromwich, M. (1991) *Financial Reporting, Information and Capital Markets*, Pitman.

Bromwich, M. and Hopwood A.G. (eds) (1992) *Accounting and the Law*, Prentice Hall/ICAEW.

Ernst and Young (1992) *UK GAAP: Generally Accepted Practice in the UK*, Macmillan.

Leach, R. and Stamp E. (eds) (1981) *British Accounting Standards: The First Ten Years*, Woodhead Faulkner, Cambridge.

Sangster, A. (1991) *A Workbook of Accounting Standards*, Pitman.

ESSAY AND DISCUSSION TOPICS

1. Why has the accountancy profession become involved in promulgating accounting standards?
2. How can accounting standards be enforced effectively?
3. In what ways, and for what reasons, did the Accounting Standards Committee fail? In what ways did it succeed?
4. What reasons are there for supposing that the Accounting Standards Board will be more successful than the Accounting Standards Committee?
5. How can 'creative accounting' be minimized? Does it matter?
6. Discuss the view that the efficient markets hypothesis eliminates the need for mandatory accounting standards.
7. Discuss the case for accounting standards being 'flexible'.
8. In what ways does society benefit from the involvement of the accountancy profession in the setting and enforcement of accounting standards? In what ways would society benefit if it were left to government legislation?

REFERENCES

Benston, G. J. (1981) *in British Accounting Standards, The First Ten Years* (eds R. Leach and E. Stamp), Woodhead-Faulkner, pp. 201–14.

Dearing, R. (1990) Accounting standards: the new approach, *Accountancy*, June, 86–7.

Griffiths, I. (1987) *Creative Accounting*, Unwin.

Hope, T. and Gray, R. H. (1982) Power and policy making in the development of an R & D standard, *Journal of Business Finance and Accounting*, Winter.

Lafferty, M. (1981) How good are the standards we now have?, in

Nobes, C. (1991) Cycles in UK standard setting, *Accounting and Business Research* **21**(83), Summer, 265–74.

Perks, R. W. and Radcliffe, G. (1982) The implementation of SSAPs with particular reference to SSAP 15, *AUTA Review*, Autumn, 38–64.

Stamp, E. (1981) A view from Academe, in *British Accounting Standards, The First Ten Years* (eds R. Leach and E. Stamp), Woodhead-Faulkner.

Stamp, E. and Marley, C. (1970) *Accounting Principles and the City Code: The Case for Reform*, Butterworths.

Watts, R. L. and Zimmerman, J.L. (1986) *Positive Accounting Theory*, Prentice Hall, p. 178.

Watts, T. R. (1981) *Setting Accounting Standards*, Accounting Standards Committee.

7 A conceptual framework

THE NEED FOR A CONCEPTUAL FRAMEWORK

In our earliest attempts to learn financial accounting we rapidly get used to the idea that there are 'right' answers. If the balance sheet does not balance, then it must be wrong. If it does balance, we like to assume that it is right, and prefer not to question any assumptions made about such things as depreciation, goodwill or stock values. We learn that financial statements that do not comply with the requirements of the Companies Acts or with accounting standards are 'wrong', and we are imbued with the notion that our accounts should be 'right'. In many areas there are 'rules' which, if carefully followed, will give the 'right' answers.

It is relatively easy to establish bookkeeping rules that ensure that the books will balance; that enable a balance sheet and profit and loss account to produced; that enable all entries in the accounts to be audited and traced back to their source; that enable us to keep track of debtors and creditors; that facilitate the discovery of most errors; and that enable us to reconcile our accounts with statements produced by banks and other outside parties. But there are many areas of difficulty, such as those dealt with by accounting standards, that remain uncertain and unresolved. The idea of having certain and correct answers to all of these problems is quite appealing, but at present there is no basic set of principles from which definite, lasting, comprehensive and consistent answers to these problems can be produced.

The idea of having a conceptual framework that underlies financial accounting principles and which provides a basis for dealing with all financial accounting problems is very appealing for a number of reasons.

1. It would provide a basis for setting accounting standards, and for deciding between different ways of treating particular items. This would apply both in producing new standards, and in dealing with a number of existing unsatisfactory situations. Some standards, for example, allow two different methods of dealing with a particular item, or permit an alternative treatment in circumstances that are not well defined. There is considerable scope for 'creative accounting', and the definition of fundamental accounting principles could help to clarify the boundaries of acceptable creativity. It could also provide guidance on problem areas that emerge where no standard has yet been developed.

2. It could enable accounting standard setting bodies to present their work as proceeding in an orderly manner in refining and applying principles, rather than as an unplanned 'fire-fighting' exercise where the impression given is that the standard setters rush from one issue to another, without any particular plan, dealing with whatever seems to be causing most concern at a particular time.

3. It would avoid conflicts between various different accounting standards by providing a basis for all to be set on a consistent basis. At present it sometimes seems as if each problem is tackled afresh, without taking into account theoretical assumptions that underlie existing accounting standards. There are recurring theoretical issues underlying the development of accounting standards. For example, is it the economic substance of an item that should determine its treatment, or is it the legal form of that item? Does the requirement to match income with expenditure over-ride the need for prudence? Is profit determined through the profit and loss account, with the balance sheet as the residual; or is profit an 'all inclusive' concept, determined in relation to the increase in net assets on the balance sheet, where the profit and loss account is the residual?

4. It might eliminate the need for detailed guidance on problems with the implementation of accounting standards, or allow it to be reduced very considerably. There would be no need to specify in detail the requirements for many different circumstances. The conceptual framework would provide the general principles, and each detailed case would be dealt with as an application of those principles.

5. It could reduce or eliminate political interference in the setting of standards. It is clear that with a number of standards (e.g. research and development; investment properties), companies that were likely to be affected by particular standards were able to lobby and influence the standard setting body to permit treatments that they favoured. The current standard setting

process has been criticized as being too subject to political lobbying instead of establishing a sound theoretical framework as a basis for accounting rules.

6. It would be appealing to have answers to fundamental questions about what we are trying to do in financial reporting, if only as a justification for all the effort and expense involved. Why and for whom are financial reports produced? On what principles are they based? What information do the various users want from them? How can reports be produced that will meet those needs?

7. It could add to the credibility of professional accountants and the statements that they produce. Objectivity and verifiability are particularly important to accountants, and if accounting principles and statements were seen as being objectively and verifiably derived from an established theoretical framework, then their credibility, and the legitimacy of the profession that produces them, would be enhanced.

8. It could enhance the status and academic respectability of the subject of accountancy in colleges and universities. If accountancy is seen merely as a practical technique, like bookkeeping, then it is difficult to justify its place in an academic curriculum. If we claim that accounting is an academic discipline, then we cannot ignore theoretical and conceptual issues. It seems that accountants, particularly academics, suffer from an inferiority complex when they compare themselves with economists, or scientists, who have sophisticated theories, concepts and principles, and seem to be able to build a whole vision of the world based upon them.

Many expectations of what a conceptual framework might deliver are unrealistically high. Some of the difficulties are discussed on pp. 171–174.

ATTEMPTS AT DEVELOPING A CONCEPTUAL FRAMEWORK

The quest for a conceptual framework is most closely associated with the work of the American Financial Accounting Standards Board (FASB) which began in 1973, but the origins of such work go back at least as far as 1940.

Early attempts

In the United States Paton and Littleton's (1940) work was intended to be a theoretical basis for developing a coherent and consistent set of accounting standards, and a series of comparable studies was published in the following decades – though none provided the basis that seemed to be required. A series of Accounting Research Bulletins (ARBs) was published and in 1953 the 42 that had been produced were consolidated into ARB No. 43. A further eight ARBs followed, but they failed to solve many important accounting problems of the day, or to produce an acceptable theoretical framework from which solutions might be derived.

In response to widespread criticism the Accounting Principles Board was established 1959 to replace the former Committee on Accounting Procedure and the Committee on Terminology. In response to the report of their Special Committee on Research (1958) the American Institute of Certified Public Accountants (AICPA) appointed its first director of research, Maurice Moonitz. In the first of a series of Research Studies that followed it was recommended that

> an immediate project of the accounting research staff should be a study of the basic postulates underlying accounting principles generally. There should also be a study of the broad principles of accounting ... The results of these, as adopted by the Board, should serve as the foundation for the entire body of future pronouncements by the Institute on accounting matters. (Moonitz, 1961)

Research studies Nos 1 and 3 outlined the principles proposed, but they proved to be too controversial in advocating current cost accounting for example, and moving away from the realization principle (by allowing stocks to be shown at net realizable value, even if this was above cost). Instead, Research Study No. 7 was adopted, which was no more than a catalogue of generally accepted principles that had already been accepted. This did not provide a basis for subsequent Opinions of the Accounting Principles Board.

FASB

In response to continued criticism the AICPA set up two study groups, one on the establishment of accounting principles, and one on the objectives of financial statements. The first produced the Wheat Report (for which Solomons takes much of the credit), which led to the Accounting Principles Board being replaced by the Financial Accounting Standards Board in 1973. The second produced the Trueblood Report which outlined 12 objectives of financial accounting. The principal one was that 'the basic objective of financial statements is to provide information useful for making economic decisions'. The Trueblood Report and the establishment of the Financial Accounting Standards Board marked the beginning of the conceptual framework project which was prominent in the 1970s and 1980s.

In 1978 the Statement of Financial Accounting Concepts (SFAC) No. 1 on the Objectives of Financial Reporting by Business Enterprises was published. It was based on the Trueblood Report and emphasized that the main aim of accounting statements as being useful in making economic and business decisions. It recognized a wide range of potential users of financial statements, but concentrated on the needs of investors and creditors in making rational investment, credit and similar decisions. It recognized that, in making such decisions, it is necessary to assess the amounts, timing and uncertainty of prospective cash inflows. In accepting this it flirted with the idea that cash flow information might be more useful than accruals based accounting information, and that forecasts of the future might be more useful than reports of the past. But nothing so radical was recommended! The case for cash flow accounting, including the publication of forecast cash flows, is beyond the scope of this book. But it is worth highlighting a basic dilemma of accounting: if users really want to know about future cash flows, and accountants report the past on an accruals basis, then accounting is bound to fall short of users' expectations. No amount of criticism of the profession, or reform by the profession, can change this basic dilemma: decision-making requires information about the future; accounting reports about the past can be improved; they can even be changed so that predictive ability becomes the main criterion for selecting accounting principles. But most accountants do not have crystal balls, cannot know the future,[1] and their reports are bound to be inadequate for user needs – even if they manage to produce a tolerable representation of the past.

SFAC 1 is important in that it marked a shift in emphasis away from stewardship as a primary objective of financial accounting towards decision-making, with profits and cash flows being particularly emphasized. This suggests a turning point in the role of accountancy in society and, in turn, reflects and influences a change in emphasis in the role of directors and of companies. The idea of stewardship suggested that directors were responsible for the custodianship of assets that belonged to shareholders; and that they were accountable to shareholders in fairly general terms for the way in which they carried out their stewardship of the company. SFAC 1 reflects a much narrower emphasis: shareholders are assumed to be interested almost exclusively in profits and cash flows, and, provided they are satisfied with the performance of their companies in that respect, other aspects of directors' responsibilities and their custodianship tend to be ignored.

SFAC 2 dealt with the qualitative characteristics of accounting information by presenting a hierarchy of accounting qualities. The pervasive constraint is that the benefits from producing financial statements should be greater than the cost of producing them. The first quality specified is understandability; the qualities that follow are decision usefulness and reliability, both of which require comparability (which includes consistency). Relevance comes next and this requires predictive value, feedback value and timeliness. This is followed by reliability

---

[1] Although, in a sense, accountants' reports can **create** the future. If a company is in financial difficulties, and the annual report highlights this fact, publication could tip the balance and provoke financial collapse. Similarly, if the report paints a (credible) rosy picture, creditors are likely to be reassured and the company may then be able to survive the immediate crisis, and perhaps improve its financial position. Accounting reports can create their own truth only if they are believed; credibility is therefore very important to accountancy, and attempts at producing a conceptual framework are intended to enhance credibility. Whether or not there is a 'truth' that exists independently of what people negotiate and believe is a philosophical question that has important implications for the nature of accounting.

which requires verifiability, neutrality and representational faithfulness. And, finally, materiality is the threshold for recognition. In addition the convention of conservatism or prudence was discussed, but the idea of any deliberate under-statement of assets or profits was rejected. Such general statements of desirable characteristics tend to be relatively acceptable; serious problems do not usually arise until particular applications are considered, and theoretical arguments deriving from a conceptual framework are used to change current practice.

The next step was to define the elements of financial statements which was done in SFAC 3 (subsequently revised in SFAC 6 to include non-profit organizations). It defined assets and liabilities, with equity as the residual; it also defined 'comprehensive income' which is an all-inclusive, balance sheet approach to income measurement. Revenues and expenses were defined, and also gains and losses which arise from peripheral or incidental transactions. Comprehensive income was made up of the excess of revenues over income, plus the excess of gains over losses. This step in developing a conceptual framework was more problematic. Many of the definitions of elements in financial statements were derived from definitions of other elements and tended to be tautologous. The approach emphasized income being derived from an increase in net assets, with the profit and loss account as the residual. This was controversial. There are problems in determining the value to be attributed to assets, and many accountants would favour the opposite approach, with the balance sheet being seen as the residual after profit has been measured using the conventions of the profit and loss account. And there were problems with some items that were excluded by the specific definitions; some items of deferred expenditure, for example, would normally be included on a balance sheet, but do not strictly fall within the definition of an asset. Once a conceptual framework project has to deal with specifics it tends either to fall apart in the face of various critics, or to dodge the issues and produce statements that are generally acceptable, but provide no real guidance on future development.

The next stage was the most difficult. SFAC 5 (1984) dealt with the problems of recognition and measurement in financial statements, particularly with regard to assets and liabilities, revenues and expenses, and so of profit. It accepted that five different approaches were used in practice: historical cost, current cost, current market value, net realizable value and present value of future cash flows. It did not, however, recommend in favour of one approach rather than another; it accepted that the five different approaches would continue to be used, and stated that income concepts will continue to be subject to the process of gradual change without indicating any preferred direction of change. The whole approach is descriptive rather than prescriptive. It may play a role in educating accountants, but it was inconclusive and does not provide an adequate basis for the development of accounting standards.

Interest in theoretical issues came rather later in the UK. The Accounting Standards Steering Committee was established in 1969 and soon recognized the desirability of an overall theoretical framework for the development of consistent accounting standards. But pressures and problems were such that they had to proceed with ad hoc solutions to particular problems before such a framework could be developed.

SSAP 2 (1971), which dealt with the disclosure of accounting policies, included what may be seen as a first, preliminary attempt at developing such a framework. It specified four 'fundamental accounting concepts', broad basic assumptions that underlie financial accounts, namely the going concern concept, the accruals concept, the consistency concept, and the concept of prudence. But this was an inadequate basis for further development, not least because the concepts conflicted with each other. SSAP 2 itself recognized one such conflict in recommending that 'where the accruals concept is inconsistent with the "prudence" concept, the latter prevails'. It is not difficult to think of other conflicts between the four concepts that are likely to arise in practice, and it is usually not much help to refer to these four concepts in search of a solution to a particular problem; often one of the concepts will suggest a particular approach to a problem, while another of the concepts will suggest a quite different approach.

The UK accounting profession's *Corporate Report* (July 1975) was a remarkable attempt at producing a conceptual framework and included some interesting proposals to improve and extend annual reports. It began by stating that corporate reports should seek to satisfy, as far as possible, the information needs of users. It then identified seven user groups (some of which were so broad as to include almost everyone!), and 15 items of information that users might need and which corporate reports might be able to provide. It specified seven desirable characteristics of corporate reports (they should be relevant, understandable, reliable, complete, objective, timely and comparable), and then reviewed the state of financial reporting at that time. Its section on 'Measurement and Method' recommended the publication of 6 additional statements (see Chapter 2, p. 37). It recognized that there were different approaches to the measurement of capital maintenance, profit and so on, and concluded that no single method would meet all user needs. It therefore suggested that further research be conducted on the feasibility of multi-column reporting to show income on several different bases, although it was recognized that this might impair understandability.

In many ways the *Corporate Report* was a commendable attempt at developing a conceptual framework for accountancy. Where it came up against difficulties that could not easily be resolved it recommended the publication of additional information and statements, and/or that further research should be carried out. It did not indicate how such research should be conducted; it seems unlikely that it was expected to find underlying truths that had not previously been discovered. The research was intended to find feasible[2] and acceptable[3]

---

[2] Para. 8.15.
[3] Para. 6.47.

solutions; this suggests that a recognition that financial accounting principles depend more on pragmatism and political expediency than on verifiable scientific propositions.

The *Corporate Report*'s impact was short-lived; it was almost immediately overshadowed by the publication of the *Sandilands Report* (September 1975) and the inflation accounting debate which followed.

The British accounting profession, and interested academics, continued to monitor the American conceptual framework project to see what could be learned from it. The ASC commissioned the Macve Report (1981) to review recent literature and form preliminary conclusions as to the possibilities of developing an agreed conceptual framework for setting accounting standards. The report concentrated on the problems that arise in determining profit and net assets, and on what constitutes useful accounting information. It highlighted the fact that there are many different potential users of accounting information, and that they are likely to have different and conflicting information needs. The report concluded that, in this situation, reaching agreement on the form and content of financial statements is as much a political process as it is a search for solutions that are technically best. It concluded that the continuing attempts to develop recognition criteria and measurement rules that can both command general acceptance and have an impact in settling particular accounting disputes were likely to be unsuccessful. It recommended that further research should be carried out, and, in due course, the Accounting Standards Committee commissioned a further report, the *Solomons Report* (1989).

The *Solomons Report* followed much the same steps as previous conceptual framework projects, several of which had been strongly influenced by Solomons himself and like-minded academics, whether directly or indirectly. The steps followed were as follows:

1. defining the purposes for which financial statements are produced;
2. defining the users of those financial statements;
3. defining the information needs of those various users;
4. establishing how those information needs are met at present;
5. defining the elements included in financial statements;
6. defining the qualitative characteristics that should apply to such statements;
7. specifying the rules of recognition and measurement of balance sheet and profit and loss account items.

Solomons favoured the primacy of the balance sheet over the profit and loss account, using a current cost approach, but with constant purchasing power adjustments. While many of the earlier parts of his recommendations could command widespread agreement, current cost accounting, and variations on it, had proved to be unpopular and so unacceptable.

Another recent study, by the Institute of Chartered Accountants of Scotland, *Making Corporate Reports Valuable* (1988) was equally wide-ranging, but favoured the use of net realizable values on the balance sheet. This also proved not to be generally acceptable.

In many ways all of the various conceptual framework projects are very similar. There is widespread agreement at the early stages: lofty statements of objectives, serving the needs of users, and specifying desirable characteristics of financial statements cause few problems. We are all in favour of virtue, at least in theory. But when it comes to recommendations on the definition and measurement of profit, and of assets and liabilities, conceptual framework projects seem to fall apart. It may be that professional accountancy bodies will have to continue with such projects. Much of the bread and butter work of professional accountants is in producing and auditing balance sheets and profit and loss accounts. We cannot afford to admit that we have no basis for defining and measuring assets, liabilities and profits, other than (constantly changing) custom and practice, and what we can get away with!

If accounting has no fundamental truths or principles waiting to be discovered, and if any conceptual framework depends on negotiation and agreement, then it is worth asking who should do the negotiation, and who should have the power to determine what is 'agreed'. At present there is an interplay between professional bodies and the accountants and auditors who they represent, the representatives of companies who have an interest in the way in which their financial performance is presented, and academics with their theoretical ideas, often derived from the subject of economics. The government and its representatives are somewhere in the background, with the professional bodies trying to keep them there. But who represents the public? If accounting principles are academic, arcane, and irrelevant to society, then it does not matter. But if accounting principles influence the distribution of resources in society, then others may legitimately seek to influence the nature and application of such principles.

PROBLEMS OF DEVELOPING A CONCEPTUAL FRAMEWORK

Although the American Financial Accounting Standards Board has devoted substantial resources to their conceptual framework project, and this has to some extent been mirrored in the UK, we still do not have anything like a conceptual framework that fully meets the expectations of the profession or the public as outlined at the beginning of this chapter. There are a number of reasons for this.

1. Financial reports may be used by various parties with very different interests. Even if a conceptual framework could be devised to meet the requirements of one group, it would probably not be appropriate for other groups. Financial reports are variously expected to serve investor needs, guide dividend

decisions, predict future prospects, provide a basis for taxation, portray economic reality and so on. Any conceptual framework that is developed is likely to be more appropriate for some purposes than for others, and therefore to be unsatisfactory in some ways.

2. Attempts at producing definitions (for example of profit, assets, liabilities) have so far produced formulae that are capable of being interpreted in different ways to support different views of what is an asset or a liability, for example. Attempts to operationalize such definitions by asking specific questions (such as should goodwill, employees, development costs, brand names or capitalized interest be included within the definition of assets?) cannot succeed if definitions are too permissive. Attempts to make definitions more specific are likely to prove unacceptable to those who find that particular accounting treatments which they favour are thereby not permitted. It is virtually impossible to produce definitions that are acceptable to all the various interested parties, except in such general terms that they offer little guidance on specific treatments.

3. To suggest that accounting standards can be derived from a conceptual framework is to misunderstand the accounting standard setting process. It is a political, bargaining process with different interested parties, each with its own power position and interests, both of which change from time to time; and the interests and power positions of the different parties are likely to change from one issue to another. There may be some individuals involved in the process who, at times, seek to deal with particular issues by referring to some sort of elusive fundamental principles of a conceptual framework. But outcomes are determined more by the political and economic interests of the most powerful parties in a bargaining process than by appeals to principle.

4. In the light of 3 above it would be more realistic to see a conceptual framework as being a cloak of respectability, an intellectual justification for practices that have been adopted for other reasons. It is easier, or more respectable and legitimate, to defend the capitalization of development expenditure on the grounds that 'it really is an asset', than on the grounds that 'our profits will suffer if we don't'.

5. To suggest that accounting principles can be derived from a conceptual framework, or that such a framework can be produced that is demonstrably true, is to misunderstand the nature of accountancy. Accountants may seek scientific credentials, but accountancy is not a science in that sense; it is more like law or a social science where truth and fairness are relative and subject to change, not absolute.

6. Although accountants may like their principles to have the aura of scientific accuracy, they do not want to become mere technicians who unthinkingly apply a set of clear-cut rules. Their status is enhanced by the need to apply 'professional judgement' in deciding the accounting treatment that should be applied in particular cases. A conceptual framework that did not go beyond

general principles might preserve, or even enhance, the need to apply highly regarded, and highly paid, professional judgement; and this may be what many accountants want. But there is likely to be resistance to a conceptual framework from which clear standards and rules logically follow, so that the accountant becomes a mere technician.
7. Many companies and their directors would also resist any conceptual framework that led to more clear-cut accounting standards. There are powerful interest groups in favour of maintaining a degree of creative accounting that enables them to present their companies' results in the way that they choose.

The apparent failure of conceptual framework projects is due largely to unrealistic expectations of them. Such expectations are in part due to a lack of understanding about the nature of accountancy. It is also due to the need for such a framework to be **agreed** by parties with very different interests. The various interested parties have little difficulty in agreeing fine-sounding phrases and intentions, but are unlikely to agree to implement principles when they see these as being against their interests.

The debate over conceptual frameworks, and the development of accounting principles, is sometimes conducted **as if** it were possible to develop accounting standards that were technically correct, and in accordance with some fundamental principles. Where one statement contradicts another, Tweedie, Chairman of the Accounting Standards Board, seems to take the view that one must be 'wrong' (Tweedie, 1992, p. 30). It may be that, from an academic economist's point of view, standards can come up with definitions of income that they regard as being theoretically correct. But such theoretical definitions tend to ignore measurement problems. Accountancy has to be a practical subject that can produce defensible, verifiable and reasonably objective figures every day, regardless of theoretical shortcomings. Whether 'technically correct' accounting standards would solve the problems of creative accounting we will probably never know. But to defend the present accounting standards arrangements on the basis that we are working towards technically correct standards based on a sound theoretical framework is a strategy for the profession that has some advantages.

It seems unlikely that a theoretical framework will ever be developed that meets all of the expectations that were discussed in the first part of this chapter. In some ways the quest for a conceptual framework from which accounting standards can be derived is rather like the quest for a code of ethics from which a country's laws can be derived. It may be relatively easy to agree general, fine-sounding principles, as we saw with the early stages of the various conceptual framework projects; but almost impossible to get agreement when we seek to apply these principles to particular issues. We can all agree that it is wrong to kill, for example; but when we seek to apply this principle to the killing of animals to eat, or of foreigners in a war, or of unborn babies, or of murderers by capital punishment, then general agreement disappears. But we still find the Bible, or some other form of general ethical principles, being invoked by each side in the controversies referred to. A holy war sounds better than murdering foreigners, divine justice sounds better than killing criminals, and so on. The Bible and other sources of ethical principles are fine in theory, but offer little guidance in current practical issues. A conceptual framework could be rather like the Bible in a number of ways: it would spell out lofty principles most of which would command widespread agreement, but offer little guidance on specific problems; and it can be interpreted in different ways to support different viewpoints. It is more realistic to compare the problems of accounting principles and standards with ethical principles and the law, than it is to seek scientific credentials.

CONCEPTUAL FRAMEWORKS, PROFESSIONAL KNOWLEDGE AND THREATS TO THE PROFESSION

Professional accountancy bodies have sought to establish a conceptual framework for accountancy in the expectation that this could raise the status of accountants and their work. If we see the accountancy profession as being very successful in society, in such things as status, credibility and the remuneration of its members, a conceptual framework could be the icing on the cake – the little something extra that makes a solid foundation in professional practice look smooth and impressive. A different view would be to see the profession as already succeeding in superficial appearances, but constantly threatened by its lack of a firm foundation. Hines (1989) suggests that 'the major rationale for undertaking CFs was not functional or technical, but was a **strategic manoeuvre** for providing legitimacy to standard-setting boards and the accounting profession during periods of competition or threatened government intervention'.

Four main threats to the profession are outlined.

1. Accounting knowledge is the residual of a political process

Most literature on professions assumes that a formal body of knowledge is the fundamental trait of Western professionals; to some extent this knowledge is socially constructed; to some extent it is modified by professionals themselves in their application of it; but to some extent it is the **image** of possessing such a body of knowledge that is fundamental to society's construction of a profession.

Historically the earliest accountants were more dependent on personal attributes and skills than on having a formal knowledge base. These characteristics were such things as penmanship (the art of writing), arithmetic, bookkeeping, diligence, honesty, accuracy, orderliness, negotiation and arbitration. Although some knowledge of the law was required, particularly in relation to bankruptcy, there seemed to be no distinct body of knowledge associated with professional accountants as opposed to lawyers.

Accounting standards and principles emerge from a political process that involves accountants, major companies, academics, analysts, government, bankers and other users. The 'knowledge' that they produce is acceptable and pragmatic, rather than true. Most professionals, other than accountants, have a body of knowledge that is produced and verified by research. Medical treatments and engineering constructions, for example, can be seen to succeed or fail on the basis of reasonably objective observation and measurement. The professional knowledge of medics and engineers is more matter of verifiable scientific fact than of something which has to be negotiated with, and acceptable to a wide variety of different interest groups. Legal knowledge is different in that it is socially constructed, not scientifically determined, but its status is enhanced because it does have the imprimatur of government (and the courts) to give it acceptability. Accounting knowledge appears to be no more than what can be negotiated between interested parties.

2. Arbitrariness of accounting standards and practice

Conceptual frameworks are sought on the grounds that there is a need for accounting information to be comparable, complete and consistent; in the absence of such a framework these qualities are presumably absent. It is suggested that accounting standard setters tackle only those problems that there is a high likelihood that they can be resolved. Standards tend to be ad hoc, and increasingly concerned with detail rather than principle, and with identifying and trying to prevent avoidance of the requirements of standards. The move towards detailed rule setting, avoidance and monitoring is, in a sense, deprofessionalizing accountancy.

3. Expansion and diversification of accounting work

The origins of the accountancy profession lie in bankruptcy work and bookkeeping and today financial accounting, auditing and taxation are the bread and butter work of most professional practices. But there has been substantial diversification, particularly into management consultancy, including advice on mergers, marketing and management, and a wide range of services including economic forecasting, recruitment consultancy and design of everything from information systems to transport systems and interior decoration. Accountancy is increasingly referred to as a business or even an industry rather than a profession. Given the vast range of services that are now offered by the largest firms of accountants, it is difficult to identify a unique of formal body of knowledge that accountants 'profess'.

4. Problematic nature of auditing and financial accounting

Auditing is probably the core of accountants' claim to be a profession, but is also the source of a good deal of criticism. When companies fail, or major fraud has been perpetrated, it is often pointed out that the auditor has recently given the company a clean bill of health, and the expertise, authority and independence of auditors is called into question. The 'expectations gap' in auditing was discussed in Chapter 3.

Hines (1988) questions the idea that it is meaningful for auditors to certify that a company's accounts are 'true and fair'. The idea relies on a realist conception which assumes a correspondence between the business's 'real' performance and position, and the accounting significations that are used to represent them. She argues that financial accounts cannot independently and neutrally 'measure' the structure and performance of businesses; they do not signify an entity that exists concretely and independently of the accounting conventions that are used to represent them. She sees financial accounts as playing a crucial role in the reflexive construction of business enterprises; that in attempting to communicate reality accountants are in some ways creating that reality. Accounting cannot be an independent and neutral activity if its reports are involved in creating that which they are assumed to portray.

Hines's arguments may be criticized in a number of ways. The attempt to relate the timing of CF projects to times when the accountancy profession was under threat follows Peasnell (1982) who concluded that

> There have been a number of attempts by the profession to develop a CF. All were undertaken at a time when the standard setting programme had run into trouble. None of them seems to have been of obvious value to the standard setters.

It is, however, difficult to identify a time when the standard setting programme was **not** under threat. The standard setters have been subject to continuous criticism; and conceptual framework projects have been undertaken almost continuously. It is therefore fairly meaningless to suggest that CF projects are undertaken only at times when the profession is under threat.

The argument that accountancy lacks a body of knowledge is also somewhat overstated. Accountants (should) know how to interpret and apply legislation concerning taxation, and the legislation and professional pronouncements concerning published accounts. Such knowledge is, of course, 'socially constructed', but is no different in this respect from the knowledge of the legal profession. A more important issue is to ask who should do the social constructing? Should it be Parliament on behalf of society, rather than the accountancy profession? Legal knowledge (principles and so on) is created both by Parliament and by the courts. Accounting principles do influence resource allocation decisions in society, and the distribution of income and wealth. In view of this it is reasonable to argue that this function belongs more to the state than to a professional body that is, directly or indirectly, financed and largely controlled by the rich and powerful in society. Conceptual framework projects may be seen as one of a number of strategies that add legitimacy to this basic position.

It would be too simplistic to portray the knowledge base of most other professions as being entirely scientific. Accountancy is probably more dependent on custom and practice, and what seems to be generally acceptable than most other professions. But all professionals to some extent interpret their knowledge in varying ways, and frequently rely on custom and practice and what seems to be generally acceptable. Medical practice in the United States of America is presumably based on the same body of knowledge as in the UK, but applications are frequently quite different. In the United States, for example, delivering babies by Caesarian section, and circumcising boys, is the usual practice, whereas these procedures are more exceptional in the UK. Explanations of such variations have more to do with the social construction of knowledge, and professional self-interest, myth and mystique, than they have to do with scientific fact.

The work of Hines may be seen as a criticism of the accountancy profession's version of knowledge, or perhaps of their failure to be academic philosophers. A major conclusion of the 1988 ICAS *Making Corporate Reports Valuable* was that 'financial reports ought to portray **economic reality**' (emphasis added). But Hines seriously questions the assumptions about accounting knowledge that are made by such a statement and challenges the notion that there is such a thing as 'econimic reality' waiting to be portrayed. It may be that accounting knowledge is **inevitably** a social construction rather than having an independent existence. Professional accountants and academics may struggle to determine what assets, liabilities and profits **really** are. But perhaps they are no more than what we choose to say that they are. And this has a number of important implications. The terms will mean different things to different people, and professional accountancy bodies can do no more than add credibility to particular uses of these terms. It also implies that the meaning of these terms will change from time to time – they are socially constructed by different parties whose power and interests change from time to time. It may be that there is no absolute truth; there are only different versions of the truth, each of which has varying degrees of credibility.This philosophical view of the nature of accountancy was explored by Lukka (1990), particularly in relation to profit. He concluded that profit is basically contractual by nature; that any concept of profit must inevitably be based on some notion of value,which is itself a socially constructed concept; that profit cannot refer to something existing objectively 'out there'; and that profit is essentially a concept created by human consciousness and explicit or implicit collective agreements in society. But the concept of profit does have considerable argumentative power and so it is of some importance. But the idea that profit can be objectively defined and measured is a myth.

SUMMARY AND CONCLUSIONS

A conceptual framework cannot be a mathematical proposition from which all accounting standards can be derived. And it is unlikely to comprise a set of propositions that can be proved to be true. In this sense accounting is not a science, and the idea of perfect objectivity, to which accountants might aspire, is not attainable. The notion of a 'framework' is fairly ambitious; it implies a substantial, rigid structure which can support various additions. But Stamp's (1982) expectations of a conceptual framework were relatively modest. He did not see it as solving the problems of truth and fairness; it would be no easier than the development of a system of laws and legal administration that secures justice for all. The comparison is interesting. He seems to be arguing that if our legal system cannot deliver justice for all, then we cannot expect financial accounting to be true and fair. This seems to assume very low expectations of accountancy and does not deal with the question why truth and fairness are not delivered. The answers are in part to do with the nature of accountancy. Perhaps there can be no fundamental accounting truths. Profit and value have no 'real' existence other than as the outcome of the definitions and measurement rules that we (or 'they') choose to adopt. The answer is also in part a result of the distribution of power in society: accountancy reflects the interests of those who are most powerful, and their version of what is true and fair.

Conceptual framework projects have been unsuccessful in delivering some of the most ambitions expectations from them. It may be that the profession will continue the search with some members hoping that it will deliver what they want; others may be more cynical: they cannot afford to admit that financial accounting practice is devoid of principle, and is no more than the product of interaction between powerful interested parties, with CF projects as an attempt to cover this with a cloak of respectability. Perhaps a conceptual framework can be no more than a framework for debate, a point of reference in dealing with current problems. Peasnell (1982) argues that

> the CF could be intended to do no more than provide very broad general
> objectives for financial reporting to which no one could take serious
> objection; the aim would be to 'raise the moral tone' of the profession ... the
> CF would be expressed in sufficiently general terms as to avoid cramping the
> [standard setters'] style ...

Perhaps we can expect no more than this from a conceptual framework.

FURTHER READING

Accounting Standards Steering Committee (ASSC) (1975) *The Corporate Report.*
ICAS (1988) *Making Corporate Reports Valuable*, Institute of Chartered Accountants of Scotland.

Macve, R. (1981) *A Conceptual Framework for Financial Accounting and Reporting: The Possibilities for an Agreed Structure*, ICAEW.
Solomons, D. (1989) *Guidelines for Financial Reporting Standards*, ICAEW.

ESSAY AND DISCUSSION TOPICS

1. Why does the accountancy profession have an interest in producing a conceptual framework?
2. What are the main difficulties in developing a conceptual framework?
3. Produce definitions of 'asset', 'liability', 'income', and 'expense'. Try to think of items that (a) fall just outside your definition, but that you think should be included; (b) that would be included in your definition, but that you think should be excluded. Can there ever be satisfactory definitions?
4. Does it matter (a) to the accountancy profession, and (b) to society, if conceptual framework projects fail?
5. What are the main threats to the credibility of the accountancy profession? Are there comparable threats to other professions?

REFERENCES

Hines, R. D. (1988) In communicating reality we construct reality, *Accounting, Organizations and Society*, **13**(3), 251–62.
Hines, R. (1989) Financial accounting knowledge, conceptual framework projects and the social construction of the accounting profession, *Accounting, Auditing and Accountability Journal*, **2**(2), 72–92.
ICAS (1988) *Making Corporate Reports Valuable*, Institute of Chartered Accountants of Scotland.
Lukka, K. (1990) Ontology and accounting: the concept of profit, *Critical Perspectives on Accounting*, **1**(3), 239–61.
Macve, R. (1981) *A Conceptual Framework for Financial Accounting and Reporting: The Possibilities for an Agreed Structure*, ICAEW.
Moonitz, M. (1961) *The Basic Postulates of Accounting*, Accounting Research Study No. 1, AICPA.
Paton, W. A. and Littleton, A. C. (1940) *An Introduction to Corporate Accounting Standards*, Monograph No. 3, American Accounting Association.
Peasnell, K. V. (1982) The function of a conceptual framework for corporate financial reporting, *Accounting and Business Research*, Autumn, 243–56.
Solomons, D. (1989) *Guidelines for Financial Reporting Standards*, ICAEW.
Stamp, E. (1982) First steps towards a British conceptual framework, *Accountancy*, March, 123–30.
Tweedie, D. (1992) Interview by Lis Fisher, *Accountancy*, July, 28–30.

Chapter

8 The power of accountants and accountancy

INTRODUCTION

The power of accounting and of accountants has been an important underlying theme in each chapter of this book. The first chapter dealt with the nature of professions and one of its concerns was to identify the attributes of professions that make them prestigious and powerful in society. The second chapter was concerned with accountability, and particularly the power relationship between the directors and the shareholders of companies. The third chapter dealt with auditing which may be seen as being a part of the accountability process that is intended to restrict the powers of directors and to enable shareholders to exercise some control over their companies. Chapter 4 (on corporate social reporting) dealt with the accountability of organizations such as companies in relation to society more generally. This may be seen as an exploration of the potential power of accountancy in controlling the activities of powerful organizations such as companies, and making them more accountable to society. Society's concerns are not restricted to profitability alone: wider aspects of performance are important. Chapter 5 examined the role of performance indicators and value for money auditing in monitoring and controlling organizations, particularly in the public sector, and in making those organizations accountable to society. The study of VFM auditing and of performance indicators is, in a sense, a study of how power is asserted to determine what aspects of performance are highlighted and deemed to be important in financial reporting. Chapter 6 suggested that the form and content of financial reports are of some importance in influencing the distribution of resources in society and examined who has the power to determine the content of accounting standards and the extent to which they are enforced. Chapter 7 assessed the search for a conceptual framework upon which accounting standards can be based and suggested that such a basis is unlikely to exist; that accounting is socially constructed rather than rational; that the idea of a rational economic basis for accountancy is a myth, albeit a powerful one; and that accounting 'principles' reflect the interests of powerful forces in society.

THEORETICAL PERSPECTIVES OF POWER

But what exactly do we mean by 'power'? This question will be tackled using insights from a number of different theoretical perspectives.

Power may be defined as the ability to exercise control over resources in such a way that one individual or group has effects on others (adapted from Clegg, 1979, p. 95). At its simplest we can see power being exercised where A is powerful enough to get B to do something that B otherwise would not do (adapted from Dahl, 1957, pp. 202–3). It is possible to study the power of accountants and accountancy in this way, and various case studies illustrate the involvement of accountants and accountancy in the exercise of power in, for example, decisions on whether coal mines should be closed (Berry *et al.*, 1985; Hopper and Lewis, 1991) or whether accounting standards should permit the capitalization of research and development expenditure. In such cases, where conflict is explicit and one side rather than another can be seen to 'win', the exercise of power can be observed.

Much of the literature on power in relation to accountancy is concerned with identifying who has the power to assert their own interests over the interests of others. This 'subjectivist' approach is one of four paradigms on power outlined by Robson and Cooper (1989), each of which embodies a different world view. The four approaches are: (1) subjectivist; (2) integration; (3) historical materialism; and (4) the analytics of relations of power.

1. The Subjectivist approach

This deals with the question 'who has power?'. The most naive subjectivist approach would be to assume that with regard to any particular issue there are a number of interested parties; that each is aware of its own interests; that each has a good prospect of influencing the outcome in any particular conflict; and that decisions are based on rational (perhaps economic) criteria that are openly debated; and that the 'best' case wins. Conflicts over particular issues in setting accounting standards are sometimes presented as if these assumptions apply.

Within the subjectivist paradigm Robson and Cooper identify three different views about patterns of power and social relations. The naive **pluralist** approach

assumes that each different group in society is able to influence the outcome
when there are conflicts of interest. It is perhaps more realistic to assume that
some groups in society are more powerful or dominant than others. **Elitist**
assumptions see society as having a coherent leadership or elite, and an undif-
ferentiated mass of people with limited influence. Another approach is the **radical** view which sees society as comprising distinct groups or classes, with one
group dominant, and in conflict with the other(s). In examining the emergence
of a requirement to disclose expenditure on research and development (Willmott
et al., 1992) it was the government, in alliance with the accounting profession,
that proved to be dominant.

Subjectivist approaches to the study of power and accounting are inadequate
in a number of respects such as the following:

1. They often adopt naive, pluralistic assumptions rather than accepting that
    some groups in society are dominant over others.
2. They concentrate on observable conflicts with defined outcomes and tend to
    ignore situations where power is exercised less overtly and where conflict
    might not be apparent. Power can be most effective in its hidden form,
    producing effects in such a way that there is no conflict to observe.
3. They tend to assume that, in conflicts, the various participants are aware of
    their own interests and struggle to defend those interests; and that those who
    are most powerful secure the outcomes that they intend. But those who are
    most powerful in society are able to assert their interests, and so effectively that
    other groups are sometimes unable to identify or articulate their own interests.
    Issues can be presented in such a powerful way that the outcome is obvious
    and the weaker parties scarcely even question whether the outcomes are
    against their interests. There are often organizational patterns of responsibility
    and authority, rooted in organizational cultures, and patterns of visibility with
    established decision premises and taken for granted assumptions that are rarely
    questioned.

    It would also be more realistic to assume that what happens in society is
    usually a mix of intended and unintended outcomes of different participants:
    even those who are most powerful do not necessarily achieve the outcomes
    that they intend.
4. They study how power is exercised in its most obvious forms in society as it
    exists today. They do not consider the historical conditions that gave rise to
    existing power arrangements, or the sources of the power that is exercised.

Although the subjectivist approach has its limitations it can be a useful start-
ing point in examining the power of accountancy in society. The question of who
has power is considered later in this chapter (pp. 189–96). To what extent is it
individual accountants? Or the professional accountancy bodies? Or the major

professional accountancy firms? Or accountancy itself as a subject and practice, and the information that it produces?

But it is sometimes difficult to observe the exercise of power and to determine who has power. Power can be exercised covertly. If we continue to think of A exercising power over B, it may be that B is hardly aware of A's power over her/him, and there is no observable conflict. Debate may take place, but if A can influence the debate so that A's main interests are not attacked, and discussion is confined to matters that are unimportant to A, then A can win without being seen to do so, and perhaps without B even being aware of what has happened to her/his 'real' interests. A's power may derive largely from A having involvement in the creation and reinforcement of 'social and political values and institutional practices that limit the scope of the political process to public consideration of only those issues which are comparatively innocuous to A' (Bachrach and Baratz, 1962, p. 948). In studying the exercise of power Bachrach and Baratz argue that 'non-decisions' should also be considered, that is 'decisions that result in suppression or thwarting of a latent or manifest challenge to the values or interests of the decision-maker'. Presumably such suppression can be considered as an exercise of power. But where there is no conflict, where there is consensus on the prevailing allocation of resources, it may not be possible to observe the exercise of power.

2. The integration approach

This deals with the exercise of power in some less obvious ways. In looking at an organization or at society as a whole it assumes that individuals and groups with different interests can be integrated so that they have a common purpose. If groups of people are persuaded that they have the same objectives, for example if they are all employed in a particular organization, then there may be no observable conflict, or obvious exercise of power. But success in persuading employees that they are working for a common purpose is itself an effective exercise of power. Power exercised to bring together the interests of different groups and individuals in society to form a consensus; this legitimizes the exercise of power to enforce the pursuit of collective goals, such as the pursuit of profit, which may be presented as being for the benefit of all. The various parties undertake binding obligations to pursue those goals and, in effect, they hand over their power to others in a hierarchy. The power of those who have the capacity to ensure that the obligations are fulfilled may be seen as **authority**. With this integration approach, power can be most effective in its unseen guises, where individuals may be seen as 'unthinking dupes' (Giddens, 1984).

A systems approach which describes and accepts existing patterns is often used. Accountants are involved in designing and operating information systems and incentive schemes that emphasize superior–subordinate (or principal–agent) relationships; the assumption with this approach is that such systems can operate for the benefit of both.

In seeking to identify the sources of power of particular groups or individuals, this approach identifies such things as positions within a hierarchy, or expertise (such as managerial or professional expertise), but without questioning the legitimacy of these things. The approach is functional: arrangements that have developed are assumed to be there because they function for the benefit of the organization or of society. The concept of expertise, for example, is not seen as a political and social construction (produced by those who are powerful in order to maintain their power), but rather a reflection of those skills that are functionally required by the system, and by society.

The functionalist theme within this integration approach is problematic. Particular arrangements may well be defended because they are assumed to function for the benefit of a particular organization or society as a whole.But organizations, and society, are not integrated wholes with common objectives. The most powerful groups within an organization, or within society, are likely to talk in such functionalist and integrationist terms. In so doing they are excluding and silencing the interests of others, and making use of accountancy to do this. Accountancy portrays, promulgates and defends profit figures as being for the benefit of us all, and is involved in an attempt to integrate different interests that would otherwise be in conflict with each other. The silencing of such conflict is an effective assertion of power.

The integrationist approach offers more insights than the subjectivist approach in a number of respects. It recognizes that the assertion of power can be more effective in its unseen forms. It suggests how accounting can be powerful in society in helping to avoid conflict, for example by producing information that is assumed to reveal the 'correct' and 'best' economic decisions for an organization. Accountants are therefore involved in developing and maintaining the idea that the participants in an organization work together for the common good. But the integration approach is also inadequate in a number of respects.

1. It sidesteps the issue of conflict.
2. In assuming harmonious consensus about what is to be achieved it tends to ignore how such consensus was achieved and so does not deal adequately with such issues as unseen manipulation, gaining control of the agenda and so on.
3. It does not question the legitimacy of the power and authority of managers and others in hierarchical relationships. It makes functionalist assumptions – that such arrangements have come into being because they operate for the benefit of the organization, and so, presumably, also for the benefit of society. Questions about the basis of managerial power, and the social construction of their 'expertise', are not tackled.
4. The environment is seen as being powerful, perhaps in an evolutionary, Darwinian sense: it selects the fittest, or most functional attributes of

organizations that enable them to survive and go from strength to strength. It does not see society or organizations as being superficial alliances of individuals and groups with different and competing interests, each seeking to predominate or to win in struggles for power and the control of resources. It would be more realistic to assume that the attributes of an organization that predominate are those which are in the interest of the most powerful groups in the organization rather than assuming that what is best for the organization is what prevails.

5. The environment is also seen as being relatively unchanging and historical questions about how existing patterns of power and influence came into being and how they are changing, or might be made to change, are not dealt with.

3. Historical materialism

This is a Marxist approach that emphasizes the economic basis of power. It recognizes that although people make their own history, what they do, and how they see the existing situation and make their decisions, is largely determined by the past. Studies using this approach are explicit about being located in a particular period of time. Concepts such as 'goals' and 'management' are seen as social and political creations which reflect the economic, political and ideological structure of society at a particular time.

Historical materialism sees society as being determined largely by economic practices and identifies the dominant mode of production as being capitalist. Capitalism involves antagonisms and contradictions between capital and labour, between exchange value and surplus value, and between socialized production and private ownership. Conflicts between these can provoke crises and the possibility of significant social change. But such change requires a major, perhaps revolutionary, shift in the location of power in society. The aim is to challenge capitalism, which is represented by big business, aided and abetted by government and other institutions in society including the accountancy profession and much of the educational system. Reforms to these institutions are possible; but unless such reforms are for the benefit of such institutions, they are likely to be powerfully resisted. More radical change is therefore advocated.

Some studies in this framework emphasize the power of management over workers and trace the subordination of labour to management: workers were brought into the factory to be under the control of the capitalist. 'Management science', machinery and new technology ensured that managers controlled the work, and the workers were subordinated. Power is inherent in management control and accounting techniques, and these techniques are applied for the benefit of the capitalist. But subordination does not happen without conflict and struggle. Studies within this framework see accounting as being involved in the extraction of surplus value from labour, and in the accumulation of capital for the benefit of the capitalist class at the expense of the workers.

Within the historical materialist approach we can see the possibility of hegemonic domination. The idea of hegemony suggests that society is dominated by particular set of ideas and philosophies that determine what is seen as being normal and proper in everyday life. Hegemony is 'an order in which a certain way of life and thought is diffused throughout society in all its institutional and private manifestations, informing with its spirit all taste, morality, customs, religious and political principles and social relations, particularly their intellectual and moral connotation' (Williams, 1960). It is assumed that one class is dominant over others, and the dominant ideas in society make this appear to be normal and acceptable. Such ideas are reproduced, modified and propagated in society by various educational and other institutions, and accountancy is involved in this. In Western capitalist society hegemonic domination is associated with the acceptability of such things as private property; values and prices being determined by the market; the living standard of workers being determined by the market price of their labour; and profit being the measure of success of investment and of organizations more generally. To the extent that such ideas are accepted, conflict is avoided, and the power of capital over labour is exercised covertly. Society itself, or social structure, may be seen as reflecting such ideological hegemony.

Booth and Cocks (1990) argue that power should be understood through the 'nested and dynamic interrelationship of three concepts'. There is an overall hegemony which dominates society; within that hegemony there are 'modes of rationality' which operate like an underlying rule; and power operates within modes of rationality.

Individuals may be seen as skilled actors who have their own way of seeing and performing in the world. But individual actors are also to some extent governed by an underlying rule, or mode of rationality; a way of seeing and interpreting what happens in society. Accountancy is part of a particular way of seeing the world, a mode of rationality that makes sense of certain activities.

4. The analytics of relations of power

In this approach the relationship between knowledge and power is particularly important, and insights are drawn from the work of Foucault. Conventional wisdom suggests that information or knowledge is power. And it might be reassuring to accountants it they believe that they have knowledge, that they know the true economic facts in a given situation, or at least that they have the tools to establish those facts. Such knowledge might give them enormous power.

But Foucault has a tendency to turn questions and simplistic statements on their head. We may suggest that knowledge is power, but what do we mean by knowledge? Some sorts of knowledge, or discourse, or ways of seeing, analysing and presenting problems, are more powerful than others in society. It is too simplistic to assume that there are correct, objective facts that can form the basis for correct or best decisions. What we consider to be knowledge, our perception or way of seeing, may be the result of a powerful discourse. Power is at least as important in producing knowledge as knowledge is in producing power. Power and knowledge directly imply one another. The 'knowledge', 'truth' or 'facts' produced by accountants who are tied up with a powerful hierarchy (such as the government or the management of a major company) are more powerful than 'facts' produced by other individuals; and, in part, this is because they are seen to be more 'true'.

Foucault (1984) was concerned that we should not accept conventional or 'scientific' 'truths' at face value and he examined the 'political economy' of truth. Truth is not something which is fixed and factual for all time. He sees truth as being centred on the form of scientific discourse and the institutions which produce it, and therefore as always being subject to change. Much of his work takes an historical approach and he illustrates how what has been taken as truth can shift markedly between one century and the next. He sees truth as being subject to constant economic and political incitement; as being the object, under diverse forms, of immense diffusion and consumption, circulating through the apparatuses of education and information whose extent is relatively broad in the social body. It is produced and transmitted under the control, dominant if not exclusive, of a few great political and economic apparatuses, and he mentions specifically universities, the army, writing and the media. We should perhaps also see accountancy as being a form of discourse that takes part in this.

But that which people see as being 'truth' can be very powerful. Accountancy may be one what Foucault calls a grid of technologies which use knowledge to make individuals the object of power, subjecting them to surveillance, categorization, recording, monitoring and control, sometimes on a daily basis. These human sciences are seen as being suspect in the sense that their truth is questionable; it is a social construction to deal with what some see as problems of social order. Individuals become cases to be observed by the social scientist in accordance with the conventions and truths of the various social scientists; the 'facts' become more visible, but the power effects of the social scientists and their discourses over the individual remain invisible. This form of power may be seen as discipline: it requires individuals to conform to particular norms.

The approach is important in a number of ways.

1. It takes an historical approach: in any particular situation the participants cannot start afresh as if nothing has happened before. Their actions and ways of seeing are inevitably influenced by the effects of previous historical struggles.
2. It recognizes that power can be exercised most effectively in unseen ways. Force and violence are seen as being relatively ineffectual compared with the

discipline that can result from the combination of power and knowledge, in monitoring and controlling for example.

3. Other approaches to power, that concentrate on conflicts of interest where each party has it own intentions, are seen as being too simplistic. Instead we should concentrate on the power effects of the discourses and practices that take place. Perhaps no one has right on their side. The discourses are neither true nor false. But they are often powerful because they are accepted by many as if they are true. People can be caught up in discourses, accepting them and their consequences without understanding the effects of what they are doing. Discourses can be more powerful than individual people. In any conflict people may know what they are doing; they may even know why they are doing it. But they are unlikely to know the effects of what they do. Somehow they are caught up in powerful discourses that lead to particular effects that they may never have intended.

Summary

In studying the power of accountancy, valuable insights can be provided by appreciating that very different theoretical assumptions about power are made. Many such studies do not make their assumptions explicit; there are often taken-for-granted theoretical assumptions which are typically subjectivist or integrationist. Studies with more radical assumptions are often more explicit and specify the theoretical frameworks within which they are operating; they highlight power relationships and conflicts in society and advocate major change.

This chapter provides insights from a number of very different perspectives, but is not intended to advocate any single particular perspective. However, it is not possible to be neutral and it may be helpful if the assumptions, biases and preferences are made more explicit; this is done in the following two paragraphs.

Subjectivist approaches are seen as being rather simplistic and naive, particularly if pluralist assumptions are made. But insights can be gained from asking the question: who has power? However, it should be recognized that power can be most effectively exercised in hidden ways that make it difficult to answer this question. The integration approach may be an abuse of power, involving accountants in persuading people that they are working for a common interest; but it is important to be able to see when this is happening if we are to understand the exercise of power. The historical materialist approach suggested that there are some valuable insights to be gained from Marxism, and we should not underestimate the role of capitalism if we are to understand the exercise of power in society. But the approach in this book is reformist, not revolutionary. Radical changes are needed if capitalism is to be made more accountable to society, and if accountancy is to serve wider interests in society than it does at present. Such changes would in part need to be institutional, enhancing auditor independence for example; and in part to do with accounting knowledge itself. Accounting knowledge is the creation of powerful interests in society and it tends to serve their interests. A wider distribution of power in society is required if accounting knowledge is to serve wider interests.

WHO HAS POWER?

In this section it is assumed that accountants and accountancy are relatively powerful in society. A distinction will be drawn between the power of (1) individual accountants, (2) the professional accountancy bodies, (3) the accountancy firms and (4) accountancy as a subject, a practice and a way of seeing things, and accounting information. How and why each can be powerful is examined and illustrated.

1. Individual accountants

Accountants are often powerful as individuals. As members of a professional body they have many of the attributes and advantages outlined in Chapter 1. For example, they tend to be middle-class graduates with high educational attainment in terms of examination success, and they are often well-placed, well-connected and well-paid. Their power is indicated by their ability to control resources in both their jobs and their private lives. Accountants are at least as likely as any other group to rise to the highest positions in organizations and to become directors or chief executives. Accountancy can help individuals to achieve powerful positions, just as expertise in engineering, marketing, the law and so on helps others. To some extent it is accountancy or other expertise and professional attributes that make some individuals powerful; and to some extent it is their own personal characteristics such as ability, motivation and charm. But once individuals have risen to positions of power it is also the position itself, whether as manager, director, minister, chief executive or chairman, and the organization in which they operate, that maintains the individual accountant's power.

2. The professional accountancy bodies

Chapter 1 examined the attributes of professions, many of which enhance their power position of professional bodies. The accountancy bodies appear to have been powerful in a number of important respects, perhaps more so than other professional bodies. They have more than 100 000 members, many of whom are in important and influential positions. They have prestigious buildings, located close to powerful government offices and city institutions in London (and in Edinburgh in the case of ICAS). They have access to a wide range of expertise and have representatives on many influential bodies. And they are regularly and formally consulted by governments on a wide range of industrial and commercial matters, including taxation and company law.

In the 1980s, the accountancy profession consolidated and strengthened its position in spite of various external threats and serious criticisms. Thatcherism attacked professional monopolies, but the accountancy profession's monopoly of auditing survived. In spite of many accounting scandals, and crises of confidence in accounting standards, the profession succeeded in retaining its control over the setting of accounting standards. The EC threatened to replace dependence on 'a true and fair view', the pillar of the British audit 'opinion', with a requirements for more specific reporting. But the professional accountancy bodies succeeded in fighting this off these threats, preserved their own flexible approaches, and continued to grow.

3. The accountancy firms

Professional accountancy practice is dominated by six major firms of accountants, each with annual fee income amounting to several hundred million pounds in the UK alone. In the United States of America the same firms' annual fee income amounts to thousands of millions of pounds.

The largest UK accountancy firms are shown in Table 8.1

Table 8.1 The largest UK accountancy firms

	Fee income (1991) £m	% of top 500 audits
1. Coopers & Lybrand	577	19.4
2. KPMG Peat Marwick McLintock	495	21.6
3. Price Waterhouse	400	15.9
4. Ernst and Young	399	13.5
5. Touche Ross	350	9.3
6. Arthur Andersen	331	3.6
7. Grant Thornton	118	2.6
8. BDO Binder Hamlyn	114	4.6
9. Pannell Kerr Forster	86	1.2
10. Stoy Hayward	68	0.8

Source: *Accountancy*, July 1992, 16–17; *Accountancy Age*, 22 Oct. 1992, 14–15.

For a number of years the accountancy profession was seen as being dominated by the 'big eight', but as a result of a number of mergers (Coopers & Lybrand with

Deloittes being the biggest), we now have the 'big six'. These major firms are in a different league from their rivals. As can be seen from the table above the smallest of the big six is more than twice as large as the next biggest firm. It could be argued that there are still eight major firms, with BDO Binder Hamlyn and Grant Thornton being substantially larger than the next largest rival.

If we look at who audits the largest UK companies, the dominance of the largest accountancy firms is even more marked, as can be seen from Table 8.1. The big six audit 83.3 per cent of the 500 largest UK companies. If only the very largest companies are considered, we would see that 94 per cent are audited by the top five alone.[1]

Moreover, the dominance of the big six is increasing. A study by Beattie and Fearnley (1992) showed that the top eight accountancy firms audited 64 per cent of listed companies in 1987, but by 1991 this had increased to 79 per cent.[2] There were still a number of practices with only one listed client, but the number of audit firms who had one or more listed clients fell by 39 – although the number of listed companies increased by 428. It seems that the large accountancy firms are in an increasingly dominant position with regard to larger clients.

The big six appear to be in an unassailably powerful position. According to Ian Hay Davison[3] no new firm will be formed through megamergers because recent experience has shown that such regroupings reduce partnership profitability, clients are lost through conflicts of interest, and economies of scale are not attained; no new firm formed through mergers within the second tier will ever be able to catch up because institutional investors in companies place their faith in audits by the big six, and any move of audits away from them would require explanations, and the company's share price might suffer; and the big six have a substantial revenue advantage because they are much more profitable than second tier firms. Such claims might seem somewhat arrogant, but it does seem that the big six are very powerfully placed in a number of ways.

They dominate the market for auditing, accountancy and related services, particularly among larger clients, as indicated above. Their size, status and dominance also enable them to obtain a range of large consultancy undertakings from major organizations, particularly the government, advising on matters as diverse as privatization, organization of the health service and education, and aid programmes to Eastern Europe in developing capitalist economies.

The big six have a major influence on the professional accountancy bodies. The larger firms are more able to spare staff to take part in the activities of the professional bodies, including the setting of accounting standards. The councils of the main professional bodies do not generally give undue representation to the largest firms, but in the plethora of subcommittees and working parties, and

[1] Source: *Accountancy Age*, 22 Oct. 1992, based on the companies that make up the *Financial Times* 100 Index.

[2] This was partly due to mergers between existing audit firms.

[3] Source: *Accountancy*, Nov. 1992, 12. Ian Hay Davison was formerly senior partner at Arthur Andersen.

where there is a need for partial or total secondment (for example in carrying out the tasks of president), it is the large firms that are more able to afford the resources, and so to extend their power and influence.

The power of the large firms was seen in a recent attempt to merge the Institute of Chartered Accountants of Scotland with the Institute of Chartered Accountants in England and Wales. It was prompted in part by the fact that a few of the larger firms were considering using ICAEW training for their trainees in Scotland. If that had happened to any significant extent it would have cast serious doubts on the future of ICAS. The proposed merger was in fact defeated by the votes of ICAS members, but the lesson was clear: both ICAS and ICAEW have to ensure that their training schemes are attractive to the large firms, and the institutes have to be responsive to their needs.

The source of the power of the large accountancy firms derives largely from their professional status, and from their size and economic power. The attributes of being a profession that contribute to the power of accountants were considered in Chapter 1. They include such things as skill based on theoretical knowledge, extensive education, testing of competence, codes of professional conduct, legitimacy and status. But most of these things apply to a greater extent to the larger firms. They are able to recruit the 'best' graduates, and their size and economic power enable them to have a much wider range of expertise and specialisms than is possible in a smaller firm. They are therefore able to take on more ambitious assignments, and to grow and become still more powerful.

The larger firms may also be seen as giving more status and credibility to the tasks that they undertake. Financial statements, cash flow forecasts, audit opinions, consultancy reports, tax computations and 'expert' opinions that carry the imprimatur of an international firm of accountants are likely to carry more weight than those produced by the sole practitioner working in her/his front room, the small high street practice, or even a large firm that is not in the top ten or twenty. Accountancy firms are usually well aware of their standing in the size rankings and it seems that the greater their size, the greater the perceived value of their work and the higher the fees they can charge.

Large firms also have their own technical departments that carefully inter-pret accounting standards and produce their own firms' recommendations on whether particular accounting treatments are acceptable. The companies that they audit are often concerned about particular accounting treatments that allow them to portray their company's financial results in the light that they choose; the most helpful technical departments are those that can find creative ways of presenting financial results that do not appear to be specifically banned by company law or accounting standards. When such treatments are devised or approved by the technical department of a large auditing firm, it is likely that similar treatments will be adopted by other companies that the firm audits. Once a number of large companies adopt a particular accounting treatment it becomes more acceptable because it has become part of 'Generally Accepted

Accounting Practice'. The large professional accountancy firms can thus be powerful in determining and changing what accounting practices are acceptable.

The larger firms are also more likely than the smaller firms to have the resources and financial strength to weather any storms. Firms of accountants are increasingly likely to be sued by clients when things go wrong, particularly in the United States. The sums involved are often greater than insurance cover that can be obtained. One US firm, Laventhol and Horwath, has folded in the face of a mass of litigation, and some of its partners have gone bankrupt. It seems likely that the largest firms are better placed than the smaller ones to (a) establish procedures that make such litigation less likely; (b) devote adequate resources to defending themselves successfully in the event of such litigation; and (c) find the resources required in the event of successful litigation against them. As the largest accountancy firms tend to have the largest clients they are also likely to be subject to the largest claims in litigation. But they are more likely than a smaller firm to be able to survive a major disaster.

The major accountancy firms are also becoming larger than most of their clients. Their annual fee income of each of the largest two, in the UK alone, is greater than the annual turnover of all but a few hundred British companies. If the fee income of the major accountancy firms is measured worldwide, they are larger than most of their listed clients, and veritable giants compared with their mass of unlisted clients. If size alone were the determinant of power, then we could say that the major accountancy firms are more powerful than most of their clients. But as the clients have a major say in determining the firms' fee income, the large firms are in many ways in a subordinate position, particularly in relation to large companies.

When one of the big six is the auditor of a medium-sized company, their relative power positions could be quite complex, or even the reverse of what would at first be expected. It might be, say, Coopers & Lybrand that audits the accounts, provides forecasts to banks and other financial institutions, and acts as an intermediary in raising funds; that deals with any decision on conversion to a plc and on flotation; that provides taxation advice, and advice on capital expenditure, including acquisitions of other businesses; and that generally acts as the link between the company and the outside financial world, including the government, the shareholders, the City and financial institutions generally. In such a situation the directors of the company might feel unable to make any significant financial decisions without the approval of Coopers & Lybrand. In this position they might be forgiven for asking, 'Who has the power around here? Who makes the decisions? Is it us, or is it Coopers & Lybrand?' At present such a scenario may seem slightly amusing, but with the big six increasingly being seen as major international businesses, and with the possibility of them converting to plc's themselves, it might not be long before many medium-sized businesses are, in effect, controlled by the big six.

It seems that the power of the large international firms of accountants, particularly the big six, is substantial and increasing, and shows every sign of continuing to do so.

4.   Accountancy and accounting information

The subject matter of accountancy, as promulgated by the professional accountancy bodies, and to a large extent adopted in university courses, can in itself appear to be powerful in specifying, justifying and legitimating decisions on the allocation of resources in society. It is based on a set of calculative techniques which tend to produce unique and 'correct' solutions to problems. 'There is little room for alternative conceptualisations of problems and their resultant solutions. This encourages students to accept their solutions as objective and absolute, instead of acknowledging that objectivity is only possible through ideological bias' (Tinker *et al.*, 1982). In part the power of accountancy lies in its ability to produce unique and apparently objective solutions to problems. Let us return to the idea that power is exercised when A gets B to do something that B would otherwise not do: A can use accountancy to define problems, and produce 'solutions' which do not deal with B's interests, and which make it difficult for B to see or to argue for alternative formulations to the problems or solutions to them. Accountancy can be as powerful in what it excludes as in what it includes.

We have seen (p. 186–187) that the old adage that 'information is power' is too simplistic. The implication of such a statement is that possession of 'the facts' makes an individual more powerful. If, for example, the management of an organization wish to close a particular production facility on the grounds that it is uneconomic, it is likely that management has the facts; and that if anyone wants to argue against the closure they will need the facts to show whether or not the facility is uneconomic. If the press, the local community or the workers or their representatives were able to show that management were presenting an untrue picture, and that the particular production facility was 'really' economic, then management would lose the argument, and the production facility would not be closed. The assumption is that decisions in society are based on rational economic criteria, and that the 'best' argument on this basis will win.

There are at least two problems with the above assumptions. In the first place managers and other decision-makers do not necessarily operate in accordance with the economic criteria that would lead to the 'best' economic consequences for themselves or for the organization for which they work. There is often a political agenda, more or less well concealed. This agenda may be to do with relative power positions: a decision-maker is likely to be at least as concerned with the effects of that decision on her/his own power position as with the economic consequences of that decision. Secondly, economic principles do not necessarily lead to a single correct decision: any data, and any case presented in support of a particular decision are inevitably based on particular (often unintended, unspecified) assumptions; those who present the case may not even be aware of those assumptions. If different assumptions were made, there would be different conclusions. The power of management to determine which information counts is at least as effective as the power of information itself. Just as information can create power, so power can create information and make it effective.

Examples can be quoted that illustrate the power of management in creating the knowledge that is powerful and effective in decision-making. The National Coal Board's version of which pits were 'uneconomic' (and so should be closed) predominated, although it was powerfully demolished by academics (Berry *et al.*, 1985; Hopper and Lewis, 1991). The financial case for the conversion of the Abbey National Building Society into a bank and a plc, and its subsequent flotation, was powerfully demolished by Abbey Members Against Flotation, and by the Building Societies Commission, but the directors still won the battle (Perks, 1991). I was also involved in a case where an educational institution proposed the closure of a major site on financial grounds. Subsequent questioning of the figures showed that the financial case was suspect, misleading or false. The financial arguments fell. But the decision was not changed. The site was closed on 'educational' grounds.

To managers and others in positions of power, accountancy and its techniques are an appealing and powerful way of presenting a case in favour of a particular decision. The approach appears to be objective and correct, and accountancy arguments are difficult to penetrate, especially to non-accountants. But it is not necessarily accountancy presentations that are powerful. Power usually lies with those who request and control those presentations. In the previous paragraph we saw examples where the accountancy presentations of the National Coal Board, the Abbey National Building Society and of an educational institution were effectively undermined. Rebel groups arguably produced 'better' accountancy presentations, but did not win the battles. Where there are open conflicts that can be observed, we can see that the most powerful parties are the ones that succeed, and that their opponents are not sufficiently empowered by the use of accountancy arguments. In this sense, accountancy does not seem to be particularly powerful.

We could imagine a scenario with two parties in conflict with each other, each with equal power. It may then be that if one uses accountancy arguments to present its case, and the other does not, then the accountancy would be just sufficient to tilt the balance in favour of the side that uses it. But such equality is unlikely. More usually one party is much more powerful than its opponents, and it wins the battles, often making use of accounting information in the conflict. But it would usually be a mistake to assume that it is accountancy that provides the power to the victors.

When it comes to open conflict it is power that wins, not accountancy and its arguments, techniques and presentations. The power of accountancy lies in avoiding such conflicts; in presenting a version of the 'facts' that is credible and legitimate; that is seen to be true and fair; that excludes the interests of the least powerful; and that is difficult to penetrate and argue against.

What conclusions can we draw from this? In the first place management, or others in a position of power, are likely to have, and to work to maintain, their control over the production of official, legitimate data for the activities for which they are responsible. To the extent that they can ensure that theirs is the only version of events that counts, their power position is maintained. Those who wish to change a particular decision can use accounting information to present a different case, and perhaps to destroy the case presented by those in power. But destroying the official case with 'better' information does not necessarily win. Those who are in power are well placed to add legitimacy and credibility to their own case, and to undermine that of their opponents. They are even likely to want to be seen to win, regardless of the merits of the different cases, so as not to undermine their credibility and their power positions. And they can change the arguments. Any set of facts can be presented and interpreted in many different ways. A study of the power of accounting should include an examination of how particular versions of 'the facts' have more credibility and legitimacy than others.

Information is rather like ammunition to be used in a battle. Having more ammunition or information does strengthen your power position. But it takes more than a good supply of ammunition to win a war. Having **access to** information or to ammunition is an indication of your power position, and the one who has most access to information (including the power to create it) is likely to be the most powerful and to win. If someone else succeeds in getting hold of that ammunition, or of more and better information, that does not take away a managers ability to create more information and so to 'win'. Those who control most resources, including the ability to employ accountants and barristers, and to use computers and sophisticated presentation techniques, are likely to be best placed to 'win'. The role of accounting can be seen in selecting, shaping, presenting and adding credibility and legitimacy to the official story or version of events in such a way as to make it difficult for opponents to penetrate or to create and gain acceptance for any different version of events. In this sense power involves the control of resources, and accounting resources in particular.

SUMMARY AND CONCLUSIONS

It seems that accountants and accountancy play a powerful role in society, although perhaps not in the most obvious ways. Often accountants and accountancy have the **appearance** of being powerful. But the power of individual accountants derives largely from the powerful organizations and other interests that they serve. If accountants operated as individuals, or as part of rebel groups divorced from their powerful employers, much of their power would disappear. Similarly, accounting information appears to be powerful when it is used by powerful interest groups to defend their position. We have seen occasions when the accountancy arguments seem to fall, but the power position still wins. It does not matter how good the accountancy argument is, it is unlikely to be accepted by those in positions of power if it is against their interests.

Accountancy is powerful in less obvious ways. The chapter began by outlining four perspectives of power. The first ('subjectivist') approach tries to identify who has power by observing conflicts. But the power of accountancy is not readily observable in such conflicts. The second ('integrationist') approach suggested that accountants are involved in persuading employees and others in society that we can all be integrated together for a common purpose (such as making organizations more profitable), which will be for the benefit of us all. This is a powerful notion that is difficult to challenge, and the power of accountancy can be seen in contributing to this myth, and, as a result, in avoiding conflicts.

The third approach ('historical materialism') was useful in highlighting the dominance of economic power, the power of capitalism, and showing how accountancy is involved in the control and subordination of workers so that profits can be generated. It also brought out the idea of hegemonic domination, and suggested how powerfully accountancy ideas are associated with dominant ideas in society, and particular ways of seeing things. The fourth approach, following Foucault, indicated some of the limitations of our ideas about truth, and suggested how power can be effective in creating knowledge. The power of accounting lies particularly in its ways of seeing, which are highly selective, and in contributing to what is seen as being correct and true and fair, by adding legitimacy and credibility to particular versions of events, or 'stories'.

Some of this argument may seem obscure. We will continue to see accountants and accounting statements as being powerful in society. But it is worth asking why they are powerful. Power is there in unseen ways. But when we think of accountants and accountancy as being obviously powerful, it is worth asking to what extent are they powerful because they represent interests that are in any case powerful.

FURTHER READING

Chua, W. F., Lowe, T. and Puxty, T. (1989) *Critical Perspectives in Management Control*, Macmillan, Basingstoke and London.

Cooper, D. J. and Hopper, T. M. (eds) (1990) *Critical Accounts*, Macmillan, Basingstoke.

Tinker, T. (1985) *Paper Profits*, Holt, Rinehart & Winston.

ESSAY AND DISCUSSION TOPICS

1. In what ways is the power of accountants and accountancy explicit and observable? In what ways is it effective, but difficult to observe?
2. Compare and contrast the subjectivist and the integrationist approaches to power with particular reference to the involvement of accountancy in each.
3. To what extent do the various participants in the organization in which you work or study have common objectives? Discuss the role of accountancy in forming and reinforcing those objectives, and in monitoring their achievement.
4. Select a controversial issue where accounting/ financial arguments are used (e.g. the closure of a local factory or educational institution; the installation of new automated equipment).

   (a) What 'taken-for-granted' assumptions underlie the financial arguments?
   (b) If you, as a student or local resident, could demonstrate that the financial arguments are flawed, and that there is a better financial case for the opposite decision, what do you think the outcome would be? Why?

5. To what extent is accounting information powerful because it is 'true'? To what extent is it accepted as being 'true' because it supports the interests of powerful groups in society?
6. Which of the following appear to be becoming more powerful in society: (a) individual accountants; (b) the professional accountancy bodies; (c) the accountancy firms; (d) accounting information? Have any of these become too powerful? How could their power be reduced?

REFERENCES

Bachrach, P. and Baratz, M. S. (1962) Two faces of power, *American Political Science Review*, 947–52.

Bachrach, P. and Baratz, M. S. (1963) Decisions and nondecisions: an analytical framework, *American Political Science Review*, 641–51.

Bachrach, P. and Baratz, M. S. (1970) *Power and Poverty: Theory and Practice*, New York, Oxford University Press.

Beattie, V. and Fearnley, S. (1992) *The Changing Structure of the Audit Market in the UK*, ICAEW Research Board.

Berry, T., Capps, T., Cooper, D., Hopper, T. and Lowe, T. (1985) NCB accounts – a mine of misinformation, *Accountancy*, Jan., 10–12.

Booth, P. and Cocks, N. (1990) Power and the study of the accounting profession, in *Critical Accounts* (eds D. J. Cooper and T. M. Hopper), Macmillan, Basingstoke, pp. 391–408.

Clegg, S. (1979) *The Theory and Power of Organisation*, Routledge & Kegan Paul, London.

Dahl, R. A. (1957) The concept of power, *Behavioural Science*, 201–15.

Foucault, M. (1980) *Power/Knowledge: Selected Interviews and Other Writings* (ed. C. Gordon), Harvester Press, Brighton.

Foucault, M, (1984) *The Foucault Reader* (ed. P. Rabinow), Penguin, Harmondsworth.

Giddens, A. (1984) *The Constitution of Society*, Polity Press, Cambridge.

Hopper, T. and Lewis, L. (1991) National Coal Board Report and Accounts 1983/4, in *Case Studies in Financial Reporting* (eds P. Taylor and S. Turley), Oxford, Philip Allan, pp. 236–67.

Perks, R. W. (1991) The fight to stay mutual: Abbey Members Against Flotation versus Abbey National Building Society, *Annals of Public and Co-operative Economics*, **62**(3), 393–429.

Robson, K. and Cooper, D. J. (1989) Power and management control, in *Critical Perspectives in Management Control* (eds W. F. Chua, T. Lowe and T. Puxty), Macmillan, Basingstoke and London, pp. 79–114.

Tinker, A. M., Merino, B. D. and Neimark, M. D. (1982) The normative origins of positive theories; ideology and accounting thought, *Accounting, Organizations and Society*, 167–200.

Williams, G. (1960) The concept of 'egemonia' in the thought of Antonio Gramsci: some notes on interpretation, *Journal of the History of Ideas*, 586–99.

Willmott, H. C., Puxty, A. G., Robson, K., Cooper, D. J. and Lowe, E. A. (1992) Regulation of accountancy and accountants: a comparative analysis of accounting for research and development in four advanced capitalist countries, *Accounting, Auditing and Accountability Journal*, **5**(2), 32–56.

Conclusion

So what can we conclude about the role of accounting in society?

The emphasis in most of the book has been critical, but it should be recognized that existing conventional accounting practice is of value to some in society, otherwise it would not continue to exist. Those who continue to make use of accountants, and arrange for them to be paid, must have good reasons for doing so. It could be argued that the employment of accountants as auditors takes place for no better reason than that it is required by law. But legal and auditing requirements came into being – and have been regularly revised and extended – because they are intended to serve the interests of some groups in society. Some may even adopt the democratic myth that parliamentary enactments represent the will of the people and are intended to benefit society as a whole. It is more realistic to assume that legislation is passed in Parliament by different people with different intentions regarding which groups in society will benefit; and that the main beneficiaries in practice may not be the main intended beneficiaries. Pressure for more extensive accounting and auditing requirements may come from shareholders and creditors who want protection from deception, fraud, and loss; from politicians who want protection from the accusation of failing to act when scandals and abuses become public; and from directors who want to be protected from the accusation that they are mavericks, subject to no effective controls. Others, such as employees, journalists and competitors may also benefit from accounting disclosures.

It is tempting to ask which groups in society are the greatest beneficiaries from accounting. But the answer is that different groups gain and lose in different ways, sometimes at the expense of other groups. Debates about changes in the role of accounting in society are about shifting the balance of advantage between different groups in society.

Any examination of the role of accounting in society should not be confined to the accounting and auditing functions in companies. Accountants are employed in a wide range of different roles in all kinds of organization. Those who choose to employ accountants in these various roles presumably do so because they believe that it is in their interest to do so, or in the interests of those that they serve, to make use of accountants. Much of what accountants do can be justified on functionalist grounds: in most organizations activities like credit control and cash management are seen as necessary functions that accountants are well placed to perform. But there is always also a political element in the role of accounting. In part this is to do with the effects of accounting activities on the distribution of wealth and resources in society. With credit control, for example, organizations that have the most effective credit controllers are likely to gain control of cash and other resources at the expense of those that have the least effective credit controllers. The political element is also to do with power relationships. For example, managers who are supported by accountants, and the information that they produce, are likely to be more powerful than those who are not.

In examining the role of accounting there is little distinction between its effects on (1) wealth distribution, and (2) power relationships. Power and wealth are two sides of the same coin: both are to do with the control of resources.

The use of accountants and accounting can have an effect on the distribution of wealth and power in society: and those who choose to use them presumably do so with the intention of enhancing or reinforcing the wealth and power of who- ever they are acting for – often themselves. Because accountants are relatively expensive to employ it is usually only those who are already relatively rich and powerful who are in a position to make use of them. This seems to lead to the conclusion that accountants are used by the rich and powerful to enhance their own wealth and power. Although this is often the case it would be an unduly restricted and cynical interpretation of the role of accounting in society, and it needs to be qualified in a number of important respects.

1. Although those who choose to employ accountants may do so because they see it as being in the interests of whoever they are acting for, they are not necessarily acting merely in their own interests. There are still many individuals who see their role in terms of public service, or acting for the benefit of other groups in society, perhaps particularly disadvantaged groups. There is still a substantial public sector, and a range of charitable and voluntary organizations, that are committed to wider objectives than merely making profits or enhancing the power and wealth of those who control them. In such organizations accountants and their practices can be used to justify many different activities that might benefit and empower a wide range of individuals and groups in society, not merely the rich and powerful. Evidence of accounting serving a wider public can be seen in both central and local government where the possibility of exposure to scrutiny by independent auditors, whose findings may then be highlighted by local councillors, MPs and the media, can act as a powerful deterrent to abuse. But there is always the danger that accountants and their restricted ways of seeing, selecting, presenting and legitimating, will also enhance the power positions of those who are already powerful.

2. Where accounting is used mainly to enhance the power and wealth of those that who recruit and control the accountants, it is unlikely that this would be admitted; and there is always room for different interpretations of what is taking place. Various credible justifications for the use of accounting can be presented. And individuals who choose to use accounting may not even be aware of the consequences of what is happening. We saw in Chapter 8 that the integrationist approach to power sees accountancy as supporting the myth that an organization's activities are really for the benefit of us all.

3. Accountants are not always employed by the rich and powerful: they are often employed on behalf of the rich and powerful who are then able, directly and indirectly, to ensure that the accountants act in their interests. Company audits are supposedly conducted primarily for the benefit of shareholders, and it is shareholders' money that is used to pay the audit fees. But the appointment and remuneration of auditors is determined by the directors of a company who are able in many ways to influence auditors, and the whole accounting function so that it tends to support their position. Those who can succeed in employing accountants, using someone else's resources, to act in their own interests, are clearly in a powerful position. Indeed power itself may be seen as including the ability to use other people's resources to enhance one's own wealth and power.

4. Wealth and power, however defined, are not fixed in quantity. Those who accumulate increasing wealth and power do not necessarily do so at the expense of others. One of the main defences of capitalist economies is that they increase the total wealth of society, and so can increase the wealth of everyone. It is something of a illusion to suggest that everyone could benefit from an increase in wealth in society; and the definition and measurement of wealth are problematic. In a sense wealth is no more than the arithmetic product of whatever measurement rules are selected by those in a position to do so. But there is an established view that if companies, directors and shareholders become more prosperous, this is good for society as a whole.

5. The status and value of accountancy depends to an important extent on it being seen as a respectable profession, and professions are expected to fulfil some desirable social role.

Accountancy is a profession that is in some ways like many others, with relatively high incomes and status for its members. But it is also a particularly successful profession. Accountancy practices, accountancy ways of thinking, seeing and presenting things and professional accountancy firms, are all increasingly influential in many areas of society that were previously relatively insulated from such bias. And it is usually private sector accounting approaches that predominate, with their emphasis on profit, short-term financial performance that is relatively easy to measure, and on control. The major accountancy firms have been remarkably successful, with growth rates often in excess of 25 per cent per annum in the 1980s and still some growth in the depressed early 1990s.

Other professions in society are often easier to defend. Most of us tend to be in favour of such things as justice, health, education and research, and good buildings, and so the contribution to society of the legal, medical, teaching, academic and architecture professions may seem fairly obvious. Such professions are, of course, no more above criticism that the accountancy profession, and it may be most professions are open to criticisms similar to those made of accountancy in Chapter 1.

But what desirable social goals are served by accountancy? In Chapter 1 it was suggested that professional accountancy might be defended as protecting shareholders and creditors; preventing and detecting fraud; making individuals and organizations 'accountable'; providing information that influences share prices, and so, in turn, the allocation of resources in the economy; and providing information to make organizations more 'efficient'. Much of the rest of the book may be seen a critical assessment of the extent to which these roles are fulfilled in practice.

Accountancy does offer some protection to shareholders and creditors. In the absence of official accounting and auditing requirements they would be dependent on whatever information directors chose to disclose; they would have no basis for comparing the risks of investing in one company with risks elsewhere; and they would have no basis for judging the reliability of the information that directors chose to disclose.

Although some companies choose to disclose information voluntarily, perhaps in the hope or expectation of influencing their share price, shareholders and creditors cannot rely on voluntary disclosure. The development of official accounting and auditing requirements has resulted mainly from abuses and scandals, and there is plainly a need for compulsory accounting disclosure and auditing in all organizations.

Accounting systems and auditors also play a role in preventing and detecting fraud. The limited nature of auditors' responsibilities with regard to fraud has been criticized; but existing accounting and auditing systems, and the possibility that they will detect and expose fraud, at least act as a deterrent. And when frauds and scandals occur, there should be enough information to uncover most of what has actually gone wrong.

Some of the other defences of accountancy do not stand up so well, particularly in relation to companies. Accounting is assumed to play an important role in accountability: in ensuring that the directors of companies are effectively accountable to their shareholders. But, in practice, it is not difficult for directors to influence the auditors so that they defend the interests of the directors rather than the shareholders.

There are also problems with the idea that resources in the economy are allocated on the basis of accounting information. Accounting information is often flawed, easily manipulated and distorted, and is not based on any defensible definitions or conceptual framework. Moreover it tends to assume that profit is a measure of efficiency, particularly when it is measured in relation to capital employed. In this respect accounting serves to defend the interest of investors rather than the interests of others in society such as employees, consumers, or those who are concerned about the environment.

But profit is not the only approach to performance measurement. Chapter 5 explored performance measures that go beyond profit. But the measures that are chosen and come to be prominent, credible and influential often do so as the result of a political process in which the most powerful parties are likely to ensure that emphasis is given to the performance measures that support their interests. Indeed, the same argument could be applied to most accounting and other information that is disclosed. Those who are rich and powerful in society are likely to be able to influence which version of events appears to be most credible, influential and even 'true'. And professional accountants can play an apparently powerful role in supporting such versions of the truth.

The relationship between power and accountancy has been a recurring theme. It has been assumed that accountancy is powerful at least in the sense that it has real effects in the world on the distribution of income, wealth and power. Annual reports, their form and content, the official version of an organization, can have real effects, and so it is important how their content is determined. The accountancy profession appears to play a significant role in this respect. In issuing and revising accounting standards to make them appear more effective in curtailing the worst abuses of creative accounting, while at the same time leaving considerable flexibility in the hands of directors, the accountancy profession is playing a significant role in society.

But how powerful is the accountancy profession, and the role of accounting more generally? It appears to be most powerful when it is allied with and supporting organizations that are already powerful, particularly major companies and central government. The use of accountancy by these organizations is a contribution to their power, and a symptom of it: they could not employ accountants unless they had the resources to do so.

With most organizations, particularly those in the public sector, it is generally accepted that there is a need for effective accountability mechanisms. In the private sector it is sometimes argued that there is no need for compulsory accounting and auditing requirements because 'the market' will take care of these matters, ensuring that only efficient companies survive, and that high audit fees are dependent on high reputations for competence and integrity. Experience of scandals and abuses, with regular extensions of official requirements as a result, indicates that market forces alone are not sufficiently effective.

A second argument against extending compulsory accounting and auditing requirements is that we can rely on the personal qualities of the individuals involved. The accountancy profession argues that independence is a state of mind and has resisted effective mechanisms to guarantee it. With regard to corporate governance more generally, the Cadbury Committee believed that

> The way forward is through clear definitions of responsibility and an acceptance by all involved that the highest standards of efficiency and integrity are expected of them ... The machinery is in place. What is needed is the will to improve its effectiveness. (para. 7.4)

It is understandable that company directors and chartered accountants would resist effective restrictions on their activities, and assume that society can rely on their personality, their state of mind, and their will to implement existing mechanisms more effectively. But self-regulation has weaknesses, and there is a need for more effective mechanisms. Corporate governance is too important to society to be left to chartered accountants and company directors to deal with in their own ways.

Power may be seen as being either

1. restricting the actions of others, coercive, controlling, taking away freedom of action, disempowering; or
2. liberating, enabling or empowering individuals or groups in society.

In the first sense we can see accounting as enhancing the power of directors of companies, and those who control other powerful organizations, at the expense of employees and others in society. It is as if the amount of power in society is limited, and any gain by one group is at the expense of another.

In the second sense we can view education, increased understanding and access to information as empowering. The more that people know and understand about themselves and the world in which they operate, the more they are empowered to determine their own lives. While accounting provides only a blinkered and distorted view of the world, yet a powerful and legitimate view, it forces people to see, think and act in particular ways, instead of being able to determine their own ways. But accounting could have a liberating and creative role; even if at present it is mainly controlling and repressive, and a support mechanism for those who are already powerful.

Accounting can be powerful in both ways. In companies it is more likely to strengthen the directors at the expense of workers and others. In government, accountability is more likely to operate in the interests of a much wider range of groups and individuals in society, and accounting can make a contribution to this.

The approach in this book has generally been critical. The aim has been to encourage readers to form their own views about how accountancy 'really' operates, and to increase understanding, rather than to put forward a particular view point. But it is too easy to be negative and critical, to find fault with whatever professions, mechanisms and systems are in operation. Academics can always claim that their responsibilities do not go beyond promoting understanding, that the nature of their activity is to be critical rather than to propose solutions to problems, and this book is intended to contribute to such understanding. But, it is not entirely negative and a number of suggestions for improvement have been made, for example in relation to auditors' responsibilities and independence, and accountability more generally.

It can be argued that companies owe a duty of accountability to society; that there is some kind of social contract between companies and society; and that companies 'should' therefore provide information about the social effects of their activities. And some of the more socially aware companies do so. But if CSR is seen as being something that can be achieved by company directors and the accountancy profession working together to produce more detailed and enlightened annual reports, then social accountability will not be effective. If society wants to change corporate behaviour in relation to such issues as pollution, employment practices or safety of products, there is a need for legislation with sanctions for offenders. Corporate social reports enable the most enlightened companies to boast of their achievements, to present glossy public relations material and to enhance their image. They will do little to change the behaviour of those companies that are more interested in profits than social performance. In presenting a mask of social acceptability they may even facilitate anti-social behaviour. Voluntary corporate social reporting may do more harm than good.

There is, however, a case for forcing companies to make specific social disclosures, both by legislation, and by shareholder action. Where society has determined, through legislation, that specific, measurable and reportable social performance is required, with legal penalties for transgressors, accountability and enforcement can be strengthened by requiring annual reports to include detailed information. Where society has determined that particular records should be kept regarding such things as industrial accidents, pollution emission levels, or numbers of disabled employees, such information should be available to the public directly; it should not be a matter for cosy arrangements between public officials and company officials.

Shareholder action could also force better social disclosures by companies. Companies are supposed to be owned by their shareholders, and company directors are supposed to be accountable to their shareholders. But, as we have seen, accountability mechanisms are weak, and tend to be used to support, legitimate and strengthen directors rather than to control them. The assumption is that shareholders are interested only in profits, dividends and the price of their shares; as long as directors succeed in these respects, social considerations are of little importance. Even activities that are against the law seem to be acceptable provided the companies are not prosecuted, or that the profits generated from such activities are greater than any penalties imposed. Attempts by individual 'small' shareholders to change company behaviour are easily defeated by directors with all the powers and resources at their disposal – and with the proxy votes of the major institutional investors in their pockets.

But shareholders could be more powerful and effective in making directors socially accountable. Although it is still small, there is a growing ethical investment movement. A number of specifically ethical investment trusts are willing to invest only in companies that appear to behave ethically in accordance with the particular ethical, social and environmental criteria adopted by each trust. There are also pressures for other institutional investors to adopt ethical investment criteria. The bulk of latent shareholder power is in the hands of institutional investors such as pension funds; and the managers of these funds tend to support directors. But the managers of investment institutions should be accountable to the investors whom they represent. The Robert Maxwell saga has demonstrated the abuses that can occur when the managers of pension funds are left to do as they please. There are signs that members of pension funds, and the trade unions that represent them, are taking an increasing interest in the investment policies of those funds. Similarly some more politically aware institutional investors, such as churches, charities and some local authorities, are concerned to invest only in companies that comply with their particular social, environmental and other ethical criteria.

There would be an impact on share prices if enough investors insisted on investing only in companies which complied with particular ethical and social criteria. The effect could come from a combination of individual investors, ethical investment vehicles, and pressure on pension funds and other institutional investors. If it became clear that the share prices of companies that are popular with ethical investors were significantly higher than those of less socially responsible companies, this would be a very effective pressure for all companies to improve their social performance. They might be doing so for purely market-driven, financial reasons: to increase their share price. But the market can be a very powerful influence.

If ethical investors are to influence share prices, and so also to influence corporate behaviour, it is essential that their investment decisions are based on relevant and reliable information. It is very easy for companies to publish annual reports that give impressive accounts of their socially responsible activities, especially in the permissive, flexible or creative accounting and auditing environment with which the accountancy profession colludes. If ethical investors are to rely on information produced by companies there is a need for it to be verified by auditors who are clearly independent from the directors.

The problems of auditor independence were discussed in Chapter 3. As with corporate reports we can not rely on the professional accountancy bodies to solve the problems. They can do no more than sanctify with cloaks of respectability which conceal their members' multifarious related income generating activities. The accountancy profession's view of independence may seem like an immovable object, but there are irresistible forces: legislation and the market. The British government's relationship with the accounting profession seems to be too close to lead to effective change. They appear to have a mutually supportive alliance. It is still possible that the EC will require auditors to be more effectively independent from directors. But a market solution may have better prospects.

There is a need for a Campaign for Independent Auditors. If there is a real demand from shareholders, creditors, and perhaps others in society, for credible auditors who are genuinely independent from directors, at present they have nowhere to turn. A successful Campaign for Independent Auditors could lead to some auditors realizing that they could actually expand their businesses by abandoning non-audit work. It could also encourage companies and other organizations, in increasing numbers, to use genuinely independent auditors if they wanted their annual reports to be credible.

More effective auditing could make the information produced by companies more reliable, but this would not be sufficient to meet the information needs of ethical and socially aware investors who want to change the behaviour of companies. They need more relevant information, and they are not likely to obtain this while company directors, accountants and auditors act as intermediaries, selecting, editing and presenting information in their own way. It is unrealistic to expect the information needs of many different interested parties to be met through a single annual report. Indeed, the whole baggage of accounting and auditing may be seen as a means of **restricting** the information that is disclosed, and enabling directors to stay in control. A more liberating approach to accountability would be to allow shareholders, creditors and other interested parties, freedom of access to all information about a company. This would have to be restricted with regard to personal information about identifiable individuals. But the issue was explored in Chapter 2 and there is little substance to most other objections to freedom of access to information.

These arguments should be applied not just to companies, but also to other powerful entities in society, including local and central government. But in some respects the public sector already offers a model for the private sector – albeit a model that the private sector is in some ways already invading. It can be argued that all powerful organizations in society, including major companies and the accountancy profession, should be under direct public control or ownership. But this is not the argument advocated here. Instead, ways are sought whereby individuals and groups in society can use accounting and accountability mechanisms to alter the distribution of power in society, and to make organizations more socially responsible. In the public sector, open access to information can work; public accountability can lead to local councillors, MPs and governments losing office; and many different groups can influence policy and the distribution of wealth and power in society. As a model, parliamentary democracy still leaves much to be desired; and governments are increasingly using the techniques of the accountancy profession to enhance their power positions and limit the effectiveness of accountability mechanisms.

Those who advocate making powerful organizations in society more 'account-able' should be aware of the limitations of the conventional professional accoun-tancy model of accountability, and should consider other approaches. But accounting can play a role not only in making companies and other organizations more accountable, but also in making governments and all powerful entities more socially responsible.

Index